Data-Driven Reservoir Modeling

Data-Driven Reservoir Modeling

Top-Down Modeling (TDM)

A Paradigm Shift in Reservoir Modeling
The Art and Science of Building Reservoir Models
Based on Field Measurements

Shahab D. Mohaghegh
Intelligent Solutions Incorporated and West Virginia University
As of this printing:
http://intelligentsolutionsinc.com/Products/IMagine.shtml
2017

Society of Petroleum Engineers

© Copyright 2017 Society of Petroleum Engineers

All rights reserved. No portion of this book may be reproduced in any form or by any means, including electronic storage and retrieval systems, except by explicit, prior written permission of the publisher except for brief passages excerpted for review and critical purposes.

Printed in the United States of America.

Disclaimer

This book was prepared by members of the Society of Petroleum Engineers and their well-qualified colleagues from material published in the recognized technical literature and from their own individual experience and expertise. While the material presented is believed to be based on sound technical knowledge, neither the Society of Petroleum Engineers nor any of the authors or editors herein provide a warranty either expressed or implied in its application. Correspondingly, the discussion of materials, methods, or techniques that may be covered by patents implies no freedom to use such materials, methods, or techniques without permission through appropriate licensing. Nothing described within this book should be construed to lessen the need to apply sound engineering judgment nor to carefully apply accepted engineering practices in the design, implementation, or application of the techniques described herein.

Learn more about SPE events and volunteer opportunities at: www.spe.org
Order books using your SPE member discount at: www.spe.org/store

ISBN 978-1-61399-560-0

First Printing 2017

Society of Petroleum Engineers
222 Palisades Creek Drive
Richardson, TX 75080-2040 USA

http://www.spe.org/store
service@spe.org
1.972.952.9393

Dedication

This book is dedicated to Turgay Ertekin. He was, is, and will always be my mentor and role model. I consider myself fortunate to have known him and to have worked under his supervision as a graduate student. What I have learned from him has guided me not only in reservoir engineering, but in life.

Acknowledgments

I would like to acknowledge and thank my colleagues at Intelligent Solutions Incorporated, Razi Gaskari and Mohammad Maysami, for their invaluable contributions throughout the many years that we have worked together.

I would like to acknowledge and thank all my graduate students throughout the past 25 years. They have enriched my life, and many have become life-long friends.

I am thankful to Narges for her unwavering support and for putting up with my tough schedule, and I am thankful to Dorna for giving my life meaning.

Foreword

Data-Driven Reservoir Modeling is intended to introduce a technology that is relatively new to petroleum engineers and geoscientists whose day-to-day job responsibilities always bring them to junctures where critical technical decisions need to be made and strategies need to be established. The technology covered in this book adds another decision-making tool to the arsenal of upstream technologists of the petroleum industry. This book should also be useful to petroleum engineering and geosciences undergraduate students in their junior or senior year, as well as to graduate students with some degree of exposure to the principles of petroleum engineering field operations, petroleum geology, and petroleum geophysics.

The aim of this book is to present a methodology that is rather new to the petroleum engineering community and is particularly suited to the application of data analytics to physical problems of reservoir engineering for tracking the state of dynamics with the goal of strengthening the decision-making process. With the help of the pragmatic approach provided in this book, data-driven modeling can be effectively used in field planning and development studies.

In today's field practices, zillions of bytes of information are generated daily. Every piece of data carries key signatures about the physical properties of the system being studied and about the ongoing physical and thermodynamic processes. The collected data can be so massive that they overwhelm manpower, while the available computational power may not permit conducting a comprehensive analysis. In addition to these issues, if we are dealing with data that are generated by relationships that are not understood or, at best, vaguely understood (i.e., all the physics and thermodynamics of the ongoing processes are not well known), reservoir analysis becomes even more challenging. In times like these, machine-learning-based algorithmic protocols (intelligent systems) come to the rescue. These systems are knowledge-based intelligent systems that emulate not only human intelligence but also the reasoning and decision-making aspects of human intelligence. In our daily operations, we are always confronted with uncertain data; here, the strategy is to exploit imprecision and uncertainty to achieve tractable, robust, and low-cost solutions. This is why capturing associations and discovering existing regularities in a big data set can become a reality even if the diversity of the data is large and the relationships between independent and dependent variables are understood only dimly.

The book assumes some degree of familiarity with the upstream petroleum industry vocabulary and the physics of flow in porous media. In order to maximize the benefits from the book, one also needs to be knowledgeable about transport processes and the thermodynamics of oilfield fluids. With that knowledge bank in place, it will be possible to critically analyze the results generated. Being conversant with computers on various platforms will be helpful if the reader is interested not only in using this class of solutions but also in developing such a catalogue of solutions.

The author of the book, Shahab Mohaghegh, is a leading authority in the application of data analytics in petroleum engineering. His writing style is extremely lucid and informative. Each chapter of the book is well structured and possesses logical continuity, clarity, and thoroughness. In my view, the book brings a wonderful opportunity to explore new modeling frontiers that are applicable to hydrocarbon reservoirs. No matter what type of reservoir or production engineering problem you are working on, Big Data analytics, when applied properly, has the potential to guide and streamline the solution work flow. Here, I present a summary of how the author covers topical areas of data-driven reservoir modeling.

Chapter 1 briefly reviews the reservoir models that are currently used in studies related to reservoir management and discusses the challenges of history matching, which is a critically important and notoriously difficult application for reservoir characterization. The chapter continues with a discussion of top-down modeling (TDM) and discusses how physical processes and geological characteristics collectively play an important role in generating the response function from the field (typically, pressure-transient and/or rate-transient data).

Chapter 2 provides a succinct review of the theory of data-driven problem-solving methodology. This chapter stresses the importance of powerful domain expertise in applying machine learning and pattern recognition to the class of problems studied in the book.

Chapter 3 outlines the historical progression of reservoir modeling and discusses the critical juncture where a decision needs to be made on the levels of accuracy and computational overhead that are faced during a full-fledged simulation study. What makes the decision even more challenging is that engineers who are conducting reservoir simulation studies almost always find themselves in the middle of a sea of uncertainties.

Chapter 4 concisely covers Big Data analytics methodologies, including data mining, artificial intelligence, artificial neural networks, and fuzzy logic, with greater emphasis on the last two. This chapter should be especially useful for readers who do not have great familiarity with data analytics practices.

Chapter 5 accentuates the importance of good understanding of the conventional reservoir-modeling techniques and principles of machine learning to appreciate the advantages and disadvantages of each of these two broadly dissimilar approaches.

Chapter 6 reminds the reader that there are empirical models that use the data collected in analyzing the performance of a hydrocarbon reservoir (e.g., decline curve analysis). This chapter also discusses some of the weaknesses that we face in the application of such empirical methodologies.

Chapter 7 introduces the concept of TDM as a new work flow in data-driven reservoir-modeling applications. The principal strength of TDM is recognized in terms of its encompassing approach, such that all available field measurements can be integrated in a seamless manner. What is more striking here is that even if we do not have a complete understanding of the dynamics of the ongoing physical phenomena, the TDM protocol is capable of generating a representative comprehensive model that incorporates all of the available data.

Chapter 8 discusses the spatio-temporal nature of the data base that is inevitably faced in reservoir engineering studies. The nonlinear nature of the process dynamics and parameters that are involved in the processes undoubtedly makes reservoir modeling even more challenging. The matters that need to be addressed at this stage typically include further simplification of the model. However, most of the assumptions that are used in such simplifications may not be compatible with the nature of the data collected, because these data internally carry many critical implications of the nonlinearities. Along these lines, the impact of static and dynamic parameters on the response functions is discussed.

Chapter 9 addresses the nonunique nature of inverse solutions (in this case, history-matching protocols). Like any other inverse model, a model that matches the history successfully cannot guarantee the accuracy of the predictions; however, a good-quality history match increases the level of confidence about the performance of the model. In a history-matching application spatio-temporal properties are accommodated with the help of artificial neural networks. In this process, a critical step is the correct prioritization of the relevance of such parameters. This enhances the overall optimization of the process that is being studied.

Chapter 10 covers the importance of conducting a critical analysis of the results of the TDM. Such an analysis will provide an opportunity to optimize the process that is being modeled and at the same time will establish realistic bounds to the results that are being generated. These limitations can be accommodated by keeping realistic and practical bounds on the operational parameters. In view of the high computational speeds that can be achieved by the TDM approach, it will be possible to conduct an expansive Monte Carlo simulation study using a large number of scenarios. In this chapter, the dynamic nature of the TDM is reiterated, just to ensure that the user does not forget to update the overall structure of the TDM whenever necessary.

Chapter 11 presents a compendium of three case studies involving mature oil fields from different corners of the world.

Chapter 12 discusses the limitations of data-driven reservoir modeling, indicating the importance of the representative nature of the data available in developing the model. This becomes especially important because the data used also carry vital information about the physical processes within the system.

Chapter 13 provides a discussion based on the author's extensive experience about what one might expect to see in the future concerning the use of data-driven reservoir modeling. One potential area where this type of modeling will be handy is in the analysis of fiber-optic data-collection systems that are finding applications in long horizontal wellbores. For example, it is believed that even small temperature variations captured in the horizontal well will provide critically important information about the identification of the producing and nonproducing zones.

Finally, extensive references are provided for any reader who is interested to learn more about data-driven reservoir modeling.

We hope you now have a good idea of what this volume is all about and what it can do for the problems that you are working on. I am confident that this book will equip you with what you need to know in order to develop realistic solutions for problems you may have thought that you would not be able solve. Here is your opportunity.

Turgay Ertekin
Professor of Petroleum and Natural Gas Engineering
Pennsylvania State University
University Park, Pennsylvania, USA
26 November 2016

Table of Contents

Dedication v
Acknowledgments vii
Foreword ix
1 Introduction 1
   1.1 Reservoir Models for Reservoir Management 1
   1.2 What Is Top-Down Modeling? 3
      1.2.1 Role of Physics and Geology 4
      1.2.2 Formulation and Computational Footprint. 4
      1.2.3 Expected Outcome of a Top-Down Model. 5
      1.2.4 Limitations of TDM. 5
      1.2.5 Software Tool for the Development of TDM. 5
   1.3 Paradigm Shift 5
      1.3.1 Drilling Operation. 6
      1.3.2 Mature Fields. 6
      1.3.3 Smart Completions, Smart Wells, and Smart Fields. 7
      1.3.4 Production From Shale Assets. 7
      1.3.5 Reservoir Simulation Models. 7
2 Data-Driven Problem Solving 9
   2.1 Misunderstanding Data-Driven Reservoir Modeling 10
3 Reservoir Modeling 13
4 Data-Driven Technologies 17
   4.1 Data Mining 17
   4.2 Artificial Intelligence 18
   4.3 Artificial Neural Networks 18
      4.3.1 Structure of a Neural Network 19
      4.3.2 Mechanics of Neural Network Operation 20
   4.4 Fuzzy Logic 23
      4.4.1 Fuzzy Set Theory 24
      4.4.2 Approximate Reasoning 26
      4.4.3 Fuzzy Inference 27
5 Pitfalls of Using Machine Learning in Reservoir Modeling 29
6 Fact-Based Reservoir Management 31
   6.1 Empirical Models in the E&P Industry 33
      6.1.1 Decline Curve Analysis 34
      6.1.2 Capacitance/Resistance Modeling 34
7 Top-Down Modeling 35
   7.1 Components of a Top-Down Model 41
   7.2 Formulation and Computational Footprint of TDM 44
   7.3 Curse of Dimensionality 47
   7.4 Correlation Is Not the Same as Causation 48
   7.5 Quality Control and Quality Assurance of the Data 50
      7.5.1 Inspecting the Quality of the Data. 52
      7.5.2 QC of the Production Data. 55

8 The Spatio-Temporal Database 59
8.1 Static Data 63
8.2 Dynamic Data 64
8.3 Well Trajectory and Completion Data 65
8.3.1 Two-Dimensional vs. Three-Dimensional Reservoir Modeling 68
8.4 Resolution in Time and Space 69
8.4.1 Resolution in Space 70
8.4.2 Resolution in Time 76
8.5 Role of Offset Wells 77
8.6 Structure of the Spatio-Temporal Database 79
8.7 Required Quantity and Quality of Data 83

9 History Matching the Top-Down Model 87
9.1 Practical Considerations During the Training of a Neural Network 92
9.1.1 Selection of Input Parameters 93
9.1.2 Partitioning the Data Set 94
9.1.3 Structure and Topology 95
9.1.4 The Training Process 98
9.1.5 Convergence 102
9.2 History-Matching Schemes in TDM 103
9.2.1 Sequential History Matching 104
9.2.2 Random History Matching 107
9.2.3 Mixed History Matching 108
9.3 Validation of the Top-Down Model 109
9.3.1 Material Balance Check 109

10 Post-Modeling Analysis of the Top-Down Model 111
10.1 Forecasting Oil Production, GOR, and WC 111
10.2 Production Optimization 112
10.2.1 Choke-Setting Optimization 113
10.2.2 Artificial-Lift Optimization 113
10.2.3 Water-Injection Optimization 114
10.3 Reservoir Characterization 115
10.4 Determination of Infill Locations 115
10.5 Recovery Optimization 117
10.6 Type Curves 118
10.7 Uncertainty Analysis 118
10.8 Updating the Top-Down Model 120

11 Examples and Case Studies 123
11.1 Case Study No. 1: A Mature Onshore Field in Central America 124
11.2 Case Study No. 2: Mature Offshore Field in the North Sea 127
11.3 Case Study No. 3: Mature Onshore Field in the Middle East 136
11.3.1 Data Used During the Top-Down-Model Development 136
11.3.2 Top-Down-Model Training and History Matching 139
11.3.3 Post-Modeling Analysis 148
11.3.4 Performing a "Stress Test" on the Top-Down Model 152

12 Limitations of Data-Driven Reservoir Modeling 155
13 The Future of Data-Driven Reservoir Modeling 157
References 159
Index 163

Chapter 1

Introduction

We are living in an interesting time. Let us put the speed at which technology is changing our world in perspective. Take the example of the printing press vs. electronic mail or email. The printing press was invented in the fifteenth century and changed how people communicated. It was the most common mode of communication for more than 25 generations.[1] It still is an integral part of our lives. But no one doubts that many of its functions are now performed by new technologies such as email, the Internet, eBooks, eNews, and so on. Furthermore, email became popular only after the 1990s. It quickly grew to become the most used mode of communication among people of all persuasions. However, now, in less than only one generation, it is losing its prominent position in human communications to other newly invented communication modes. The new generation hardly uses email. Email is now being replaced by text messages and social network communications. Email, such a step-change in our communications, is ready to relinquish its prominence in less than one generation. This is the speed at which the technology is moving forward.

The modern oil industry is a bit more than one hundred years old.[2] Most technologies that are currently in use by petroleum engineers and geoscientists can be traced back to their development for the oil industry during the mid-twentieth century.[3] Some of our newer technologies (e.g., horizontal wells, seismic survey, measurement while drilling) are less than a few decades old. This book presents an example of a new and quite recent technology that is making its way into the oil and gas industry. This book is dedicated to application of artificial intelligence and data mining in the upstream oil and gas industry, and specifically to their application to build comprehensive reservoir models.

1.1 Reservoir Models for Reservoir Management

It has been said that all models are wrong, but some models are useful (Box 1976). One of the objectives of reservoir engineers is to build reliable reservoir models to be used by reservoir managers in order to make decisions. The uniqueness and complexity of each hydrocarbon reservoir make the accomplishment of this objective quite challenging. For the purposes of this book, we define the problem as follows:

*Building full-field models that have **practical** utility for managing complex reservoirs. In order to fit this mold, the full-field reservoir model must be **accurate** and have a **small computational footprint**.*

Complementary stipulations for such a model include incorporation of all available information about the reservoir, including detailed information about all wells. The two attributes that are emphasized in the above definition are accuracy and small computational footprint. The model has to be

---

[1] Each century can be counted as four to five generations.
[2] Actual oil production for commercial use goes back to the mid-1820s in Imperial Russia.
[3] Darcy's law goes back to 1856, and Arp's decline curves were introduced in 1945.

accurate so that it can honor the past (history matched) before any comments can be made regarding its predictive capabilities. Furthermore, to be considered a viable reservoir management tool, the model's computational footprint should be small enough to warrant sensitivity analyses, quantification of uncertainties, and exploration of large solution spaces for field development planning.

The importance of accuracy of a full-field reservoir model should be obvious. Nevertheless, it must be emphasized that by history matching the past performance of the reservoir, which is usually preserved in the form of production history, one develops confidence in the utility of the model for further analyses. As the number of dynamic measurements in the field increases, so too does the complexity of the history-matching process. For example, when flowing bottomhole pressure or production rates are the only measured dynamic properties that are to be history matched (usually one of the two is used as the constraint, while the other one is calculated), the reservoir modeler has a much easier task to accomplish (and a better chance of success) as compared to the cases where other dynamic data such as Gas Oil Ratio (GOR), Water Cut (WC), time-lapsed saturation and static reservoir pressure (as a function of time) have been measured (and are present) in the history and need to be simultaneously history matched.[4]

The importance of the computational footprint cannot be overemphasized. It strikes at the heart of the problem: the model utility. This is a practical issue. No matter how accurate a full-field reservoir model is, a large computational footprint can make it useless in practice.[5] Reducing the computational footprint of numerical models is the main reason companies have moved toward supercomputers and clusters of parallel central processing units. The never-ending race between larger models (high resolution in space and time) and faster computers continues to preoccupy many of our colleagues in the larger companies.

Tasks such as sensitivity analysis and quantification of uncertainties associated with the geological (static) model (the backbone of any reservoir model) are complex and time-consuming undertakings. As the run time (time for execution after the development is completed) of a model starts increasing to more than a few hours, performing such analyses becomes impractical. The solution is either to cut corners or to come up with tricks to perform fewer runs and make the most out of the results. This last exercise (reducing the number of runs) starts introducing limitations in the analyses. We pay a price by reducing the number of runs. Sometimes unjustifiable assumptions of linearity must be made in order to make certain approaches work. There is very little we can do. It is simply a conundrum that we cannot simplify our way out of. As long as we live by the laws of the current paradigm,[6] there is only so much that we can do.

Equally complex and puzzling are field development and planning problems. As the number of wells (both producers and injectors) and the type of constraints increase, so too does the solution space that needs to be searched for optimal (or near-optimal) solutions. *Solution space* in this context is defined as the number of possible combinations of wells and their associated constraints that can form a solution (combinatorial explosion). Any optimization routine, no matter how smart it may be, requires examining a large number of solutions in order to find the optimal or the near-optimal solutions. Each solution in the case of a development plan means at least a single run of the reservoir model. It is easy to see that as the execution time (computational footprint) of a reservoir model increases, its utility as an objective function for planning is compromised. Again, many

---

[4]Needless to say, just because a model can history match the past does not mean that its predictive capabilities are guaranteed. Those familiar with the history-matching process are well aware that history matching is an art as much as a science. Unfortunately, performing unreasonable tuning and modification of parameters to reach a history match is not an uncommon practice in our industry. A history-matched model is a nonunique model, by definition.

[5]Especially in the eyes of reservoir managers, who most of the time are the primary users of reservoir simulation models as a tool.

[6]The current paradigm, known as the computational paradigm, states that building models includes development of governing equations using first-principles physics and then using discrete mathematics to numerically solve the governing equations.

reservoir engineers continue their quest to build proxy models that are simplified versions of the more-complex models, so that they can be used for such purposes, but there is always a price to pay. Sometimes the price we end up paying is so severe that it undermines the original efforts of building such complex and detailed numerical reservoir models from the very start.

Are there solutions for problems such as those mentioned above? Yes and no. For as long as we are sticking to the traditional paradigm of building reservoir models, there are no solutions. Here, by the traditional paradigm, we are referring to the well-known sequence of building the geological (static) model and then using the principles of fluid flow in porous media to develop a dynamic model based on the numerical solutions of the partial-differential equation that governs fluid flow in porous media, the so-called numerical reservoir simulation and modeling, and finally modifying the static model in order to history match the dynamic model.

As long as we adhere to these core principles, we are simply pushing the envelope. There are, and continue to be, successes and failures. Incremental gains are made here and there. But if we want to remove this serious practical shortcoming altogether, we need to move beyond the traditional paradigm of building reservoir models. The solution requires a paradigm shift. This paradigm shift and its manifestation in reservoir modeling are the subjects of this book.

This is not a general book that discusses the virtues and capabilities of data-driven analytics and indicates areas of the upstream oil and gas industry that can benefit from machine learning and data mining. This book is very specific. It has identified one specific area in our industry, namely reservoir modeling, and provides ample details on how this new and exciting technology (artificial intelligence and data mining) can be used to build new reservoir models. From that point of view, it is the only book of its kind in the oil and gas industry that provides step-by-step details in how to build a data-driven reservoir model, also known as a Top-Down Model (TDM). The following section is a summary of what can be expected in this book.

1.2 What Is Top-Down Modeling?

To efficiently develop and operate a petroleum reservoir, it is important to have a model. Currently, numerical reservoir simulation is the accepted and widely used technology for this purpose. Data-driven reservoir modeling (also known as top-down modeling or TDM[7]) is an alternative (or a complement) to numerical reservoir simulation. TDM uses a Big Data solution (machine learning and pattern recognition) to develop (train, calibrate, and validate) full-field reservoir models based on field measurements (facts) rather than mathematical formulations of our current understanding of the physics of the fluid flow through porous media.

Unlike other empirical technologies, which only use production data as a tool to forecast production,[8] or only use production/injection data for its analysis,[9] TDM integrates all available field measurements in order to forecast production from every single well in a field with multiple wells. The field measurements that are used by TDM to build a full-field reservoir model include well locations and trajectories, completions and stimulations, well logs, core data, well tests, seismic, and production/injection history (including wellhead pressure and choke setting). TDM combines all the information from the sources mentioned above into a cohesive, comprehensive, full-field reservoir model using artificial intelligence technologies. A top-down model is defined as a full-field model within which production [including gas/oil ratio (GOR) and water cut (WC)] is conditioned to all the measured reservoir characteristics and operational constraints. TDM matches the historical production (and is validated through blind history matching) and is capable of forecasting a field's future behavior on a well-by-well basis. Imagine a decline curve analysis technique that covers the entire field, well by well, and incorporates reservoir characteristics and operational constraints and

---

[7]Throughout this book "data-driven reservoir modeling" and "top-down modeling" are used interchangeably.
[8]Decline curve analysis
[9]Capacitance/resistance model

accounts for interaction between wells whether they are only producers or a combination of producers and injectors. TDM is such a tool.

The novelty of data-driven reservoir modeling stems from the fact that it is a complete departure from traditional approaches to reservoir modeling. Fact-based, data-driven reservoir modeling manifests a paradigm shift in how reservoir engineers and geoscientists model fluid flow through porous media. In this new paradigm, current understanding of physics and geology in a given reservoir is replaced by facts (data/field measurements) as the foundation of the model. This characteristic of TDM makes it a viable modeling technology for unconventional (shale) assets where the physics of the hydrocarbon production (in the presence of massive hydraulic fractures) is not yet well understood.

1.2.1 Role of Physics and Geology. Although it does not start from the first principles of physics, a top-down model is very much a physics-based reservoir mode. The incorporation of physics in TDM is quite non-traditional. Reservoir characteristics and geological aspects are incorporated in the model insofar as they are measured. Although interpretations are intentionally left out during the model development, reservoir engineering knowledge plays a vital role in the construction of the top-down model. Furthermore, expert knowledge and interpretation are extensively used during the analysis of model results. Although fluid flow through porous media is not explicitly (mathematically) formulated during the development of data-driven reservoir models, successful development of such models requires a solid understanding and experience in reservoir engineering and geosciences. Physics and geology are the foundation and the framework for the assimilation of the data set that is used to develop the top-down model. The diffusivity equation has inspired the invention of this technology and was the blueprint upon which TDM was developed.

1.2.2 Formulation and Computational Footprint. The top-down model is built by correlating[10] flow rate at each well and at each timestep[11] to a set of measured static and dynamic variables. The static variables include reservoir characteristics such as well logs (e.g., gamma ray, sonic, density, resistivity), porosity, formation tops and thickness, and others at the following locations:

1. At and around each well
2. The average from the drainage area of each well
3. The average from the drainage area of the offset producers
4. The average from the drainage area of the offset injectors

The dynamic variables include operational constraints and production/injection characteristics at the appropriate timestep when production is being calculated (estimated), such as

1. Wellhead or bottomhole pressure, or choke size, at timestep t
2. Completion modification (e.g., operation of inflow-control valve, squeeze off) at timestep t
3. Number of days of production at timestep t
4. GOR, WC, and oil production volume at timestep $t-1$
5. Water and/or gas injection at timestep t
6. Well stimulation details
7. Production characteristics of the offset producers at timestep $t-1$

---

[10]Correlation that is conditioned to causation will be discussed in more detail in subsequent sections of this book.

[11]The length of timesteps in TDM is a function of the production characteristics and the age of the reservoir as well as the availability of data. It is usually either daily, monthly, or annual.

The data (enumerated above) that are incorporated into the top-down model show its differences from other empirically formulated models. Once the development of the top-down model is completed, its deployment in forecast mode is computationally efficient. A single run of the top-down model is usually measured in seconds or in some cases in minutes. Size of a top-down model is determined by the number of producer and injector wells. The small computational footprint makes TDM an ideal tool for reservoir management, uncertainty quantification, and field development planning. Development and deployment costs of TDM are a small fraction of that for numerical reservoir simulation.

1.2.3 Expected Outcome of a Top-Down Model. Data-driven reservoir modeling can accurately model a mature hydrocarbon field and successfully forecast its future production behavior under a large variety of operational scenarios. Outcomes of TDM are forecast for oil production, GOR, and WC of existing wells as well as field development planning and infill drilling. When TDM is used to identify the communication between wells, it generates a map of reservoir conductivity that is defined as a composite variable that includes multiple geologic features and rock characteristics contributing to fluid flow in the reservoir. This is accomplished by deconvolving the impact of operational issues from reservoir characteristics on production.

1.2.4 Limitations of TDM. Data-driven reservoir modeling is applicable only to fields with a certain amount of production history; for this reason, TDM is not applicable to greenfields and fields with a small number of wells and short production history. Another limitation of TDM is that it is not valid once the physics of the fluid flow in a field goes through a complete and dramatic change. For example, once a top-down model is developed for a field under primary recovery, it cannot be applied to enhanced- recovery phases of the same field.

1.2.5 Software Tool for the Development of TDM. Top-Down Modeling was pioneered by Intelligent Solutions Incorporated (ISI). ISI has recently released a software product for the development and deployment of Top-Down Model, called IMagine™. At the time of publication of this book, no other company has announced a similar product for the development of top-down models.

1.3 Paradigm Shift

Paradigm shift, a term first coined by Thomas Kuhn (1996), constitutes a change in basic assumptions within the ruling theory of science. According to Kuhn, "A paradigm is what members of a scientific community, and they alone, share" (Kuhn 1977). Jim Gray, the American computer scientist who received the Turing Award for his seminal contribution to computer science, once said, "Originally, there was just experimental science, and then there was theoretical science, with Kepler's Law, Newton's Law of Motion, Maxwell's Equations, and so on. Then for many problems, the theoretical models grew too complicated to solve analytically, and people had to start simulating. These simulations have carried us through much of the last half of the last millennium. At this point, these simulations are generating a whole lot of data, along with a huge increase in data from the experimental sciences. People now do not actually look through telescopes. Instead, they are 'looking' through large scale, complex instruments which relay data to datacenters, and only then look at the information on their computers.... The new model is for data to be captured by instruments or generated by simulations before being processed by software and for the resulting information or knowledge to be stored in computers.... The techniques and technologies for such data-intensive science are so different that it is worth distinguishing data intensive science from computational science as a new, *fourth paradigm* for scientific exploration" (Bell et al. 2009).

So how does this paradigm shift constitute itself in the exploration and production industry? Do we collect and/or generate (either from our simulators or from instruments) enough data to benefit from such a paradigm shift? In this book, we examine the reservoir-modeling discipline in the exploration and production industry in order to address these questions.

What is the current paradigm of building models that attempts to explore and explain fluid flow in porous media? We use analytical as well as numerical approaches both at the well level and at the reservoir level. This is the current paradigm. In our attempts at analytical solutions, where well testing is a good example, we approximate the problem in order to come to an exact analytical solution. Assumptions such as reservoir homogeneity, well-defined reservoir boundaries, and single-phase flow are among the basic assumptions that are required in order for the analytical solutions to be applicable. On the other hand, when we try to define the problem more realistically, by incorporating reservoir heterogeneity, irregular reservoir boundaries, multiple wells, and multiphase flow, then we are forced to discretize the problem in time and space and generate a large number of linear equations that can be solved numerically. Then, we use numerical solutions to solve the system of linear equations that was generated. Numerical solutions to the partial-differential equations are only approximate solutions. In other words, in attempts to minimize assumptions in the problem, we approximate the solutions. This paradigm has served our industry for decades and has resulted in many scientific and practical advances. We are not advocating that this be shelved. Data-driven reservoir modeling provides an alternative to (and in many cases a complement to) the traditional analytical and numerical approaches to modeling fluid flow in porous media. It is the paradigm shift as it is applied to reservoir modeling and reservoir management.

When it comes to reservoir modeling, we generate or collect massive amounts of data throughout the life of a hydrocarbon-producing field. Data-driven reservoir modeling proposes the use of this massive amount of data that is collected in the form of drilling characteristics, well construction and trajectories, well logs of all different natures, core data, well tests, seismic surveys, and finally production and injection histories along with pressure measurements, in order to build a reservoir model that is entirely based on these field measurements and minimizes the incorporation of our interpretations and biases into the resulting model. Let us examine examples where large amounts of data are collected during oil and gas exploration and production.

1.3.1 Drilling Operation. The modern drilling operation generates hundreds of gigabytes of data on a daily basis. Measurement while drilling (MWD) and logging while drilling (LWD), which have been around for years, generate considerable amounts of data in real time while the drilling operation is ongoing. Complementing these data with seismic surveys and geological models that are developed for a given field includes incredible amounts of information about the field that can help increase drilling efficiencies and eventually move the industry toward completely autonomous drilling operation.

1.3.2 Mature Fields. Mature fields around the world are sources of vast amounts of data and information that have been collected over decades. Mature fields usually include a large number of wells that have been drilled throughout its history. The fact that the wells have been drilled at different time periods provides valuable insight into the fluid flow as well as pressure and saturation distribution throughout the field. This includes large amounts of historical production and injection data usually with the associated wellhead pressure or choke settings. Most of the wells, if not all of them, have the basic set of well logs. Several wells will have been cored, and therefore some core analyses are also available. Usually, well tests are available, and sometimes seismic surveys have been performed (sometimes more than once).

In many cases, the size of the mature field determines the amount of data that can be expected to be available. More-prolific fields usually are blessed with larger amounts of data and more- diverse types of data. The amount and the variety of the data available on some prolific mature fields can be staggering. So much so, that it overwhelms reservoir engineers and reservoir managers. Many times in such cases large amounts of data will go unused and unanalyzed.

1.3.3 Smart Completions, Smart Wells, and Smart Fields.
Smart fields have two major characteristics. First, they include smart completions with controls and measurements taking place at different locations along the completion, and, second, installation of permanent downhole gauges provides high-resolution data streams. Even haphazardly designed smart fields have generated massive amounts of data that hardly ever are looked at, even offline.

Smart completions let engineers intervene with details of wells' operations from a distance. Smart wells transmit nearly continuous (real-time) data streams (e.g., pressure, flow rate) to the remote office providing immediate feedback on the consequences of recently made decisions and actions taken. Smart fields include multiple smart wells providing the possibility of managing the entire reservoir remotely and in real time. Smart fields generate terabytes[12] and petabytes[13] of data that are good examples of Big Data in the upstream oil and gas industry.

1.3.4 Production From Shale Assets.
We have been witnessing an incredible increase in hydrocarbon production from source rocks, such as shale, in recent years. Production from shale has been made possible by drilling long lateral wells and then stimulating them using massive, multiple stages of hydraulic fractures. During this process, operators are now collecting large amounts of data that include well-construction data, reservoir characteristics in the form of well logs, completion data including much detail about each cluster of hydraulic-fracturing procedures, and finally detailed production data. This is a massive amount of data, especially when we consider that the well count in shale assets is in the hundreds.

Furthermore, the introduction of distributed temperature sensing and distributed acoustic sensing systems is adding a whole new dimension to the important data that can be collected during oil and gas production in shale wells. Once the distributed temperature sensing and distributed acoustic sensing data can be coupled with microseismic and other reservoir and production-related data that have been collected from the shale wells, engineers and geoscientists will have a realistic shot at understanding all the complexities that are associated with hydrocarbon production from shale in the presence of coupled induced and natural fractures. There should be no doubt in anyone's mind that the only technology that has a realistic shot at making all this possible is advanced data-driven analytics, also known as "Shale Analytics."[14]

1.3.5 Reservoir Simulation Models.
It is a well-known fact that reservoir simulation models generate massive amounts of data. Actually the amount of data that is generated by reservoir simulation models is so large that in order just to look at them for analysis, special visualization tools are required. Imagine that a large reservoir of tens or even hundreds of square miles that includes multiple distinct geological layers is being modeled. Furthermore, imagine that a large number of wells has been modeled in this reservoir. Having reservoir simulation models with tens and or even hundreds of millions of gridblocks is becoming standard in today's oil and gas industry.

Now imagine generating oil, gas, and water production from the wells. Such a model generates gigabytes or terabytes of data for each of its timesteps, which include not only the static characteristics of the reservoir that has been modeled but also the resulting pressure and saturation distributions throughout the time and space for each gridblock. If the simulation is compositional, the amount of generated data increases exponentially.

---

[12] A terabyte of data is 10^{12} bytes of data.
[13] A petabyte of data is 10^{15} bytes of data.
[14] A book by this name (*Shale Analytics*) has recently been published by Springer-Verlag.

Chapter 2

Data-Driven Problem Solving

The definition that will be provided for data mining will underline the main reason behind referring to the set of activities that are presented in this book as data-driven modeling rather than data mining. It is true that we are using data mining (among other tools) to perform the analyses (building reservoir models) that are presented here, but, as will become more and more clear, our objective is not merely to identify the utility of yet another newly popularized tool in the oil industry (a task that by itself may have merit and may be treated as an academic exercise), but rather to offer a solution and a tool that can be used by professionals in our industry today. Ever since its introduction as a discipline in the mid-1990s, Data Science has been used as a synonym for applied statistics. Today, Data Science is used in multiple disciplines and is enjoying immense popularity. Application of Data Science to physics-based (such as the oil and gas industry) vs. nonphysics-based disciplines has been the cause of much confusion. Such distinctions surface once Data Science is applied to serious industrial applications rather than to simple academic problems.

When Data Science is applied to nonphysics-based problems, such as social networks and social media, consumer relations, demographics, politics, and medical and/or pharmaceutical sciences, it is merely applied statistics. This is because there are no sets of governing partial-differential (or other mathematical) equations that have been developed to model human behavior such as the response of human biology to drugs. In such cases (nonphysics-based areas), the relationship between correlation and causation cannot be resolved using physical experiments and the results of the data mining analyses are usually justified or explained by scientist and statisticians, using psychological, sociological, or biological arguments.

Applying Data Science to physics-based problems such as reservoir modeling is a completely different story. The interaction between parameters that are of interest to physics-based problems, despite their complex nature, has been understood and modeled by scientists and engineers for decades. Therefore, treating the data that are measured throughout the life of a hydrocarbon reservoir as just numbers that need to be processed in order to learn their interactions is a gross mistreatment and oversimplification of the problem, and hardly ever generates useful results. That is why many such attempts have resulted in poor outcomes, so that many engineers (and scientists) have concluded that Data Science has few serious applications in our industry.

Given the excitement that has been generated by the application of data analytics and data mining in other industries, such as retail and social media, a number of professionals have contemplated the usefulness of these technologies in the oil and gas industries. The results have been a good number of articles in several oil- and gas-related conferences, journals, and magazines. However, some of these authors lack domain expertise in the upstream oil and gas industry, while others lack a reasonable and fundamental understanding of data-driven technologies such as machine learning and pattern recognition. As such, they do not usually offer impressive studies that can be used in the industry by professionals to address their day-to-day issues and problems. Many professionals in our industry, who have listened to the presentations on the general theme of artificial intelligence and data mining in the oil industry, have expressed a common complaint. They claim that they have hardly ever heard presentations (especially from the larger operators) that have anything substantial to offer. The main theme of these presentations can be summarized in the following statements:

1. Artificial intelligence and data mining are great tools that have been used in other industries and have helped them tremendously.
2. We in the oil industry should be using this technology, too.
3. My company has been using this technology in the past several months/years and has benefited from it.

In other words, these presentations lack substance, content, and solutions. They are always too general, and many times the larger companies hide behind issues such as confidentiality of the data in order not to be specific. Such presentations have generated a notion that because most of the presenters are not domain experts, they are not comfortable to make technically specific presentations in front of domain experts. Contrary to the type of presentation that has just been mentioned and the associated publications that usually include vague statements, in this book we have a specific mission and have specific problems to solve, and therefore we present very specific solutions.

We are addressing an old problem in our industry using a completely new solution method. The problem we are planning to address is the development of all-inclusive, full-field reservoir models—models that can tell a comprehensive and yet cohesive story about how fluid flows in hydrocarbon reservoirs, models that can incorporate all the measurements in their machinery. Because measurements made in the field represent a large variety of characteristics at different scales, this task is very challenging. It is so challenging that many petroleum professionals who have been dealing with this problem for years (but using conventional and traditional techniques) are very skeptical that it can be solved.

For example, well logs look at the reservoir characteristics at a scale that is only inches away from the wellbore. Cores are taken at the scale of the wellbore and are then sampled at an even smaller scale so that they are looking at a very small portion of the rock (one or two inches in size) to examine fluid flow in a laboratory scale. On the other hand, seismic surveys measure the rock characteristics at a scale that is measured in tens of feet. Reconciling all these measurements into a seamless, single model is a giant task.

We have already come up with wonderful tools to address these problems (analytical and numerical modeling of fluid flow in the reservoir) that have provided our industry with valuable insight for decades. Nevertheless, the author cannot think of anyone (professionals, engineers, or geoscientists) who understands the depth of the problem being addressed in the day-to-day operations in our industry and is still under the illusion that we have completely, once and for all, solved the problem and therefore do not need any new inventions.

Therefore, for the purpose of this book, we define data-driven modeling as the process of applying artificial intelligence and data mining methods such as machine learning and pattern recognition in order to uncover hidden patterns in large data sets that represent fluid flow in porous media. Then, we include the patterns we have discovered into a cohesive and comprehensive full-field reservoir model with verifiable forecasting abilities that can be used to manage fields and their production.

2.1 Misunderstanding Data-Driven Reservoir Modeling

As machine learning and data-driven analytics become a prominent force in today's science and technology, it becomes difficult to undermine their inevitable role in the upstream oil and gas industry. This fact makes it hard for the "traditionalists" to completely dismiss the impact of such technologies in modern petroleum engineering. Therefore, either intentionally or (in some cases) unintentionally, the resistance towards the incorporation of this new technology in the oil and gas industry presents itself in a different manner.

In such cases, which the author has seen on several occasions, the outright rejection of artificial intelligence and data mining technology and its application to the upstream oil and gas industry stems from claiming that they are "nothing new." Obviously, this is the result of misunderstanding this new and game-changing technology. Such reactions to the application of artificial intelligence and data mining usually surface as a claim that it is not a "big deal," and is therefore not important. This is a technique that is used in order not to lose credibility or to be called a "traditionalist," which means being resistant to change and to new ideas.

This has given rise to a new group of traditional petroleum engineers (or earth scientists) who have become overnight experts in machine learning and data-driven analytics. They may (or may not) have read a paper or a book on the algorithms that are the foundation of neural networks and (maybe) have understood the mathematical structure of such techniques (as will be discussed in subsequent chapters, the mathematics behind machine learning is not complex and is easy to understand) and now feel compelled to join discussions on the topic (and sometimes even feel qualified to review related articles for journals and, of course, reject them) and dismiss the methods as a new way of doing old stuff that we have been exercising in the oil industry for decades; some even go as far as using decline curve analysis as an example and mention that data-driven reservoir modeling is not much more than an extension of decline curve analysis.

This class of traditional engineers and geoscientists, a large number of whom are found among our own reservoir engineers, reservoir modelers, and other engineers who are involved in numerical modeling of complex dynamic phenomena such as computational fluid dynamics, fails to understand that the incorporation of data analytics in modeling is a paradigm shift in modeling and not just using another technique.

This is not the difference between using finite element vs. finite difference in order to discretize the medium in which the fluid is flowing. It is not the difference between solving the system of equations implicitly or explicitly to arrive at a solution. It is not even the difference between solving the equations analytically vs. numerically. This difference can be traced back to how one views the reality. It is the philosophfical difference between Aristotelian vs. Platonic view of the world. That is why even some smart people in science and engineering still have trouble understanding the major differences between these technologies.

Chapter 3

Reservoir Modeling

Development of numerical reservoir simulation was a necessary response to an ever-growing understanding of the complexities associated with oil and gas production from hydrocarbon reservoirs. Although it had a modest beginning in terms of size and detail, it enjoyed reasonably fast growth. The computational requirements of numerical reservoir simulation made it a good candidate for mainframe computers and later for UNIX[15]-based systems. It was not until the mid-1990s to the late 1990s that a considerable increase in computational power of personal computers (PCs) opened new doors in the numerical reservoir simulation industry. Major vendors of reservoir simulators started deploying their software applications on PCs, and since that time use of mainframes and UNIX-based systems has been all but abandoned, and almost all the commercially available simulators are now PC-based.

As the computational power of personal desktop computers has increased in accordance with Moore's law,[16] so too has the level of detail that reservoir engineers and geoscientists have included in their numerical reservoir simulation analysis. Given the fact that discrete calculus is the foundation of numerical reservoir simulation and modeling,[17] the reservoir rock is divided into a large number of small cells, and the collection of all these small cells forms the geological (geocellular) model. Fluid flow through the interconnected small cells with the inclusion of wellbores as inner-boundary conditions and other rocks (with their fluid content, if any) surrounding the hydrocarbon reservoir as the outer-boundary condition forms the essence of what we know today as numerical reservoir simulation. Therefore, as the size of the reservoir increases, and the size of the cells being used to model the reservoir decreases (to include more details on reservoir and flow characteristics), the computational footprint of the reservoir simulation increases dramatically.

There has been a race between the computational power that is now offered through parallel processing of multiple central processing units (CPUs) and the number of gridblocks (cells) that is used to model complex reservoirs. Most of the numerical simulation models that are developed for real reservoirs include considerably more than a million cells. The numerical reservoir simulation model that was the subject of the author's most recent projects included an original geological model with more than 21 million gridblocks that had been upscaled to 2.5 million gridblocks for the dynamic model.

---

[15]UNIX is a family of multitasking, multiuser computer operating systems that derive from the original AT&T UNIX, developed in the 1970s at the Bell Labs research center by Ken Thompson, Dennis Ritchie, and others.

[16]The observation was made in 1965 by Gordon Moore, cofounder of Intel, that the number of transistors per square inch on integrated circuits had doubled every year ever since the integrated circuit was invented. Moore predicted that this trend would continue for the foreseeable future.

[17]Discrete calculus is used to turn the nonlinear, second-order, partial-differential equation that governs the fluid flow in porous media into a set of linear algebraic equations that are easily solved with well-known numerical techniques.

Even in a computational environment that includes tens of parallel CPUs, a single run of such a simulation model takes several hours. In some cases, when unconventional hydrocarbon reservoirs are being modeled [steam-assisted-gravity-drainage models (SAGD), or naturally fractured reservoirs that include a large number of induced fractures such as shale], the computational time of numerical models is measured in days and weeks. In other words, to achieve the accuracy and the precision that numerical reservoir simulation models provide, one must sacrifice speed and timely response to queries.

These descriptions of the computational footprint of numerical simulation models explain why it is quite understandable that many reservoir management teams do not have a favorable view of numerical reservoir simulation models as reservoir management tools. Reservoir managers need to make decisions in a timely manner, and they need tools that are accurate and fast.

1. *The reservoir management tool must be accurate.* It goes without saying that the quality of the decisions made by a reservoir manager is a function of the accuracy of the tool that is used to model the reservoir. *Accuracy* here means the degree of correctness of the responses generated by the model (tool) as a function of the details (field measurements—reservoir characteristics and operational conditions) that are involved in the analysis. For example, if decline curve analysis is the tool that is being used to make decisions, it is obvious that no reservoir characteristics and no operational constraints are used during the decision-making process. Therefore, the quality of the decisions is seriously compromised because the tools being used only approximate reality in order to achieve the required speed.

2. *The reservoir management tool must be fast.* Reservoir managers are required to make decisions for short-term, medium-term, and long-term planning of a reservoir. Furthermore, reservoir managers need to make decisions that take into account (a) multiple scenarios, and (b) uncertainties associated with many parameters involved in hydrocarbon production. Therefore, reservoir management tools need to have a small computational footprint so that they can accommodate thousands of model executions (scenarios). The large number of scenarios is then assessed in a short time period (minutes or hours, not days and weeks) to form the basis of reservoir management decisions. Large numbers of model runs (executions) are required to search large solution spaces and to quantify uncertainties.

Although they fulfill one of these two requirements (accuracy), numerical simulation models fail to accommodate the second requirement (speed) that must be met if they are to be an effective reservoir management tool. Furthermore, numerical reservoir simulation requires significant investment in time and manpower, which translates into serious budgetary considerations. The manpower must include teams of geologists, petrophysicists, geophysicists, and reservoir engineers to develop detailed static and dynamic models. Since the size of the numerical models is usually substantial, serious computational resources (clusters of parallel CPUs) are required for the execution of these models.

Once the dynamic model is developed, it almost never matches the production measurements from the field. Therefore, a long and tedious process is undertaken in order to condition the numerical simulator to match the observations (measurements) from the field. This is called history matching. The art and science of history matching should be the subject of a book, because there are very few books that specifically guide reservoir engineers on how to correctly perform history matching. Although it is easy to find a few chapters in some reservoir simulation books that explain the technical step-by-step mechanism of the history-matching process, it is hard to find books and writings that guide engineers on what to do and what not to do (which parameters are okay to change and which ones should be avoided and under what conditions, along with the consequences of some of the changes that one may make) while performing history matching. That is why reservoir managers sometimes are quite skeptical about numerical reservoir models, since not much is usually mentioned (explicitly) on how a history match is accomplished. The reason for this skepticism is not hard to understand because the fact that a model history has matched observed production does not necessarily mean that the history match has been achieved legitimately.

The general process of history matching a numerical reservoir simulation model carries within itself a major, though implicit, assumption. This assumption is so deep-seated that many reservoir engineers may not even accept it as an assumption and deal with it as a fact rather than an assumption. Nevertheless, the author believes that what is mentioned in the next paragraph is more an assumption than it is a fact. The assumption states as follows:

The governing equations for the fluid flow in porous media that is formulated in the numerical reservoir simulation software applications are unchangeable facts and are the ground truth that are applicable to the hydrocarbon reservoir being modeled; therefore, if our dynamic model does not match the field measurements (observed and measured production from wells), then the fault must be with the static (geological) model. The consequences of this assumption are that the geological (static) model must be modified until a match of the observed production can be achieved. This claim is further justified by claiming that the geological (static) model includes every cubic foot of the reservoir while our actual measurements have been performed only at discrete locations (wells). Furthermore, because the grid cells have been populated with reservoir parameters between wells by means of interpretations and/or geostatistics, they are susceptible to mistakes and need to be modified during the history-matching process. In other words, when we do not get a history match using our dynamic model (the inner working of which is the truth, 100% of the time), then it is the fault of those that have developed and delivered the static model and, therefore, it needs to be changed until we get a history match.

One should expect that the above assumption must have consequences on how we history match the numerical reservoir simulation model. One of these consequences should be that the actual measured values at the well locations should not be the subject of modification in order to get a history match. Nevertheless, changing even measured reservoir parameters at the well locations, in order to get a history match, is not an uncommon practice. That is why there is a notion in the industry that states: "The time required to get a history match for a numerical reservoir simulation model equals the deadline imposed by management." That is why it is hard to find "do's" and "don'ts" that are widely accepted among the practitioners. Even if many of the practitioners have their own "do's" and "don'ts," these rules are always applicable, as long as they help in getting a history match. If getting a history match proves to be a hard task and the deadline imposed by the management starts to get too close for comfort, then, maybe, practitioners start compromising on their own "do's" and "don'ts."

Perhaps one effective way to address these history-matching issues is for the team of reservoir engineers and the team of geoscientists who have developed the static model to meet regularly and discuss the difficulties faced during the history-matching process (this is not common because it can get very long and expensive). Then, the geoscientists should deal with some of the issues faced by the reservoir engineers and reservoir modelers during the history-matching process and should come up with new interpretations. This would require an extended amount of time and resources and flexible deadlines that are usually hard to come by, but it still does not provide any guarantees that it would solve the major and fundamental issues that are faced during the history-matching process.

Even when a history match is achieved, it is a well-known fact that it is not unique. Therefore, quantification of uncertainties associated with the geological (static) model is always an important issue to address. This requires large amounts of resources, and, in many cases, it is not performed comprehensively. Traditional proxy models that are currently used in the industry (simplified physics-based—reduced-order—models or statistics-based response surfaces) provide speed but fail to fulfill the accuracy requirements.

Smart proxies such as surrogate reservoir models (SRMs)[18] that are data-driven, highly accurate (without sacrificing the physics that has been modeled into the simulator or reducing the space and time resolution) and very fast. A single run of a smart proxy such as an SRM only takes a few seconds while its accuracy in replicating the response of the numerical simulation model is in the higher 90th percentiles. Therefore, the SRM, as a smart proxy, fulfills both requirements (speed and accuracy) of a reservoir management tool. However, development of a smart proxy is conditioned on having a functioning numerical reservoir simulation model.

The top-down model, on the other hand, provides a complete alternative to the numerical reservoir simulation model and can serve as an appropriate tool for reservoir management. The top-down model is a comprehensive, full-field, empirical reservoir model that does not modify the collection of the measured reservoir characteristics in order to history match multiple independent production variables. The remainder of this book is dedicated to the details of top-down modeling and how it achieves its objectives.

---

[18]Smart proxy modeling will be the subject of a separate book that would apply data-driven reservoir modeling to developing proxy models for numerical reservoir simulation models.

Chapter 4
Data-Driven Technologies

Data-driven technologies are a set of new techniques that rely on data rather than our current understanding of the physical phenomena in order to build models, solve problems, and make recommendations and help us make decisions. In the context of reservoir engineering and reservoir modeling, *data* are also referred to as *facts*. This is based on the assumption that the measurements made in the field actually represent facts about the reservoir and the state of the fluid flow in it. It is well understood that measurements include noise and that noise, as an integrated part of the collected data, can be handled.

4.1 Data Mining

Wikipedia (https://en.wikipedia.org/wiki/Data_mining) defines data mining as "the computational process of discovering patterns in large data sets involving methods at the intersection of artificial intelligence, machine learning, statistics, and database systems… The overall goal of the data mining process is to extract information from a data set and transform it into an understandable structure for further use." This definition explains the reason that the terms "data mining" and "knowledge discovery" are used interchangeably. Wikipedia further explains: "The actual data mining task is the automatic or semi-automatic analysis of large quantities of data to extract previously unknown, interesting patterns such as groups of data records (cluster analysis), unusual records (anomaly detection), and dependencies (association rule mining…)."

Before data-driven algorithms can be used, a target data set must be assembled. In data-driven reservoir modeling, we call this target data set the "spatio-temporal database." Because data-driven modeling can only uncover patterns that are actually present in the data, the spatio-temporal database must be large enough to contain such patterns while remaining concise enough to be mined within reasonable time. Preprocessing of the spatio-temporal database includes data cleaning (cleansing) to remove the records that contain erroneous data [erroneous data should be distinguished from simple noise that is present in any data that are handled (collected) by people] and records with missing data. Removing records with missing data can be a bit tricky and must be carried out with much care. This topic will be covered in more detail in the later sections of this book.

Data-driven reservoir-modeling development and analysis includes three phases. The first phase of the data-driven reservoir modeling, which is an exploratory analysis in nature, relates to the data mining. The second phase of data-driven reservoir modeling that is mainly concerned with the development (training, history matching, and validation) of a predictive reservoir model for the entire field is accomplished through artificial intelligence. The final phase of the data-driven reservoir modeling, which is the post-model analysis, includes a combination of both data mining and artificial intelligence. Since data mining is exploratory in nature, it mostly includes unsupervised algorithms. However, in the case of its application to reservoir engineering and reservoir modeling, some of the traditional unsupervised algorithms have been modified in order to incorporate reservoir engineering and geoscience domain expertise in the analysis.

4.2 Artificial Intelligence

Artificial intelligence has been called by different names. It has been referred to as "virtual intelligence," "computational intelligence," and "soft computing." Until recently there was not a uniformly acceptable name for this collection of analytic tools among the researchers and practitioners of the technology.[19] Today the term "artificial intelligence" is used most commonly as an umbrella term. This was not the case until recently, because "artificial intelligence" has historically referred to rule-based expert systems and was used synonymously with expert systems. Expert systems made many promises of delivering intelligent computers and programs, but these promises never materialized. Many believe that the term "soft computing" is the most appropriate term and that "virtual intelligence" is a subset of "soft computing." Although there is merit to this argument, we will continue using the term "artificial intelligence" throughout the book.

Artificial intelligence may be defined as a collection of new analytic tools that attempts to imitate life (Zurada et al. 1994). Artificial intelligence techniques exhibit an ability to learn and deal with new situations. Artificial neural networks, evolutionary programming, and fuzzy logic are among the main technologies that are classified as artificial intelligence. These techniques possess one or more attributes of "reason," such as generalization, discovery, association, and abstraction (Eberhart et al. 1996). In the last decade, artificial intelligence has matured to become a set of analytic tools that facilitate solving problems that were previously difficult or impossible to solve. The current effective use of artificial intelligence includes the integration of these tools, augmented by more-conventional tools, such as statistical analysis, to build sophisticated systems that can solve challenging problems.

These tools are now used in many different disciplines and have found their way into commercial products. Artificial intelligence is used in areas such as medical diagnosis, credit card fraud detection, bank loan approval, smart household appliances, subway systems, automatic transmissions, financial portfolio management, robot navigation systems, driverless cars, and many more. In the oil and gas industry, these tools have been used to solve problems related to pressure transient analysis, well log interpretation, reservoir characterization, and candidate well selection for stimulation, among other things.

Their use in building complete and comprehensive, full-field reservoir models is new and has been around for only a few years. This technology has tremendous potential because it can generate reservoir models in a fraction of the time and budget of traditional models while providing most of the capabilities that the traditional numerical model can provide. The fact that this technology is so young provides ample opportunities for researchers and practitioners in the field to enhance its capabilities.

4.3 Artificial Neural Networks

Much has been written about artificial neural networks. There are books and articles that can be accessed for better understanding of the topic and all relevant algorithms. The objective here is to provide a brief overview, sufficient to make the presentation of the topics in this book easy to follow. For more detail about this technology, it is highly recommended that the reader refer to the large number of books and articles that have been referenced here.

Neural network research can be traced back to a paper by McCulloch and Pitts (1943). In 1958, Frank Rosenblatt invented the Perceptron (Rosenblatt 1958). Rosenblatt proved that given linearly separable classes, a perceptron would, in a finite number of training trials, develop a weight vector

---

[19]There is a history behind the initial avoidance of the name "artificial intelligence" for many years, which has to do with the start of artificial intelligence as a purely rule-based system, before data-driven technologies were included in the collection of tools that are now called "artificial intelligence." Lack of success and the failure to penetrate the industrial market of purely rule-based artificial intelligence techniques in the 1960s and 1970s made many researchers and practitioners choose other names such as virtual intelligence, computational intelligence, soft computing, intelligent systems, and others to distinguish this new set of tools that was revitalized in the middle to late 1980s from its purely rule-based predecessor.

that would separate the classes (a pattern classification task). He also showed that his proof holds independent of the starting value of the weights. Around the same time, Widrow (1962) developed a similar network called Adeline. Minsky and Papert (1969) in a book called *Perceptrons* pointed out that the theorem obviously applies to those problems that the structure is capable of computing. They showed that elementary calculations such as simple "exclusive or" (XOR) problems cannot be solved by single-layer perceptrons. This was an important and game-changing event in the history of artificial neural networks.

Rosenblatt (1958) had also studied structures with more layers and believed that they could overcome the limitations of simple perceptrons. However, there was no learning algorithm known that could determine the weights necessary to implement a given calculation. Minskey and Papert doubted that one could be found and recommended that other approaches to artificial intelligence be pursued. Following this discussion, most of the computer science community left the neural network paradigm for 20 years (Hertz et al. 1991). Research and development, including all the available funding from state and federal sources, were funneled to rule-based expert systems. In the early to mid-1980s, John Hopfield was able to revive neural network research. Hopfield's efforts coincided with development of new learning algorithms such as backpropagation. The growth of neural network research and applications has been phenomenal since this revival.

4.3.1 Structure of a Neural Network. An artificial neural network is an information-processing system that has certain performance characteristics in common with biological neural networks. Therefore, it is appropriate to briefly describe a biological neural network before offering a detailed definition of artificial neural networks. All living organisms are made up of cells. The basic building blocks of the nervous system are nerve cells, called neurons. **Fig. 1** shows a schematic of two bipolar neurons. A typical neuron contains a cell body where the nucleus is located, dendrites, and an axon. Information in the form of a train of electrochemical pulses (signals) enters the cell body from the dendrites. According to the nature of this input, the neuron will activate in an excitatory or inhibitory fashion and provide an output that will travel through the axon and connect to other neurons, where it will become the input to the receiving neuron.

The point between two neurons in a neural pathway, where the termination of the axon of one neuron comes into close proximity with the cell body or dendrites of another, is called a synapse. The signals traveling from the first neuron initiate a train of electrochemical pulses (signals) in the second neuron.

It is estimated that the human brain contains on the order of 10 to 500 billion neurons (Rumelhart and McClelland 1986). These neurons are divided into modules, and each module contains approximately 500 neural networks (Stubbs 1988). Each network may contain approximately

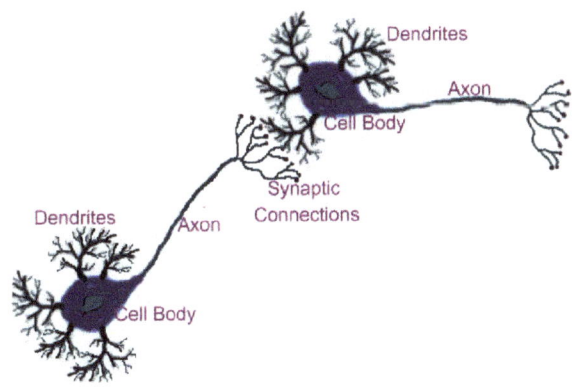

Fig. 1—Schematic of two bipolar neurons.

100,000 neurons in which each neuron is connected to hundreds to thousands of other neurons. This architecture is the main driving force behind the complex behavior that comes so natural to us. Simple tasks such as catching a ball, drinking a glass of water, or walking in a crowded market require so many complex and coordinated calculations that sophisticated computers are unable to undertake the task, and yet they are performed routinely by humans without a moment of thought.

This becomes even more interesting when one realizes that neurons in the human brain have a cycle time of approximately 10 to 100 milliseconds, while the cycle time of a typical desktop computer chip is measured in nanoseconds (approximately 10 million times faster than human brain). The human brain, although a million times slower than common desktop personal computers (PCs), can perform many tasks that are orders of magnitude faster than computers because of its massively parallel architecture.

Artificial neural networks are a rough approximation and simplified simulation of the process explained above. An artificial neural network can be defined as an information-processing system that has certain performance characteristics similar to biological neural networks. They have been developed as generalizations of mathematical models of human cognition or neural biology, based on these assumptions:

1. Information processing occurs in simple processing elements, called neurons.
2. Signals are passed between neurons over connection links.
3. Each connection link has an associated weight, which, in a typical neural network, multiplies the signal being transmitted.
4. Each neuron applies an activation function (usually nonlinear) to its net input to determine its output signal (Fausett 1994).

Fig. 2 is a schematic of a typical neuron (processing element) in an artificial neural network. Output from other neurons is multiplied by the weight of the connection and enters the neuron as input. Therefore an artificial neuron has many inputs and only one output. The inputs are summed and subsequently applied to the activation function, and the result is the output of the neuron.

4.3.2 Mechanics of Neural Network Operation. An artificial neural network is a collection of neurons that are arranged in specific formations. Neurons are grouped into layers. In a multilayer network, there are usually an input layer, one or more hidden layers, and an output layer. The number of neurons in the input layer corresponds to the number of parameters that are being presented to the network as input. The same is true for the output layer. It should be noted that neural network analysis is not limited to a single output and that neural networks can be trained to build data-driven models with multiple outputs. The neurons in the hidden layer or layers are mainly responsible for feature extraction.

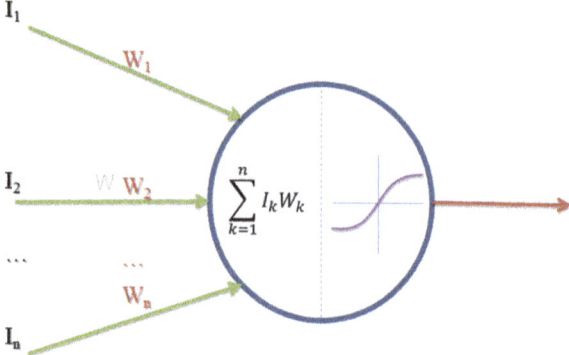

Fig. 2—Schematic of an artificial neuron or a processing element.

These neurons provide increased dimensionality and accommodate tasks such as classification and pattern recognition. **Fig. 3** is a schematic of a fully connected three-layer neural network. There are many kinds of neural networks. Neural network scientists and practitioners have provided different classifications. One of the most popular classifications is based on the training methods. Neural networks can be divided into two major categories: supervised and unsupervised neural networks. Unsupervised neural networks, also known as self-organizing maps, are mainly clustering and classification algorithms. They have been used in the oil and gas industry to interpret well logs and to identify lithology. They are called unsupervised simply because no feedback is provided to the network by the person that is training the neural network. The network is asked to classify the input vectors into groups and clusters. This requires a certain degree of redundancy in the input data and hence the notion that redundancy is knowledge (Barlow 1989).

Most of the practical and useful neural network applications in the upstream oil and gas industry are based on supervised training algorithms. During a supervised training process, both input and output are presented to the network to permit learning on a feedback basis. A specific architecture, topology, and training algorithm are selected, and the network is trained until it converges to an acceptable solution. During the training process, the neural network tries to converge to an internal representation of the system behavior. Although by definition neural networks are model-free function approximators, some people choose to call the trained network a neuromodel. In this book, our preferred terminology is "data-driven" model.

The connections correspond roughly to the axons and synapses in a biological system, and they provide a signal transmission pathway between the nodes. Several layers can be interconnected. The layer that receives the inputs is called the input layer. It typically performs no function other than the buffering of the input signal. In most cases, the calculations performed in this layer are a normalization of the input parameters, so that parameters such as porosity (which usually is represented in fractions) and initial pressure (which is usually in thousands of psi) would be treated equally by the neural network at the start of the training process. The network outputs are generated from the output layer. Any other layers are called hidden layers because they are internal to the network and have no direct contact with the external environment. Sometimes they are likened to a "black box" within the network system. However, just because they are not immediately visible does not mean that one cannot examine the function of those layers. There may be zero to several hidden layers in a neural network. In a fully connected network, every output from one layer is passed along to every node in the next layer.

In a typical neural data-processing procedure, the database is divided into three separate portions called training, calibration, and verification sets. The training set is used to develop the desired

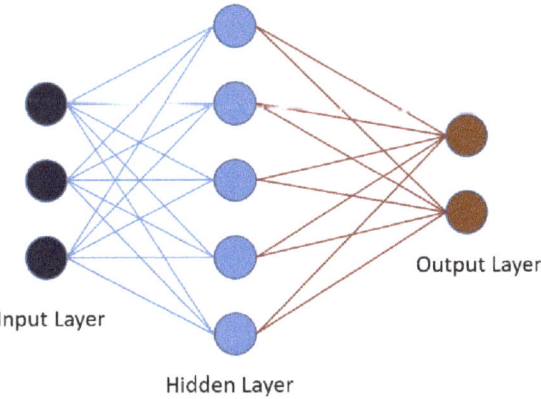

Fig. 3—Schematic of a three-layer neuron network.

network. In this process (depending on the training algorithm that is being used), the desired output in the training set is used to help the network adjust the weights between its neurons or processing elements. During the training process, the question arises about when to stop the training. How many times should the network go through the data in the training set in order to learn the system behavior? When should the training stop? These are legitimate questions, because a network can be overtrained. In the neural-network-related literature, overtraining is also referred to as *memorization*. Once the network memorizes a data set, it becomes incapable of generalization. It will fit the training data set quite accurately, but suffers in generalization. Performance of an overtrained neural network is similar to a complex nonlinear regression analysis.

Overtraining does not apply to some neural network algorithms simply because they are not trained using an iterative process. Memorization and overtraining are applicable to those networks that are historically among the most popular ones for engineering problem solving. These include backpropagation networks that use an iterative process during the training.

In order to avoid overtraining or memorization, it is a common practice to stop the training process every so often and apply the network to the calibration data set. Because the output of the calibration data set is not presented to the network (during the training), one can evaluate the network's generalization capabilities by how well it predicts the calibration set's output. Once the training process is completed successfully, the network is applied to the verification data set.

During the training process each artificial neuron (processing element) handles several basic functions. First, it evaluates input signals and determines the strength of each one. Second, it calculates a total for the combined input signals and compares that total to some threshold level. Finally, it determines what the output should be. The transformation of the input to output—within a neuron—takes place using an activation function. **Fig. 4** shows two of the commonly used activation (transfer) functions.

All the inputs come into a processing element (in the hidden layer) simultaneously. In response, the neuron either "fires" or "does not fire," depending on some threshold level. The neuron will be allowed a single output signal, just as in a biological neuron—many inputs, one output. In addition, just as things other than inputs affect real neurons, some networks provide a mechanism for other influences. Sometimes, this extra input is called a *bias term* or a *forcing term*. It could also be a *forgetting term*, when a system needs to unlearn something (McCord Nelson and Illingworth 1990).

Initially, each input is assigned a random relative weight (in some advanced applications—on the basis of the experience of the practitioner—the relative weight assigned initially may not be random). During the training process, the weight of the inputs is adjusted. The weight of the input represents the strength of its connection to the neuron in the next layer. The weight of the connection will affect the impact and the influence of that input. This is similar to the varying synaptic strengths of biological neurons. Some inputs are more important than others in the way they combine to produce an impact. Weights are adaptive coefficients within the network that determine the intensity of the input signal. The initial weight for a processing element can be modified in response to various inputs and according to the network's own rules for modification.

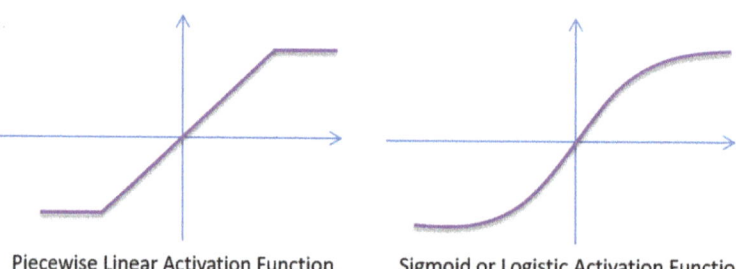

Fig. 4—**Commonly used activation functions in artificial neurons.**

Mathematically, we could look at the inputs and the weights on the inputs as vectors, such as I_1, $I_2, I_3, I_4 \ldots I_n$ for inputs and $W_1, W_2, W_3, W_4 \ldots W_n$ for weights. The total input signal is the dot, or inner, product of the two vectors. Geometrically, the inner product of two vectors can be considered a measure of their similarity. The inner product is at its maximum if the vectors point in the same direction. If the vectors point in opposite directions (180°), their inner product is at its minimum.

Signals coming into a neuron can be positive (excitatory) or negative (inhibitory). A positive input promotes the firing of the processing element, whereas a negative input tends to keep the processing element from firing. During the training process, some local memory can be attached to the processing element to store the results (weights) of previous computations. Training is accomplished by modification of the weights on a continuous basis until convergence is reached. The ability to change the weights allows the network to modify its behavior in response to its inputs: that is, to learn. For example, suppose a network is being trained to correctly calculate the initial production from a newly drilled well. At the early stages of the training, the neural network calculates initial production from the new well to be 150 BOPD, whereas the actual initial production is 1,000 BOPD. On successive iterations (training), connection weights that respond to an increase in initial production (the output of the neural network) are strengthened and those that respond to a decrease are weakened until they fall below the threshold level and the correct calculation of the initial production is achieved.

In the backpropagation algorithm (Haykin 2009) (one of the most commonly used supervised training algorithms in upstream oil and gas operations), the network output is compared with the desired output—which is part of the training data set—and the difference (error) is propagated backward through the network. During this backpropagation of error, the weights of the connections between neurons are adjusted. This process is continued in an iterative manner. The network converges when its output is within acceptable proximity of the desired output.

4.4 Fuzzy Logic

Today's science is based on Aristotle's crisp logic formed more than 2,000 years ago. The Aristotelian logic looks at the world in a bivalent manner, such as black and white, yes and no, and 0 and 1. Development of set theory in the late 19th century by the German mathematician Georg Cantor, which was based on Aristotle's bivalent logic, made this logic accessible to modern science. Then, the subsequent superimposition of probability theory made the bivalent logic reasonable and workable. Cantor's theory defines sets as a collection of definite, distinguishable objects. **Fig. 5** is a simple example of Cantor's set theory and its most common operations such as complement, intersection, and union.

The first work on vagueness dates back to the first decade of the 20th century, when the American philosopher Charles Sanders Peirce noted that "vagueness is no more to be done away with in the world of logic than friction in mechanics" (Freeman 1983). In the early 1920s, the Polish mathematician and logician Jan Łukasiewicz came up with three-valued logic and talked about many-valued or multivalued logic (Lukasiewicz 1963). In 1937, the quantum philosopher Max Black published a paper on vague sets (Black 1937). These scientists built the foundation upon which fuzzy logic was later developed.

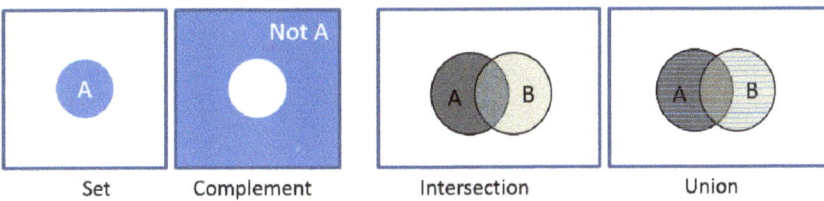

Fig. 5—Operations of conventional crisp sets.

Lotfi A. Zadeh is known to be the father of fuzzy logic. In 1965, while he was the chair of the Electrical Engineering Department at the University of California, Berkeley, he published his landmark paper "Fuzzy Sets" (Zadeh 1965). Zadeh developed many key concepts, including the membership values, and provided a comprehensive framework to apply the theory to many engineering and scientific problems. This framework included the classical operations for fuzzy sets, which comprise all the mathematical tools necessary to apply the fuzzy set theory to real-world problems.

Zadeh used the term "fuzzy" for the first time, and with that he provoked much opposition. He became a tireless spokesperson for the field. He was often harshly criticized. For example, R. E. Kalman said in a 1972 conference in Bordeaux, France, "Fuzzification is a kind of scientific permissiveness; it tends to result in socially appealing slogans unaccompanied by the discipline of hard scientific work" (Kosko 1993). It should be noted that Kalman is a former student of Zadeh's and the inventor of famous Kalman filter, a major statistical tool in electrical engineering that has also been used in computer-assisted history matching in the oil and gas industry. Despite all the adversity, fuzzy logic continued to flourish and has become a major force behind many advances in intelligent systems.

The term "fuzzy" carries a negative connotation in western culture. The term "fuzzy logic" seems to both misdirect attention and to celebrate mental fog (McNeill and Freiberger 1993). On the other hand, eastern culture embraces the concept of coexistence of contradictions as it appears in the Yin-Yang symbol. While Aristotelian logic preaches "A," *or* "Not A," Buddhism is all about "A," **_and_** "Not A"(**Fig. 6**).

Some believe that the tolerance of eastern culture for such ideas was the main reason behind the success of fuzzy logic in Japan. While fuzzy logic was being criticized in the United States, Japanese industries were busy building a multibillion dollar industry around it. By the late 1990s, the Japanese held more than 2,000 fuzzy-related patents. They have used fuzzy technology to build intelligent household appliances, such as washing machines and vacuum cleaners (Matsushita and Hitachi), rice cookers (Matsushita and Sanyo), air conditioners (Mitsubishi), and microwave ovens (Sharp, Sanyo, and Toshiba), to name a few. Matsushita used fuzzy technology to develop its digital image stabilizer for camcorders. Adaptive fuzzy systems (a hybrid with neural networks) are found in many Japanese cars. Nissan has patented a fuzzy automatic transmission that is now very popular with other makes such as Mitsubishi and Honda (Kosko 1993).

4.4.1 Fuzzy Set Theory. The human thought, reasoning, and decision-making process is not crisp. We use vague and imprecise words to explain our thoughts or communicate with one another. There is a contradiction between the imprecise and vague process of human reasoning, thinking, and decision making and the crisp, scientific reasoning of black-and-white computer algorithms and approaches. This contradiction has given rise to an impractical approach of using computers to assist

Fig. 6—The Yin-Yang symbol.

humans in the decision-making process, which has been the main reason behind the lack of success for conventional rule-based systems, also known as expert systems.[20] Expert systems as a technology started in the early 1950s and remained in the research laboratories and never broke through to the consumer market.

In essence, fuzzy logic provides the means to compute with words. Using fuzzy logic, experts no longer are forced to summarize their knowledge in a language that machines or computers can understand. What traditional expert systems failed to achieve finally became reality with the use of fuzzy expert systems. Fuzzy logic is composed of fuzzy sets, which are a way of representing nonstatistical uncertainty and approximate reasoning, which includes the operations used to make inferences (Eberhart et al. 1996).

Fuzzy set theory provides a means for representing uncertainty. Uncertainty usually results from either the random nature of events or the imprecision and ambiguity of information we have about the problem we are trying to solve. In a random process, the outcome of an event from among several possibilities is strictly the result of chance. When the uncertainty is a result of the randomness of events, probability theory is the proper tool to use. Observations and measurements can be used to resolve statistical or random uncertainty. For example, once a coin is tossed, no more random or statistical uncertainty remains.

Most uncertainties, especially when dealing with complex systems, are the result of a lack of information. The kind of uncertainty that is the outcome of the complexity of a system is the type of uncertainty that rises from imprecision, from our inability to perform adequate measurements, from a lack of knowledge, or from vagueness (like the fuzziness inherent in natural language). Fuzzy set theory is a powerful tool for modeling the kind of uncertainty associated with vagueness, with imprecision, and/or with a lack of information regarding a particular element of the problem at hand (Ross 1995).

Fuzzy logic achieves this important task through fuzzy sets. In crisp sets, an object either belongs to a set or it does not. In fuzzy sets, everything is a matter of degrees. Therefore, an object belongs to a set to a certain degree. For example, the price of oil today is USD 52.69/bbl.[21] Given the price of oil in the past few months, this price seems to be quite low.[22] But what is a low price for oil? A few months ago, the price of oil was approximately USD 100.00/bbl.

The International Energy Agency estimates that oil from shale formations costs from USD 50/bbl to USD 100/bbl to produce, compared with USD 10/bbl to USD 25/bbl for conventional supplies from the Middle East and North Africa (Arnsdorf 2014). Taking into account the costs to produce a barrel of oil in the United States, one can say that today's price is low.

If we arbitrarily decide that the cutoff for the "low" category of oil price is USD 55.00, and use crisp sets, then USD 55.01 is not a low oil price. However, imagine if this was the criterion that was used by oil company executives to make decisions. Imagine the number of layoffs that would be just around the corner. Fuzzy logic proposes the fuzzy sets for the price of oil shown in **Fig. 7**.

The most popular form of representing fuzzy set and membership information is as follows:

$$\mu_A(x) = m.$$

This representation provides the following information: the membership of x in fuzzy set A is m. According to the fuzzy sets shown in Fig. 7, when the price of oil is USD 120.00/bbl, it has a

---

[20]For decades, the term "artificial intelligence" was synonymous with rule-based expert systems as a result of historical events dating back to the early 1950s. This was the reason that, until the early the 2000s, scientists, professionals, and practitioners hesitated to use the term "artificial intelligence" to refer to their activities.

[21]This was the price of oil on Saturday, 3 January 2015.

[22]The price of oil plunged by approximately 50% during the last couple of months of 2014.

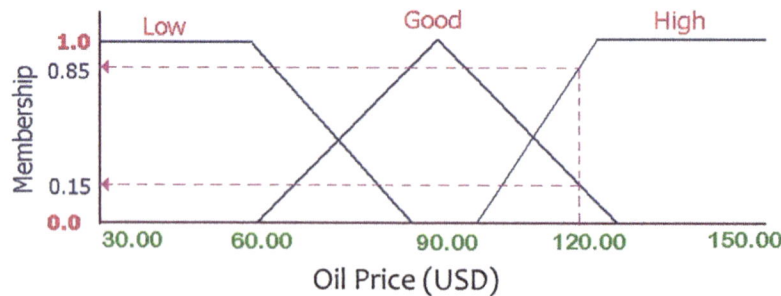

Fig. 7—Fuzzy sets representing the price of oil.

membership of 0.15 in the fuzzy set "Good" and a membership of 0.85 in the fuzzy set "High." Using the above notation to represent the oil price membership values,

$$\mu_{Good}(\text{USD } 20.00) = 0.15, \qquad \mu_{High}(\text{USD } 20.00) = 0.85.$$

4.4.2 Approximate Reasoning. When decisions are made on the basis of fuzzy linguistic variables ("Low," "Good," "High") using fuzzy set operators ("And," "Or"), the process is called "approximate reasoning." This process mimics the human expert's reasoning process much more realistically than the conventional expert systems. For example, if the objective is to build a fuzzy expert system to help us make a recommendation on enhanced recovery operations, then we can use the oil price and the company's proven reserves to make such a recommendation. Using the fuzzy sets in Fig. 7 for the oil price and the fuzzy sets in **Fig. 8** for the company's total proven reserves, we try to build a fuzzy system that can help us in making a recommendation on engaging in enhanced recovery operations, as shown in **Fig. 9**.

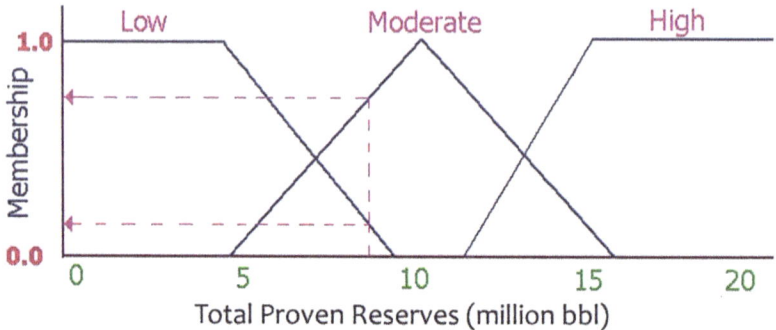

Fig. 8—Fuzzy sets representing the total proven reserves.

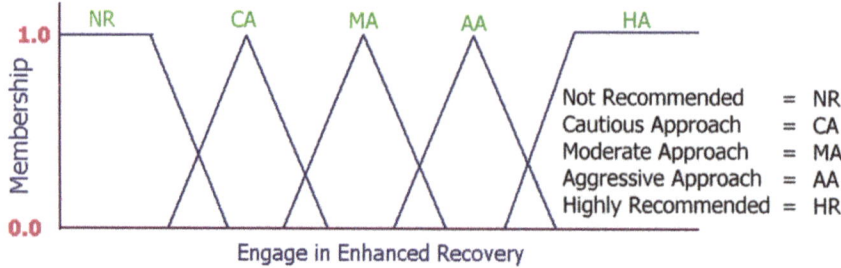

Fig. 9—Fuzzy sets representing the decision to engage in enhanced recovery.

The approximate reasoning is implemented through fuzzy rules. A fuzzy rule for the system being explained here can have the following form:

Rule No. 1: IF the **Price of Oil** is **"High"** AND the **Total Proven Reserves** of the company are **"Low,"** THEN **Engaging in Enhanced Recovery** practices is **"Highly Recommended."**

Because this fuzzy system comprises two variables and each of the variables consists of three fuzzy sets, the system will include nine fuzzy rules. These rules can be set up in a matrix, as shown in **Fig. 10**.

The abbreviations that appear in the matrix in Fig. 10 correspond to the fuzzy sets defined in Fig. 9. As one can conclude from the above example, the number of rules in a fuzzy system increases dramatically with addition of new variables. Adding one more variable consisting of three fuzzy sets to the above example increases the number of rules from 9 to 27. This is known as the "curse of dimensionality."

4.4.3 Fuzzy Inference. A complete fuzzy system includes a fuzzy inference engine. The fuzzy inference helps build fuzzy relations on the basis of the fuzzy rules that have been defined. During a fuzzy inference process, several fuzzy rules will be fired in parallel. The parallel rule firing, unlike the sequential evaluation of the rules in the conventional expert systems, is much closer to the human reasoning process. Unlike the sequential process in which some information contained in the variables may be overlooked because of the stepwise approach, the parallel firing of the rules allows consideration of all the information content simultaneously.

There are many different fuzzy inference methods. One of the popular methods is called Mamdani's inference method (Jamshidi et al. 1993). This inference method is demonstrated graphically in **Fig. 11**. In this figure, a case is considered when the price of oil is USD 120.00/bbl and the company has approximately 9 million bbl of proven reserves. The oil price is represented by its membership in fuzzy sets "Good" and "High," while the total proven reserves are represented in the fuzzy sets "Low" and "Moderate." As shown in Fig. 11, this causes four rules to be fired simultaneously.

According to Fig. 10, these rules are Nos. 1, 2, 4, and 5. In each rule, the fuzzy set operation "And," the intersection between the two input (antecedent) variables, is evaluated as the minimum and, consequently, is mapped on the corresponding output (consequent). The result of the inference is the collection of the different fuzzy sets of the output variable, as shown at the bottom of the figure.

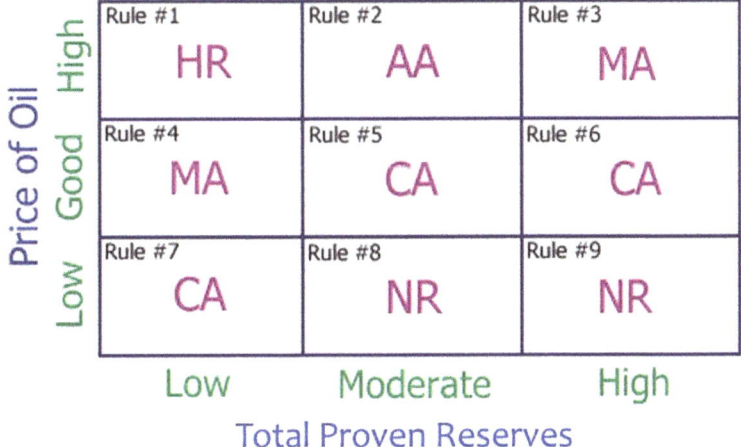

Fig. 10—Fuzzy rules for approximate reasoning.

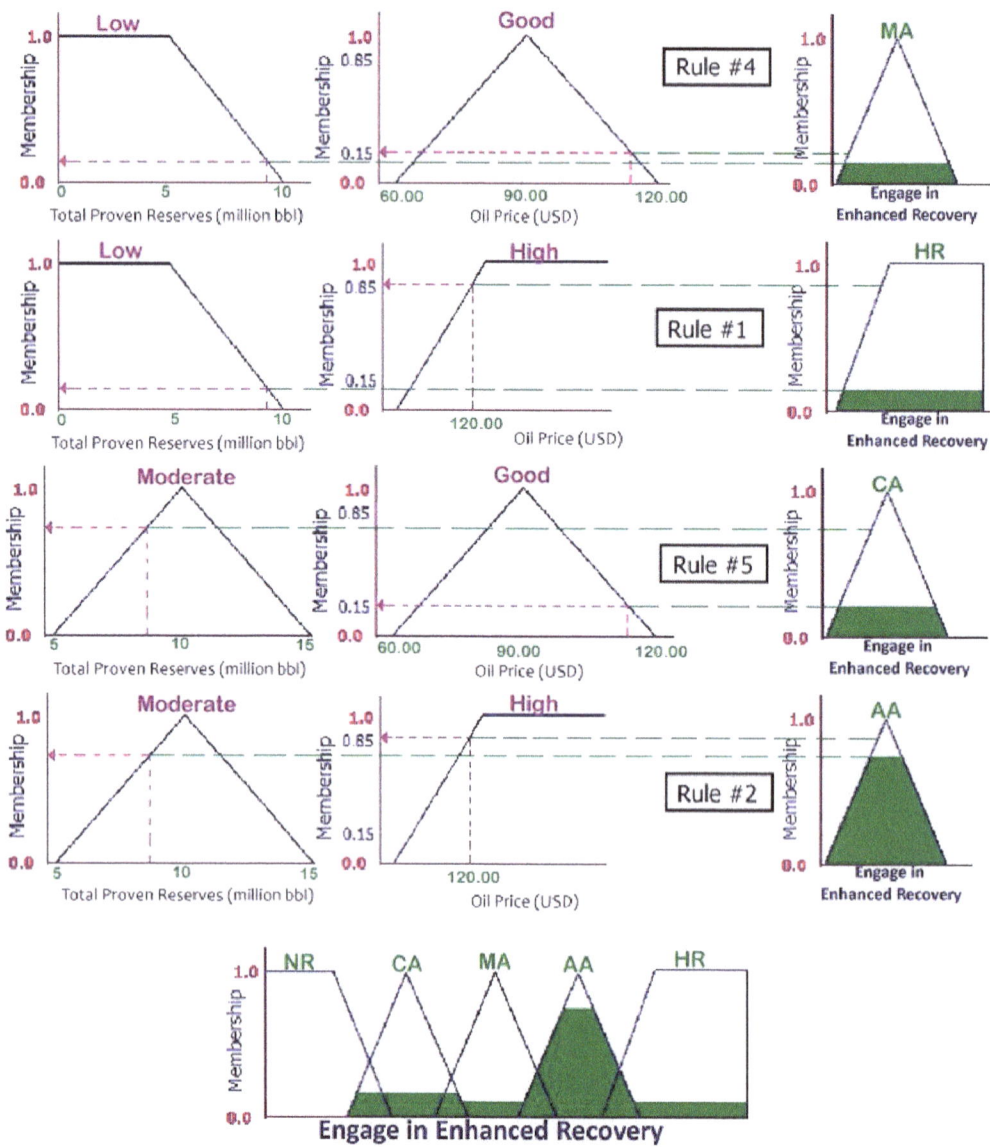

Fig. 11—Graphical representation of Mamdani's fuzzy inference.

A crisp value may be extracted from the result as mapped on the output fuzzy sets by defuzzifying the output. One of the most popular defuzzification procedures is to find the center of the mass of the shaded area in the output fuzzy sets.

Chapter 5

Pitfalls of Using Machine Learning in Reservoir Modeling

Rushing to evaluate the capabilities of a new technology as it starts to find its foothold in a new industry seems to be a common issue. Such efforts usually cut both ways. On the one hand, there are those that intentionally or unintentionally try to undermine the new technology and portray it as another fad that will fizzle away sooner or later, so they try to contribute to its quicker demise. On the other hand, there are those who with good intentions try to promote the technology, but present a superficial implementation of it and in some cases (not all) prepare the groundwork for those who will attack the technology for its lack of depth and minimal enhancements in the face of big promises.

Data-driven analytics and machine learning have not been an exception and have been the subject of such treatment. Because the author will be presenting a negative view of some published material, in order to make his point, he is hesitant to provide direct references to such publications. Instead the ideas that have been the essence of some of these publications will be discussed. Some of these ideas are considered to be incorrect when it comes to the application of machine learning to reservoir modeling, while others are considered to be less than efficient and need to be avoided for that reason.

One approach that should be avoided when using machine learning technologies in reservoir modeling[23] is to treat them as yet another curve-fitting technique. Treating machine learning as another statistics-based curve-fitting technique[24] shortchanges this technology and reduces it to a simple technique that does not promise much. Those that approach artificial intelligence and machine learning as a curve-fitting technique miss out on the fact that incorporation of this technology manifests a paradigm shift on how problems are approached and then solved. They attempt to use artificial intelligence and machine learning within the same paradigm that they have been following for the past several decades. Because this approach fails to understand the "learning process" that takes place in the human brain and then fails to grasp the idea that it is this "learning process" that is being mimicked in artificial intelligence and machine learning as an approach to problem solving, it cannot take full advantage of what artificial intelligence and machine learning have to offer.

---

[23]There are multiple applications of artificial neural networks to reservoir modeling in the literature that fall into this category. My guess is that these are mainly from individuals with good intentions but limited understanding of neural networks who became excited once they got access to a neural network software and tried to see what they could do.

[24]Please note that I did not use the term "Statistical Learning." Statistical Learning is a term that is used in other disciplines to refer to machine learning. It has a long and detailed history of agreements and disagreements between experts from disciplines such as artificial intelligence, computational intelligence, and statistics. There is a long and interesting history, including much disagreement between scientists of different disciplines, when it comes to these disciplines. This makes for interesting reading.

In order to effectively use artificial intelligence and machine learning to solve engineering problems, one needs to start thinking differently about problem solving. In this paradigm, the practitioner's job is to shape the architecture of the data such that it can be used as a teaching tool to an entity that has no prior knowledge of mathematics and physics. In data-driven reservoir modeling, we are teaching a machine geology and reservoir engineering, and the only tool available to accomplish this task is data. So we have to think long and hard, and think about the principles that the machine needs to learn in order to be able to model the fluid flow behavior in this system. For example, to be effective in building a data-driven reservoir model, one needs to ask

- How can I use the data available to me in order to teach the machine the principles of pressure interference between wells?
- How can I use the data available to me in order to teach the machine fluid displacement principles?
- How can I use the data available to me in order to teach the machine the impact of operational constraints on production and its distinction from the impact of reservoir characteristics?

Without taking such an approach to the application of artificial intelligence and machine learning to reservoir modeling, we cannot expect anything more than a superficial application of this technology that, as expected, will accomplish very little. Even good reservoir engineers that are first exposed to machine learning through some of these superficial approaches come away disappointed, quite justifiably.

Another approach that will leave the reader equally disappointed is usually performed by those who have a good understanding of statistics and machine learning, but have limited (or no) understanding of reservoir engineering and reservoir modeling. They usually attempt to collaborate with individuals with a good understanding of reservoir engineering and reservoir simulation and modeling, but what has resulted from these efforts has also been quite elementary and, for the potential capabilities of such sound technologies as artificial intelligence and machine learning, quite disappointing. Some papers in the literature that are good examples for this type of approach are those that present very simplified attempts at using artificial intelligence and machine learning to build proxy models for reservoir simulators that closely follow the train of thoughts used by statisticians in building response surfaces. They change parameters such as permeability multipliers, use experimental designs to generate several simulation runs, and try to use neural networks in order to build their models.

In summary the main pitfalls of using artificial intelligence and machine learning in reservoir modeling are

1. Not understanding the essence of the artificial intelligence and machine learning technology as a paradigm shift in problem solving and instead trying to use them as curve-fitting techniques
2. Not fully incorporating domain expertise (reservoir engineering and geoscience) when building models based on artificial intelligence and machine learning

The characteristics of artificial intelligence and machine learning are their capabilities in learning and discovery. They discover patterns that are usually hidden in the data, and they observe the system behavior through the collected data and learn the nuances of system behavior. Therefore, the data from a system should be prepared in a way that will accommodate these important characteristics and make the most of them. The main contribution of this book may be expressed as the realization of how artificial intelligence and machine learning should be used in reservoir engineering and reservoir modeling, and then the development of a strategy to implement this realization in real-life scenarios.

Chapter 6

Fact-Based Reservoir Management

This book is about data-driven reservoir modeling and its implementation by the author in the form of top-down modeling (TDM). It is important to put data-driven reservoir modeling and TDM in perspective from a reservoir management point of view. In this chapter, we visit the impact of this reservoir-modeling technology in reservoir management and call it data-driven reservoir management or fact-based reservoir management.

Reservoir management has been defined as use of financial, technological, and human resources to minimize capital investments and operating expenses and to maximize economic recovery of oil and gas from a reservoir. The purpose of reservoir management is to control operations in order to obtain the maximum possible economic recovery from a reservoir on the basis of facts, information, and knowledge (Thakur 1996). Historically, tools that have been successfully and effectively used in reservoir management integrate geology, petrophysics, geophysics, and petroleum engineering throughout the life cycle of a hydrocarbon asset. Through the use of technologies such as remote sensors and simulation modeling, reservoir management can improve production rates and increase the total amount of oil and gas recovered from a field (Chevron Corporation 2012).

Reservoir simulation/modeling has proved to be one of the most-effective instruments that can integrate data and expertise from a wide range of disciplines such as geology, petrophysics, geophysics, and reservoir and production engineering in order to model fluid flow in the reservoir. Once the reservoir simulation model is built for a particular reservoir (field), it is history matched using the pressure and production measurements from multiple wells in the asset, in order to tune geological understandings and to provide predictive capabilities on how to best operate and control the field under investigation.

Because no two hydrocarbon reservoirs are the same and each asset has its own unique geological characteristics and drive mechanisms, the art and science of reservoir simulation and modeling must be adapted to the uniqueness of each reservoir (field) in order to realistically model the past and predict the future of a hydrocarbon-producing reservoir. Although reservoir simulation/modeling remains one of the major contributors to reservoir management practices for the foreseeable future, its realistic application to reservoir management practices continues to face challenges.

These challenges are related to exploration of a very large solution space that is a required step during a reservoir management study. During the reservoir management process, it is necessary to generate, evaluate, and rank multiple potential scenarios to move forward as early as possible in the work flow. Furthermore, important practices such as quantification and analysis of uncertainties associated with the geological model as well as economic analysis and planning require a large number of scenarios to be generated and evaluated in order to assist the decision-making process. Performing reservoir management studies without such capabilities reduces the decision making to guess work (educated guess work nonetheless).

Another aspect of reservoir management is that it needs to be updated regularly. As new wells are drilled and produced (or injected into) and new measurements are made, whether they be production and injection volumes (daily or monthly), wellhead and bottomhole pressure values, new well tests, logs, or core analysis, more data and information become available. Availability of the new data provides a strong incentive to update the reservoir model and consequently the reservoir management strategies. This can result in developing more confidence in the original reservoir management plan, or modification of the original plan now that new facts are considered. Either way, frequent updating of the reservoir management plan requires the frequent updating of the reservoir model with the most recent facts and measurements. Furthermore, construction of a larger number of scenarios becomes necessary, from which the new or modified reservoir management plans are deduced. In any case, because reservoir management is an organic and regularly updated practice, all actions associated with it, including updating of the reservoir model and extensive exploration of its solution space as well as quantification of uncertainties associated with the model, need to be regularly performed during the life cycle of the asset.

Data-driven reservoir modeling, which is also referred to as "fact-based reservoir modeling," is a novel approach to building models representing fluid flow in hydrocarbon-producing porous media that are completely based on facts (field measurements). Instead of starting from first-principles physics, which results in partial-differential equations such as the diffusivity equation, data-driven reservoir modeling starts from field measurements such as well construction and configurations, well completion, well logs, core analysis, well tests, seismic, and production/injection history.

Contrary to the assessment of some critics, physics is not ignored during the data-driven reservoir modeling, when it is done properly, as is the case with TDM. Of course, when nondomain-experts initiate and/or manage such modeling exercises and practices, such concerns are valid.[25] In data-driven reservoir modeling, the role of physics is changed from that of being the architect of the governing equations to the role of providing philosophical infrastructure, guiding light, and the blueprint that provides the framework for the model development process. Data-driven reservoir modeling does not adhere to the dogma that all modeling of natural phenomena must start with physics to have credibility nor does it accept the notion of naïve statisticians that no physics or petroleum engineers are needed for modeling and that data can be the answer to all problems in the upstream exploration-and-production industry.

Data-driven reservoir modeling starts with the premise that data, especially in our discipline, carry information. Data collected during the drilling, reservoir, and production operations in an oil field include footprints, in space and time, of fluid flow in the porous media. If a large enough volume of such data is assembled in a proper fashion,[26] and appropriate tools are used in interpreting them by well-trained petroleum engineers, then there is a realistic chance of being able to build comprehensive and cohesive full-field models that not only will not violate the known physics, but will be able to shed light on complex and highly nonlinear behavior that might have been missed by a purely physics-based approach.

---

[25]It is an unfortunate fact that many operators, especially larger ones that have engaged in implementation of data-driven technologies in their operations, have started by handing over the entire data-driven operations to nondomain-experts (mostly statisticians) rather than putting a seasoned, but open-minded, reservoir or production engineer in charge. This usually results in a very long and tedious process before realizing any return on such investment and in the past has resulted in only minor advances and mediocre achievements. There are cases in which the patience of the management has been short-lived with such outcomes and the operation has been terminated, while in some others, it seems that a similar fate is currently looming. The unfortunate result seems to be to put the blame on the technology rather than on the decisions made for its implementation.

[26]This is a key notion and probably the most significant contribution of the author and his collaborators throughout the years. It is not enough to collect good data and to have the machine-learning tools to turn the final version of the data into models. The step between these two, which is the data preparation and the assimilation of that into a properly designed spatio-temporal database, and then the incorporation of the spatio-temporal database into a physically and geologically sound model are the most important steps in this process.

The reason should be clear to experienced (and consequently humble) reservoir engineers. Physics-based approaches are bound to be limited to our current understanding of the natural phenomenon, an understanding that continues to improve as a function of time. Our understanding of complexity of fluid flow in large and diverse combinations of porous media is far more advanced today than it was 40 years ago, and it is bound to advance even further in the next 40 years. But the facts that are intrinsic to (and the patterns that exist in a collection of) data are permanent and do not change with time. The question is this: Do we have the tools and the techniques, and the know-how, to extract these facts and to integrate them in the form of a comprehensive and cohesive model?

Two terms were used above to describe the quality of the data-driven model. These terms were "comprehensive" and "cohesive." Inspired by decades of experience and practice with numerical reservoir simulation models, the data-driven reservoir model must be comprehensive such that it would cover all aspects (as far as data availability permits[27]) of fluid flow in the porous medium for a given asset. In other words, a data-driven reservoir model must take into account all the wells in a given asset whether these wells are currently active or have been active in the past and now are shut-in; whether they are producers, injectors, or observer wells; whether the wells are vertical, slanted, or horizontal or a combination of all three. A comprehensive data-driven reservoir model must be able to model primary production, or waterflooding, or enhanced recovery.

The word "cohesive" refers to the interdependency of wells during the fluid flow and production/injection in the asset. A cohesive model allows for this interaction and actually models the impact of offset producers and injectors on production from every well in the field.

The first and the most comprehensive data-driven reservoir-modeling technology developed by reservoir engineers (not mathematicians or statisticians) is TDM. TDM was introduced a few years ago and has enjoyed continuous research and development to enhance its capabilities ever since. Several international oil companies, national oil companies, and independents have successfully adopted this technology and are benefiting from its results.

Data-driven reservoir management is a reservoir management process in which the key models that are used to make critical decisions are data-driven models. The main advantages of data-driven reservoir models are these:

1. They are fact-based and include minimal interpretations and human biases.
2. The time required for their development (training, calibration, and validation of the predictive models) is a small fraction of the time required for a comprehensive numerical simulation model.[28]
3. They have a small computational footprint that accommodates a large number of scenarios to be investigated in a relatively short period of time.
4. They are easy to update on a regular basis.
5. Finally, they are organic and evergreen, meaning that they improve with time and training and with new data and the lessons learned from experience.

6.1 Empirical Models in the E&P Industry

Developing empirical models has a rich history in the oil industry. This is because empirical models tend to be simpler than analytical and/or numerical models. The word "empirical" means that the solution generated is based on, concerned with, or verifiable by observation or experience rather than through theory or pure logic. As such, empirical models are developed using existing data and measurements, which are overwhelmingly production and/or injection data. Therefore, there is not much need to undergo more expense to make measurements that are required by analytical and

---

[27]This is an important issue because in data-driven modeling we are limited to the physics that is historically present in the operations and is captured by the data. More on this topic will be covered in the section on the limitations of this technology.

[28]Development of a top-down model is measured in weeks not years.

numerical techniques, such as porosity, permeability, compressibility, and so on. Furthermore, in cases where data regarding well construction and trajectory, completion characteristics, reservoir data (well logs and/or core data), and operational constraints are already available and can be readily used or incorporated in the model, most empirical models are not set up such that they can make any use of them.

The most common empirical model that has been used historically in the oil and gas industry is decline curve analysis. Another empirical model that was developed decades ago and has recently been revived is capacitance/resistance modeling (CRM). A quick look at these two techniques from the point of view of data-driven reservoir (well) models will be useful.

6.1.1 Decline Curve Analysis. Decline curve analysis was first introduced by Arps in the 1940s (Arps 1945). This is probably the most commonly used technique to analyze production from oil and gas wells. It is based on the observation that production from oil and gas wells declines as a function of time, and with visual graphical techniques, the decline can be characterized and be used to forecast the future behavior of the well. Although empirical in nature, there are no serious published documents that claim decline curve analysis to be a substitute for reservoir model of any kind. Nevertheless, as the most popular empirical technique in the oil industry, a short review of this technology is necessary here.

The reason for the extensive use of the decline curve in the industry has to do with the fact that (a) it only needs production data for its utility and (b) its simplicity of implementation. Because operators measure their production in order to have a record of their sales, chances are that production data are one piece of information that they keep track of. Therefore, if the production data are all that is needed to analyze the productivity and eventual life of an oil- and/or gas-producing well, then, the attraction of the technique becomes obvious.

However, as expected, limitations of data and information bring along limitations of accuracy and precision in analysis, and therefore in forecast. The limitations of decline curve analysis are well known in the industry and have been discussed and documented in detail in multiple books and scholarly articles (Agarwal et al. 1998). Among these limitations are lack of sensitivity of decline curve analysis to some of the most important characteristics that control production from any well and reservoir, such as reservoir characteristics and operational constraints.

Furthermore, decline curve analyses are developed for and are usually applied to single wells. This has not stopped us from applying the technology to multiple wells (groups of wells) and entire fields. Needless to say, in such cases, the result cannot be more than a first pass and a bird's-eye-view analysis of the production characteristics.

With time, several modifications of the decline curve analysis have surfaced, and most recently, with the emergence of unconventional resources such as shale, more-specific versions of decline curves have appeared in order to accommodate the peculiarities of the production from wells that produce from this source rock (Duong 2011; Lee and Sidle 2010; Ilk et al. 2010).

6.1.2 Capacitance/Resistance Modeling. Introduction of CRM in the oil and gas industry is credited to W. A. Bruce in the 1940s (Bruce 1943). This technology has recently been revived by Lake et al. (Sayarpour et al. 2009). The main premise and hypothesis of this technology is that characteristics of a reservoir can be inferred from analyzing production and injection data only. The main limitation that CRM shares with decline curve analysis is that, again, some of the most important characteristics that control production from any well and reservoir, such as reservoir characteristics and operational constraints, are absent from its analyses.

The argument in CRM is that production and injection data inherently have within them all the reservoir characteristics and operational constraints, which is true. However, once the model is checked for consistency with past production, one may not be able to analyze changes in the operational constraints, or modifications of flow paths resulting from new operational conditions or drilling activities in the future.

Chapter 7

Top-Down Modeling

To efficiently develop and operate a petroleum reservoir, it is important to have a model. Currently, numerical reservoir simulation is the accepted and widely used technology for this purpose. Data-driven reservoir modeling, also known as top-down modeling (TDM), is an alternative (or a complement) to numerical simulation. TDM uses the Big Data solution (artificial intelligence, machine learning, and data mining) in order to develop (train, calibrate, and validate) full-field reservoir models that are based on field measurements (facts) rather than mathematical formulation of our current understanding of the physics of the fluid flow through porous media.

There are empirical technologies that forecast production, such as decline curve analysis and capacitance/resistance modeling (CRM), that were briefly discussed in Chapter 6. The main problem with these technologies is that they do not make use of a large amount of data that are usually available in mature fields.

TDM integrates all available field measurements, such as well locations, well construction and trajectories, completions and stimulations, well logs, core data, well tests, seismic, and production/injection history (including wellhead pressure and choke setting) into a cohesive, comprehensive, full-field reservoir model using machine learning and pattern recognition. In other words, TDM presents a full-field model within which production [including gas/oil ration (GOR) and water cut (WC)] is conditioned to all reservoir characteristics and operational constraints that are measured. TDM matches the historical production (and is validated through blind history matching) and is capable of forecasting a field's future behavior.

The novelty of TDM stems from the fact that it is a complete departure from traditional approaches to reservoir modeling. As a fact-based, data-driven, reservoir modeling technology, TDM manifests a paradigm shift in how reservoir engineers and geoscientists model fluid flow through porous media. In this new paradigm, our current understanding of the physics and the geology in a given reservoir is supplemented with facts (data/field measurements) as the foundation of the model. This characteristic of TDM makes it a viable modeling technology for unconventional resources such as shale where the physics of the hydrocarbon production (in the presence of massive hydraulic fractures) is not yet well understood.

The most important characteristic of TDM is its practicality. Once developed and validated, TDM has almost all the functionalities that reservoir modelers have come to expect from a full-field reservoir simulator (model) that operates on an individual-well basis. It uses all the available data from a mature field and constructs a comprehensive full-field reservoir model that matches past performance of all the wells in the field and forecasts their future behavior while taking into account the interactivity of all the wells in the field. TDM provides the means to perform a large number of analyses on the field and answer some crucial questions. The small computational footprint of TDM accommodates important reservoir-modeling tasks such as quantification of uncertainties and field development planning that require millions of simulation (model) runs in order to provide meaningful results. Since the execution of a developed top-down model takes only seconds or minutes, performing such tasks becomes quite practical.

Although TDM is an empirical modeling technology, it goes far beyond pure statistical analysis of the available data, since usually the statistical analysis of the available data from a reservoir is hardly ever more than hindsight. TDM builds a bridge between the physics of the fluid flow in the porous media and the available field measurements that realistically represent the fluid flow behavior in the specific reservoir being modeled.

Traditional numerical reservoir simulation and modeling have become the industry standard for full-field modeling, analysis, and decision making in prolific assets. They are used in all phases of field development in the oil and gas industry. The routine of numerical simulation studies calls for integration of static and dynamic measurements into a reservoir model that has been formulated on the basis of our current understanding of fluid flow in porous media, generally in what is known as the diffusivity equation. Numerical solution of the diffusivity equation (and other physics such as conservation of energy, when appropriate) is then applied in the context of an interpreted geological model.

Numerical reservoir simulation is a bottom-up approach. It starts with the rock through building a geological (geocellular or static) model of the reservoir. Seismic information, when available, is used to delineate the volume of the rock that is being modeled to identify different existing layers as well as major faults or other discontinuities in the reservoir rock. Using modeling and geostatistical manipulation of the data, the geocellular model is populated with the best available (including interpretations) geological and petrophysical information. Engineering fluid-flow principles are added, and the resulting nonlinear partial-differential equations are solved numerically to arrive at a dynamic reservoir model.

The dynamic reservoir model is calibrated using the production history of multiple wells by modification of several of the parameters involved in the geological model[29] in a process called history matching, and the final history-matched model is used in predictive mode in order to strategize field development and improve recovery.

Some of the major characteristics of numerical reservoir simulation and modeling are

1. It takes a significant investment (time and money) to develop a geological (geocellular, static) model to serve as the foundation of the reservoir simulation model.
2. The high-resolution geological model is upscaled to a reasonable size (determined by the availability of computing resources in the operating company using the model) to be handled during dynamic modeling.
3. The initial (base) flow model is history matched to conform to the observed dynamic field measurements.
4. Development and history matching of a numerical reservoir simulation model are not trivial processes and require reservoir engineers and modelers and geoscientists with significant amounts of experience.
5. Numerical reservoir simulation and modeling are expensive and time-consuming endeavors.
6. Many uncertainties are associated with the results produced by a numerical simulation model.
7. A prolific asset is required in order to justify the significant investment (capital and manpower) required for a reservoir simulation model.

TDM presents an alternative and/or a complement to the numerical reservoir simulation and modeling. TDM is an innovative integration of several disciplines to build an empirical reservoir model.

---

[29]It is interesting to note that because reservoir engineers are usually the ones that perform the history matching, modifying the geological model in order to achieve a production history match comes naturally to them. This practice has hardly ever been questioned. For example, why is it that we have no problem modifying the characteristics of the geocellular model but never question the fluid-flow equations that are, at least, equally responsible for a history match (or lack of it)?

The technologies that are integrated in order to create a top-down model include reservoir engineering, reservoir modeling, statistical analysis, and advanced data-driven analytics that include artificial intelligence, machine learning, data mining, and pattern recognition.

The aim of TDM is to serve in some cases as an alternative and in other cases as a complement to traditional numerical reservoir simulation and modeling. TDM can be an alternative to numerical reservoir simulation when the asset being modeled is not prolific enough to warrant the investment required by numerical simulation and modeling, or when a quick solution is required and the management team cannot wait years for a model to be developed. Furthermore, TDM may be a complement to the numerical reservoir simulation when a numerical reservoir simulation model for the asset already exists and management wants to get a completely different perspective on the production operation in the asset, and in a short period of time.

When it is compared to numerical reservoir simulation and modeling, TDM takes quite a different and independent approach to full-field reservoir modeling. The most important distinguishing characteristics of TDM that distinguishes it from numerical reservoir simulation are

1. It does not assume that we have all the information necessary to build a fully representative geological model of the asset, understanding all the underlying complexities and the geological behavior.[30]
2. It does not assume that we fully understand and are able to formulate (using physics and mathematics) all the complexities, nuances, and intricacies of the fluid flow through porous media for the asset being modeled.
3. Therefore, it attempts to build a representative model of the field (as much as possible) by giving maximum weight to all available data (field measurements).

Please note that the principles of the physics and geology and our interpretation of their applicability to the given field are not ignored during the development of a top-down model. These interpretations are used in a different fashion. Instead of using these understandings and interpretations to form the fabric of our model, in TDM, we use them to guide our construction of the model and, once completed, to interrogate the model results.

TDM is a physics-based reservoir model. However, the incorporation of the physics in TDM is quite untraditional. Reservoir characteristics and geological aspects are incorporated in the model as much as they can be measured, while interpretations are intentionally left out during model development. Physical and geological understandings and interpretations are extensively used during the analysis of model results. Although physical principles of fluid flow through porous media are not explicitly (mathematically) formulated during the development of a top-down model, successful development of such a model is almost impossible without solid understanding and experience in reservoir engineering and geosciences.

Furthermore, there is no doubt that while constructing a top-down model, we are building a proxy of the reality. However, it must be noted that numerical simulation and modeling is also a proxy of the reality, without its ever being explicitly acknowledged. Just because we have formulated the details of a numerical simulation and are able to explicitly explain all the little details about its functionality, does not make it a realistic physical (and, therefore, not a proxy) model. Numerical simulation is always an approximation and thus a proxy of the reality. This seems to be a fact that many times is overlooked by those who are not well experienced in the art and science of numerical reservoir simulation and modeling, but who are fascinated by its well-behaved performance.

---

[30]TDM presents the best empirical model that can be built with the existing field measurements at any given time. As the amount of available information increases with time, the top-down model can be updated to include the new data and information.

In TDM, the integration of the technologies that were named above forms the foundation of a comprehensive spatio-temporal database.[31] The reason this collection of information is named a spatio-temporal database is a reflection of the use of the diffusivity equation as the blueprint and the foundation for the top-down model. Furthermore, it emphasizes the fact that the formulation of the top-down model represents the fluid flow through porous media, in space (well locations) and time (production and injection history). This database represents an extensive set of snapshots of the state of the fluid flow in the formation in space and time.

It is expected that all the characteristics that govern the complexities of fluid flow in the reservoir will be captured in this extensive spatio-temporal database. The extent to which the spatio-temporal database covers the activities in the field determines the limitations and/or the capabilities of the top-down model and its applicability.

The spatio-temporal database includes, but is not limited to, data from the field (field measurements) that cover the following parameters:

1. Well location (latitude, longitude, true vertical depth, measured depth)
2. Well construction and trajectory (e.g., vertical/slanted/horizontal, inclination, azimuth)
3. Well completion (e.g., openhole vs. cased and perforated, recompletion, squeeze-offs)
4. Well stimulation (e.g., acid jobs, workovers, hydraulic fracturing)
5. Well logs (e.g., gamma ray, density, resistivity, sonic)
6. Formation evaluation (e.g., formation tops, gross thickness, net to gross, porosity, initial saturation)
7. Core analysis (e.g., permeability, relative permeability, capillary pressure)
8. Well tests
9. Seismic
10. Operational constraints (e.g., wellhead pressure, choke size, shut-in durations, artificial lift)
11. Production and injection rates (oil, water, gas; GOR and WC)

As can be deduced from this list, TDM is far more than statistical analyses of production data to find simple correlations between injection into and production from wells. TDM is an implementation of a comprehensive and integrated set of diverse technologies that converge to build a comprehensive and well-behaved reservoir model. It is comprehensive because it can model production[32] from every individual well in a field as well as static pressure and saturation distributions throughout the field.[33] TDM integrates multiple technologies to accomplish this task. To develop TDM, a thorough and extensive understanding of reservoir engineering and reservoir modeling that is integrated with deep understanding of machine learning (how machines learn and how they should be presented with the knowledge to learn from data and later replicate system functionalities) and pattern recognition is required. One without the other is simply not enough.

TDM integrates all that is relevant in the production of the fluids from an asset into a comprehensive, full-field reservoir model. It seeks to integrate the data gathered from all these sources into a complete database that would understand and honor the differences that exist in the scale and in the nature and the sources from which the data are gathered (generated).[34] Furthermore, the spatio-temporal database must be set up in such a manner that it can represent the intricate details that are

---

[31]Given its importance, this database and how it is constructed are covered further in the following sections.

[32]Rate may be the model output when the wellhead or bottomhole pressure are the constraints, or vice versa.

[33]Obviously, some field measurements of these parameters are required to start the modeling process.

[34]For example, core analyses are made on rock samples that are 1 to 2 in. from where the well is drilled, well logs represent characteristics that are measured no more than 6 in. away from the wellbore, seismic surveys represent samples of the reservoir that are measured in feet, and well tests represent behavior that represents flow behavior anywhere from several feet to hundreds of feet away from the wellbore (depending on the type of well test performed).

crucial to modeling and history matching production of hydrocarbon from an asset. Examples of such intricate but crucial details are

1. Wells communicate with their offset wells (producer/producer as well as injector/producer).
2. Production from wells is related to how they are operated.
3. Wellbores of different character represent different wellhead pressures for similarly flowing bottomhole pressures.
4. Reservoir characteristics between two wells play an important role in how these wells communicate.
5. The same well, if completed differently, will produce differently.

Furthermore, there is some seemingly very obvious and common reservoir engineering knowledge (common sense) that is taken for granted by reservoir engineers that needs to be communicated to the computer. Such common knowledge is sometimes the hardest thing to teach a machine. For example teaching a computer that "when a well is shut-in, there will be no production," or "when a well is shut-in and has no production, the static pressure in its vicinity will increase with time" sound very obvious to a reservoir engineer, but it is not so straightforward to teach these to a computer.

The spatio-temporal database includes information regarding two major data types that represent fluid flow in porous media: the static and the dynamic data. The static data, as the name suggests, are the data that are not expected to change with time (such as formation top or formation thickness), while the dynamic data are those that are time-dependent (such as number of days of production in a month or wellhead pressure). Furthermore, the spatio-temporal database must include relevant data regarding the offset production or injection wells. Each well must be paired with a number of its closest offset wells,[35] because static and dynamic characteristics of each offset well directly impact the behavior of the well that is considered during modeling (also known as the focal well). Also it must be remembered that each well plays multiple roles in a spatio-temporal database. At times it is the focus of the analysis, while at other times it is an offset (and therefore the support) for other (usually multiple) wells.

Upon completing the assimilation of the spatio-temporal database (details of which will be covered in subsequent sections and chapters), which proves to be one of the most important steps in development of a top-down model, training and history matching of the top-down model are performed simultaneously. It must be noted that a rigorous blind history-matching scheme (validation) is required in this step of the process to ensure the robustness of the model. The blind history matching is a process through which certain parts of the production history (usually the tail end) are intentionally left out of the model development and the history-matching process. This portion of the production history is used solely for validation purposes.

Once the training and history-matching steps of the top-down model are completed, the model is deployed in the forecast mode in order to predict the production (oil production, GOR, and WC) for every individual well in the asset. The predictions made by the top-down model are compared with the production history that was left out of the modeling process in order to judge the validity (predictive capability) of the model. The top-down model accurately models a mature hydrocarbon field and successfully forecasts its future production behavior on a well-by-well basis.

The outcomes of TDM are oil production, GOR, and WC of existing wells as well as field development planning and optimum locations for infill drilling. When TDM is used to identify the communication between wells, it generates a map of reservoir conductivity that is defined as a composite variable that includes multiple geologic features and rock characteristics that contribute to fluid flow

---

[35]The number of offset wells that need to be considered is a function of reservoir characteristics and usually is not the same for all reservoirs. The more conductive (high permeability) a reservoir is, the higher would be the number of offset wells that need to be considered.

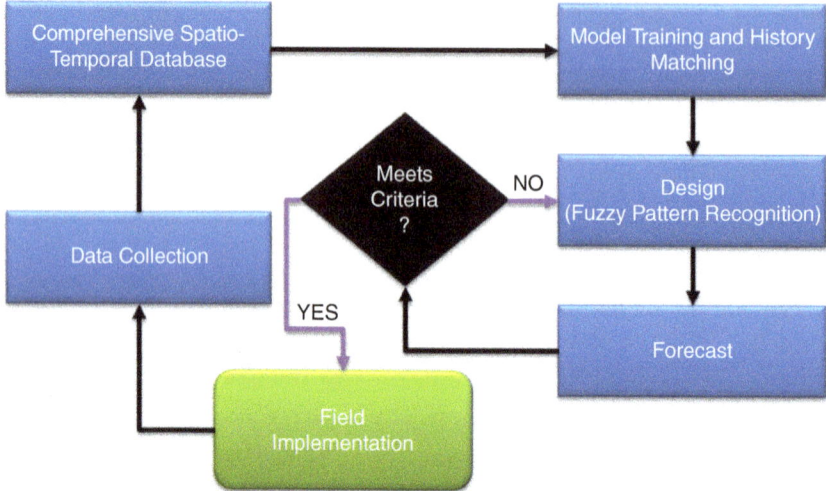

Fig. 12—A high-level and simplified flow chart for reservoir management using TDM.

in the reservoir. This is accomplished by deconvolving the changes in production behavior that are a result of operational issues from those that may be attributed to reservoir characteristics.

Upon completion of the top-down model, field development strategies are planned and tested (analyzed) using the history-matched model (in predictive/forecast mode). The plans are tested to see if they fulfill the reservoir management objectives. This process is repeated, iteratively (by planning new wells to be drilled and predicting their performance), until the reservoir management objectives are met. Of course, this process can be automated using optimization algorithms. Once the objective is accomplished, the plan is forwarded to operations for implementation.

The top-down model is an evergreen model, because it can easily be incorporated into a closed-loop process that can be updated and retrained using new data as they become available. The TDM work flow (part of which is shown in **Fig. 12**) includes the following steps:

1. Identifying the objectives of the project
2. Understanding the reservoir and its history
3. Data collection, management, and quality control
4. Assimilation of the spatio-temporal database
5. Data mining and pattern recognition to better understand the assimilated spatio-temporal database
6. Determination of the number of data-driven models required for the top-down model[36]
7. Input/output selection for each of the data-driven models
8. Training and history matching the data-driven models
9. Validating the data-driven models
10. Integration of the data-driven models into the final top-down model
11. Post-modeling analysis using the top-down model

Once the data are collected, quality controlled, and assimilated into the said spatio-temporal database, they are processed using a set of machine-learning algorithms in order to generate a complete and cohesive model of fluid flow in the entire reservoir. This is accomplished by using a set of

---

[36]This item will be covered in more detail in the next sections.

discrete modeling techniques to generate predictive models of well behavior, followed by intelligent agents that integrate the discrete models into a cohesive model of the reservoir as a whole.

The top-down, intelligent reservoir model is validated using the most recent data from existing wells and/or a set of wells that have recently been drilled in the field. The validated model is then used for field development strategies to improve and enhance hydrocarbon recovery.

TDM has been validated using synthetic cases (Mata et al. 2007; Gomez et al. 2009). In these studies, in order to validate the applicability of TDM in representing fluid flow in porous media, numerical reservoir simulation models were developed and treated as the ground truth. The numerical models were used to generate the type of data that are usually available from a real case. The generated data were used to predict the behavior of the numerical reservoir model. In other words, in these studies the objective was to see if the top-down model can understand and then reproduce the physics (and the geology) that was used to build the reservoir models.

Multiple applications of TDM applying to actual assets, both conventional (Gaskari et al. 2007; Mohaghegh and Gaskari 2009; Kalantari-Dahaghi et al. 2010; Khazaeni and Mohaghegh 2011; Mohaghegh 2011; Maysami et al. 2013) and unconventional (Grujic et al. 2010; Zargari and Mohaghegh 2010; Esmaili et al. 2012; Kalantari-Dahaghi and Mohaghegh 2011; Mohaghegh et al. 2012; Haghighat et al. 2014), have been published, extensively. Some of these applications have used only publicly available data, while others (that have been far more successful) have used more-detailed data provided by the operator.

7.1 Components of a Top-Down Model

All top-down models are not created equal. The specific structure of a top-down model is usually determined by three factors: (1) the main objective of the project, (2) the size and the age of the field being modeled, and (3) the quality and quantity of the data that are available. However, there is a main, general structure for all top-down models. This main, general structure is shown in **Fig. 13**.

The main, general structure of a top-down model always includes a spatio-temporal database as the main source of data and information. The spatio-temporal database is assimilated from the available static and dynamic data and is used for the development of the data-driven models. Other components of the general structure, as shown in Fig. 13, include an algorithm for feature selection, one or more data-driven models, means by which the quality and validity of the data-driven models are ensured, and, finally, post-modeling analysis tools and techniques.

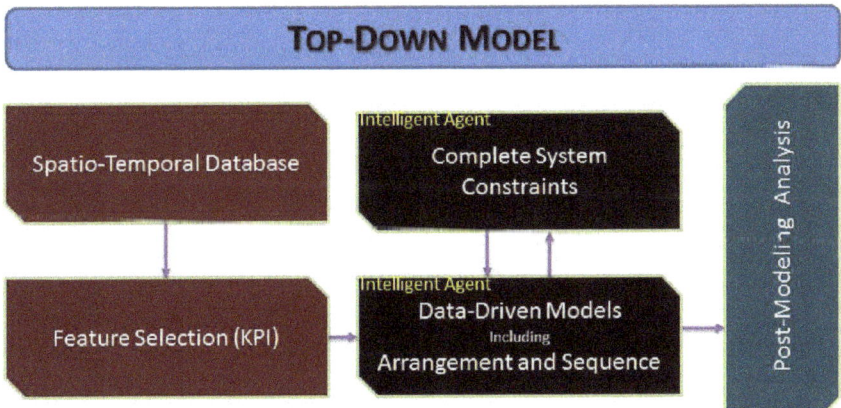

Fig. 13—The main, general structure of a top-down model. The main structure must always include a spatio-temporal database, an algorithm for feature selection, one or more data-driven models, means by which the quality and validity of the data-driven models are ensured, and, finally, post-modeling analysis tools and techniques. KPI = key performance indicator.

The spatio-temporal database and post-modeling analysis tools and techniques will be covered in more detail in later sections of this book. Other features will be briefly discussed here.

As previously mentioned, several techniques and algorithms are combined to form a final top-down model. Major components used to develop a top-down model include

1. *Feature selection using a fuzzy pattern recognition algorithm (or similar techniques)*
   As will be presented in the next several sections, development of a top-down model usually starts with the assimilation of a large database from field measurements that include static and dynamic variables. This database usually ends up being quite large. It is important to include any and all parameters that have a chance of impacting the time-dependent variables in the model. However, it is not recommended to build data-driven models with a large number of inputs.

   As the number of input parameters increases, the robustness and the validity of the data-driven model decreases. Only mediocre models include a large number of inputs. Therefore, TDM includes techniques to select the most-influential parameters from the spatio-temporal database to build the data-driven models. However, experience has shown that incorporation of techniques that combine multiple parameters to reduce dimensionality such as principal-component analysis (PCA) (or any variant of this statistically based technology) does not improve the accuracy and robustness of the data-driven models and should be avoided.

   Given the fact that the spatio-temporal database includes a large number of parameters and that a subset of these parameters must be used for the development of the data-driven models, it becomes necessary for some sort of feature reduction algorithm to be used. It is not trivial to identify and select the most-important parameters for the training of the data-driven models. Some researchers have used simple regression techniques to accomplish feature reduction (parameters are ranked on the basis of their R^2 value when correlated to the output variables), while others have chosen to use PCA. The author has been using a pattern recognition technology that is based on fuzzy set theory (see Section 4.4 Fuzzy Logic) that has the capability of identifying and ranking the most-influential parameters.[37]

2. *Data-driven models to accurately estimate the key output variables of the top-down model (usually time-dependent parameters)*
   As the reservoir being modeled becomes more realistic, nonacademic, and challenging (like most real-life problems and case studies) development (training, calibration, and validation) of multiple and interactive data-driven models will be required to satisfy the needs of a top-down model. Artificial neural networks have been used extensively as the data-driven model of choice in all top-down models.

   Multiple data-driven models are developed and arranged in a particular sequence in order to respond to the requirements of the particular project. For example, in a recently developed top-down model for an oil field in the Persian Gulf, it soon became evident that four data-driven models were required to achieve the objectives of the project. The four data-driven models were developed for static reservoir pressure, flowing bottomhole pressure (FBHP), liquid rate, and WC. **Fig. 14** shows a schematic of the "Data-Driven Models Arrangement and Sequence" module developed for this particular field.

   As shown in this figure, once the feature selection module completes its work and identifies which static and dynamic parameters should be included in the models, the development of data-driven models starts. First a data-driven model is developed for "static reservoir pressure." The output of this model is the static reservoir pressure at the location of a given well

---

[37]This is a proprietary algorithm that is part of the TDM software application called IMagine™, http://www.intelligent-solutionsinc.com/Products/IMagine.shtml.

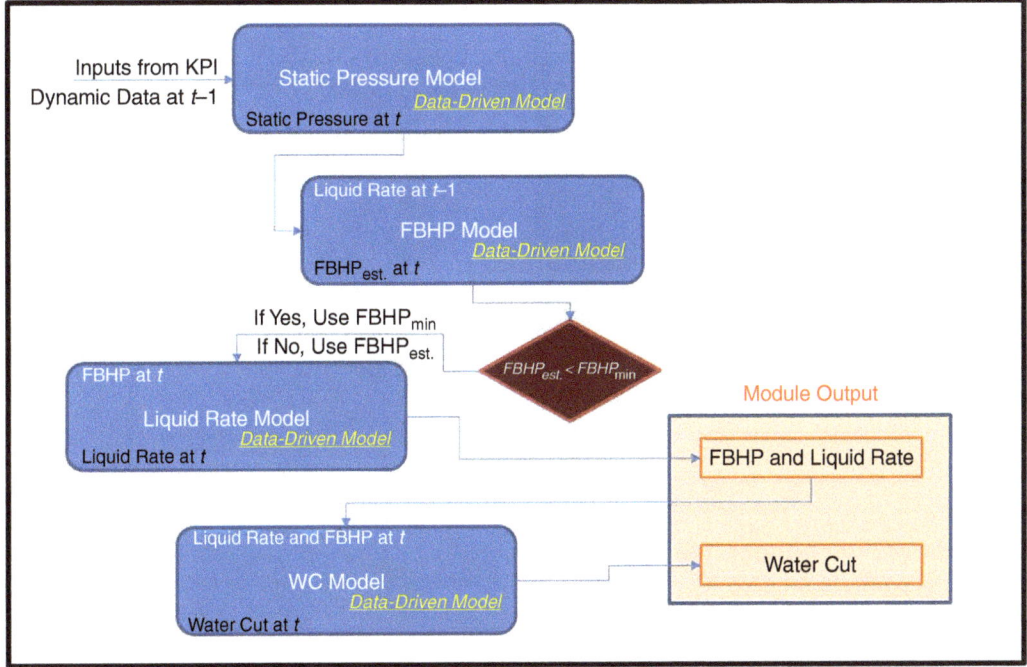

Fig. 14—Example of components of "Data-Driven Models Arrangement and Sequence" module in a top-down model developed for a mature offshore asset in the Persian Gulf. Four data-driven models were developed for this particular top-down model. This figure shows the arrangement and the sequence of these models in the context of the top-down model.

and at time t. The next data-driven model is one that estimates the FBHP for this well at time t while using the static reservoir pressure at time t and liquid rate at time $t-1$.

Because operation of wells in this field is constrained by the minimum FBHP, the estimated value of the FBHP from this data-driven model is compared with the minimum FBHP set for the field (or for the particular platform/pad). If the estimated FBHP is less than the minimum FBHP, then the minimum FBHP at time t will be used as input to the next data-driven model, which is the model to estimate the liquid rate at time t. If the estimated FBHP is equal to or greater than the minimum FBHP, then the estimated FBHP at time t will be used as input to the data-driven model for the liquid rate. The outcome of this process is a pair of FBHP and liquid rate at time t. The final data-driven model estimates the WC. The data-driven WC model can use output from all the previous models (at time t) as its input.

3. *Intelligent agents to manage the operation of the top-down model*
Intelligent agents usually act autonomously. An autonomous agent is defined as "a system situated within, and a part of, an environment that senses that environment and acts on it, over time, in pursuit of its own agenda and so as to effect what it senses in the future" (Franklin and Graesser 1997). An intelligent agent is an agent capable of making decisions about how it acts based on experience (Mills and Stufflebeam 2005). In the context of data-driven reservoir modeling and management, an autonomous intelligent agent is a computer code that evaluates the outcome of each data-driven model, makes a decision, and instructs the execution and implementation of multiple data-driven models in order to satisfy multiple constraints that are imposed on the overall field operations (**Fig. 15**).

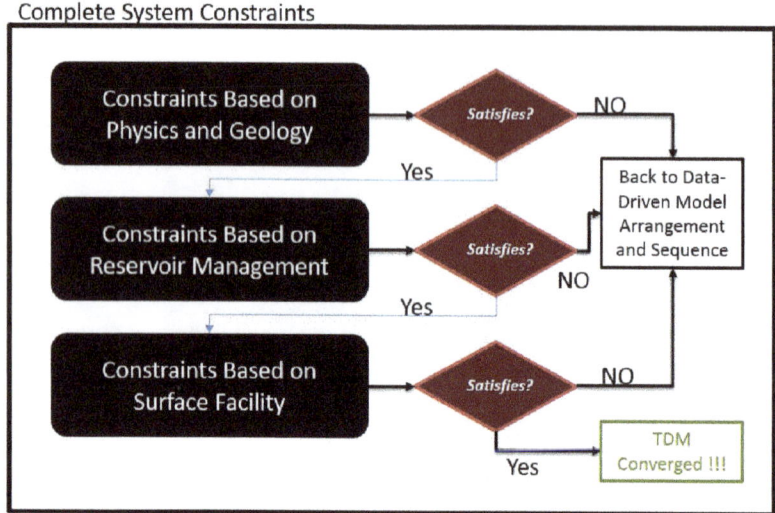

Fig. 15—The intelligent agents in TDM perform multiple tasks. One of the tasks performed is making sure that physics- and geology-based constraints, reservoir-management-based constraints, and, finally, constraints based on the surface facility are met by the estimated values from the data-driven models.

The intelligent agent's functionality can be divided into two major areas: (1) to direct traffic during the implementation of the data-driven models such as the one described in the previous section. The four developed data-driven models need to be arranged and put into a logical sequence for implementation, and (2) to impose multiple constraints dictated by physics and geology, reservoir management, and surface facilities.

The intelligent agents are usually a collection of crisp and/or fuzzy rules (including a fuzzy inference engine; see Section 4.4 Fuzzy Logic) that integrate multiple data-driven models and make sure that they are executed in the proper order to achieve the objectives that are identified for the top-down model. Furthermore, intelligent agents make sure that all imposed constraints (natural or manmade) are honored by the top-down model. The constraints could be minimum FBHP, water-handling-capacity limitation at the surface facility, or others.

7.2 Formulation and Computational Footprint of TDM

The top-down model is built by simultaneously correlating[38] production to reservoir characteristics, completion characteristics, flow characteristics, and facility constraints. Therefore, in general, a top-down model can be formulated as shown in the following equation:

$$q(s,t) = f\left(x_1, x_2, x_3, \ldots, x_n, y_1, y_2, y_3, \ldots, y_n, w_1, w_2, w_3, \ldots, w_n, z_1, z_2, z_3, \ldots, z_n\right), \ldots \ldots (1)$$

where $q(s, t)$ = production as a function of space and time,
$(x_1, x_2, x_3, \ldots, x_n)$ = parameters related to reservoir charactersitics,
$(y_1, y_2, y_3, \ldots, y_n)$ = parameters related to completion charactersitics,
$(w_1, w_2, w_3, \ldots, w_n)$ = parameters related to flow charactersitics,
and $(z_1, z_2, z_3, \ldots, z_n)$ = parameters related to surface facilities.

---

[38]The term "correlation" should be treated with much care in this context. Here, correlation is actually conditioned by causation based on physical understanding of the process. A subsequent section of this book is dedicated to discussing this issue.

In the preceding formulation, "flow characteristics" refers to facts such as interaction between wells that need to be taken into account when building a data-driven model that attempts to mimic fluid flow in the porous media. It is well-known that production from one well is impacted by production from adjacent/offset wells as well as by injection of gas and water in the wells surrounding it.

The data-driven model should somehow be taught that production and injection in other wells (offset wells) impact the production in the well that is of interest (and is currently being modeled) at any given instance in space and time. One may ask how to teach such interactions to a computer program? The answer is: with the only tool that you have—data. Here is how.

Flow characteristics are very much dependent upon reservoir characteristics (such as permeability), and therefore this interdependency must be communicated through data during the training process. Furthermore, reservoir characteristics between wells (and not only at the well location) contribute to this phenomenon. Therefore, one way to teach the data-driven model about flow characteristics is to include the following items (as variables) in each record (instance of production in space and time) during the training process:

1. Reservoir characteristics at the well location
2. Average reservoir characteristics from within the drainage area (volume) between the wells that may interact
3. Flow characteristics such as oil, GOR, and WC at the well and its offsets, one timestep behind
4. Gas and/or water injection, at the same timestep
5. Operational constraints (e.g., wellhead pressure, bottomhole pressure, choke size) at the same timestep.

To be more specific, during the development of the top-down model, several time-dependent variables such as flow rate (oil, gas, and water, and consequently GOR and WC), FBHP (or wellhead pressure, choke size, or other) at each well in the field and at each timestep[39] are correlated to a set of static and dynamic variables.

The static variables include reservoir characteristics (well logs such as gamma ray, density, sonic, resistivity, porosity, permeability, and formation thickness) at the following locations:

1. At the well location
2. The average for the drainage area (volume)
3. The average for the drainage area (volume) of the offset producers
4. The average for the drainage area (volume) of the offset injectors

Dynamic variables include operational constraints and production/injection at appropriate timesteps. Some of the dynamic variables that need to be included in the data-driven models are

1. Wellhead or bottomhole pressure, or choke size, at timestep t
2. Completion modification (e.g., operation of inflow-control valve, squeeze off, completion extension), at timestep t
3. Number of days of production, at timestep t
4. GOR, WC, and oil production (for the well being modeled), at timestep $t-1$
5. GOR, WC, and oil production of the offset wells, at timestep $t-1$
6. Water and/or gas injection, at timestep t
7. Well stimulation details

---

[39]The length of timesteps in TDM is a function of the production characteristics and the age of the reservoir as well as data availability. It is usually daily, monthly, or annual. This is covered in more detail in subsequent sections of this book.

The list of data mentioned above that is incorporated into the top-down model shows the difference of this type of modeling from other empirically formulated models such as decline curve analysis and CRM. It is noteworthy that TDM conditions production at each well and at each timestep (every month, for example) to all field measurements that are available and have shown the potential to be influential. From this vantage point, TDM is far closer to a numerical reservoir simulation than it is to empirical techniques such as decline curve analysis and CRM that only concentrate on production or production/injection data.

Therefore, a more-detailed formulation of the top-down model may be presented in the form of the following equation:

$$q_{wi,t} = f\left[\subset \left(S_{wi}, S_{OP}, S_{OI}, D_{wi,t}, D_{OP,t-1}, D_{OI,t}\right)\right], \quad\quad\quad\quad\quad\quad\quad\quad\quad\quad (2)$$

where $q_{wi,t}$ = flow rate of well (i) in timestep t,
wi = well (i),
t = timestep t,
$t-1$ = timestep $t-1$,
$\subset$ means "a subset of"

S = static characteristics of the reservoir,
$S = s(wb) + s(pb)$,
$s(wb)$ = well-based static variables,
$s(pb)$ = polygon (drainage area)-based static variable,

$S_{wi} = Static_{\text{Well}}$,
$S_{OP} = Static_{\text{Offset Producers}}$,
$S_{OI} = Static_{\text{Offset Injectors}}$,

D = dynamic characterisitcs of the well,
$D_{wi,t} = Dynamic_{\text{Well,time } t}$,
$D_{OP,t-1} = Dynamic_{\text{Offset Producers,time } t-1}$,
and $D_{OI,t} = Dynamic_{\text{Offset Injectors,time } t}$.

Once the development (training, calibration, and validation) of the top-down model is completed, its deployment in forecast mode is computationally efficient. A single run of the top-down model is usually measured in seconds or perhaps in minutes when it is deployed for calculation of the entire time domain. However, when the completed top-down model is deployed in the forecast mode, and only to calculate future events in the field,[40] a single run takes only a few seconds at the most. This allows practical and efficient reservoir management and analysis, such as field development planning and uncertainty quantification, to be performed in a short period of time.

Given the time and effort involved in the development and later in the use and implementation of a top-down model,[41] it quickly becomes obvious that once the TDM is reasonably well understood and its use has become a standard operating procedure within an organization with multiple assets, the cost-savings of TDM can be impressive. TDM has development and deployment costs, including software licensing, that are only a small fraction of the time and effort commitment required for numerical reservoir simulation.

---

[40] Such as field development planning.
[41] It soon becomes obvious that the best approach to developing top-down models is to use software applications that are specifically developed for this purpose. Just imagine developing your in-house code for numerical reservoir simulation as opposed to licensing products that are already on the market.

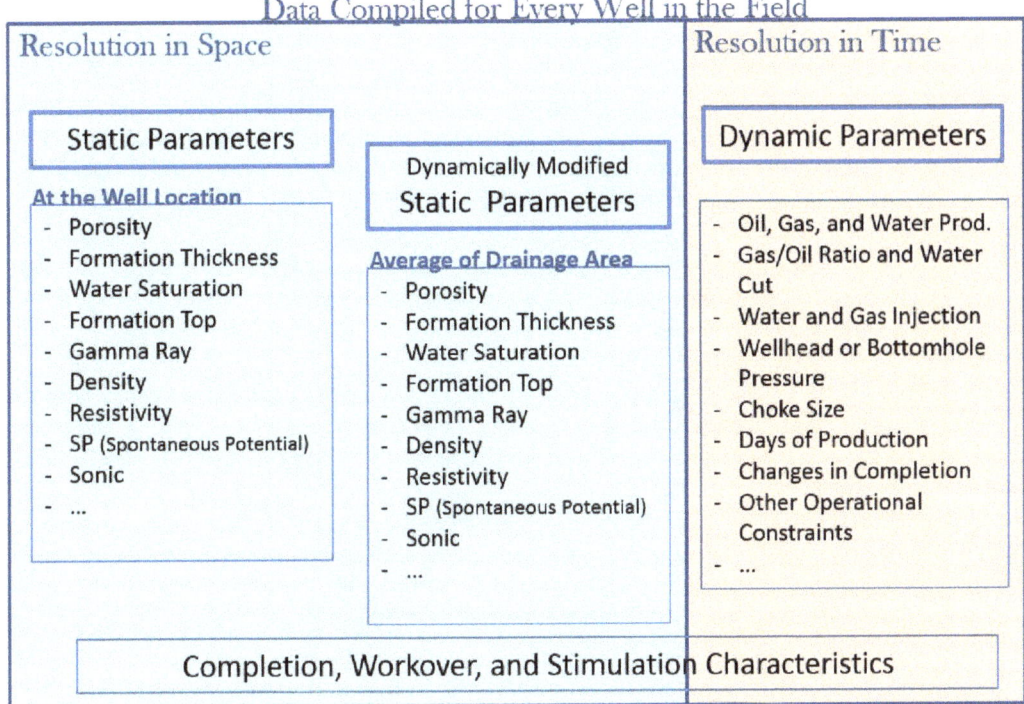

Fig. 16—A general, high-level summary of the types of data that are compiled for every well in the field.

7.3 Curse of Dimensionality

A closer look at the parameters that have been identified in Eq. 2 (a summarized list of these parameters can be seen in **Fig. 16**) reveals that the number of parameters that are prepared in the spatio-temporal database (more details about the spatio-temporal database are covered in Chapter 8) is very large. These are the parameters that have the potential to be a participant in the formulation of the top-down model. For a moderate-sized asset, the number of potential parameters that can be used as input in the data-driven models to form the top-down model can easily increase to more than several hundred.

Given the fact that "overelaboration and overparameterization is usually the mark of mediocrity" (Box 1976), the number of variables that will be used to build the top-down model (the data-driven models that eventually form the top-down model) must be small or moderate. The actual number that is finally used to develop the top-down model usually ends up being between 10 and 40 parameters (in most cases much closer to 10 than to 40). This is the reason for the "subset" notation in the formulation presented in the previous section (Eq. 2). Having a very large number of variables at the start of problems that are going to be addressed using data-driven solutions is a common problem. In machine-learning circles, this is known as "the curse of dimensionality."

The solution to the curse of dimensionality is a process known as "feature selection" or "feature reduction." The difference between "feature selection" and "feature reduction" is that the former selects a subset of features (variables, parameters) from the existing list, while the latter reduces the number of features (variables, parameters) sometimes by statistical and or mathematical combination of the features. It should be noted that there may be several parameters in the spatio-temporal database that are already a combination (using mathematical formulations that make physical sense) of several other parameters. Calculation of "net thickness" (multiplying gross thickness by net-to-gross ratio) and calculation of "volumetric reserves" (multiplying net thickness by porosity and hydrocarbon saturation) are good examples of these composite parameters. Such composite parameters that are the result of domain expertise on the part of the model developer should not be mistaken by statistical combination for features such as those achieved using PCA.

The activity known as feature selection or feature reduction is a key component of developing a top-down model. On the basis of the experience gained from years of developing data-driven models, the author has concluded that feature reduction techniques such as PCA and its many variants fail to deliver the type of results that are expected from a robust reservoir model. The author has learned that when it comes to building data-driven reservoir models, feature selection is the better approach to reducing the number of parameters that need to be used in the development of data-driven models. This can be achieved through elimination of some features and identification of KPIs. The preferred feature selection technique for a top-down model is fuzzy pattern recognition,[37] a process that uses fuzzy cluster analysis in order to identify the most-influential parameters in the database for a given time-dependent variable.

As mentioned before, if certain composite parameters are known (through domain expertise) to be beneficial and serve specific purposes in fluid flow through porous media, then using such combinatorial/composite parameters is recommended. But this must be done without sacrificing the fundamental parameters that are used to generate the composite parameter. We present both the fundamental and the composite parameters to the TDM process and let the top-down model's feature selection (fuzzy pattern recognition) algorithm decide which ones should be used during the model-building process.

To clarify this process, we will look at it through an example. We know that original oil in place is a contributor to the fluid flow through porous media. Therefore, in addition to parameters such as formation thickness, porosity, and water saturation, we can create a composite parameter called hydrocarbon pore volume (HPV). HPV is calculated by multiplying formation thickness by porosity and by one minus the water saturation. In assimilation of the spatio-temporal database, we present all four parameters (formation thickness, porosity, water saturation, and HPV) and let the top-down model's feature selection algorithm decide which parameter it should use.

7.4 Correlation Is Not the Same as Causation

One of the most contentious issues brought up by engineers and scientists, when presented by statistical analyses, is the relationship between correlation and causation and the fact that they are not necessarily the same. In other words, just because two variables correlate, does not mean that one is the cause of the other. **Figs. 17 through 19** are three examples that clearly demonstrate this phenomenon.

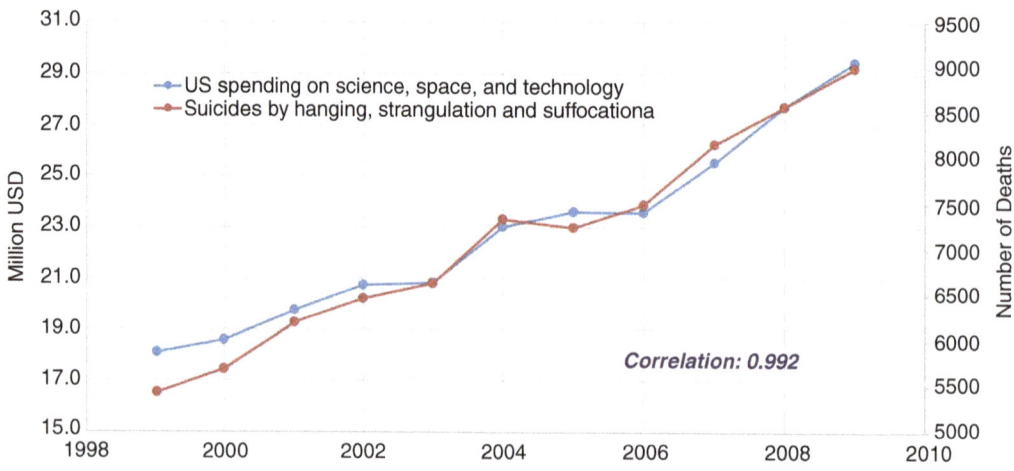

Fig. 17—An example of lack of relationship between correlation and causation: US spending on science, space, and technology highly correlates with number of suicides by hanging, strangulation, and suffocation.

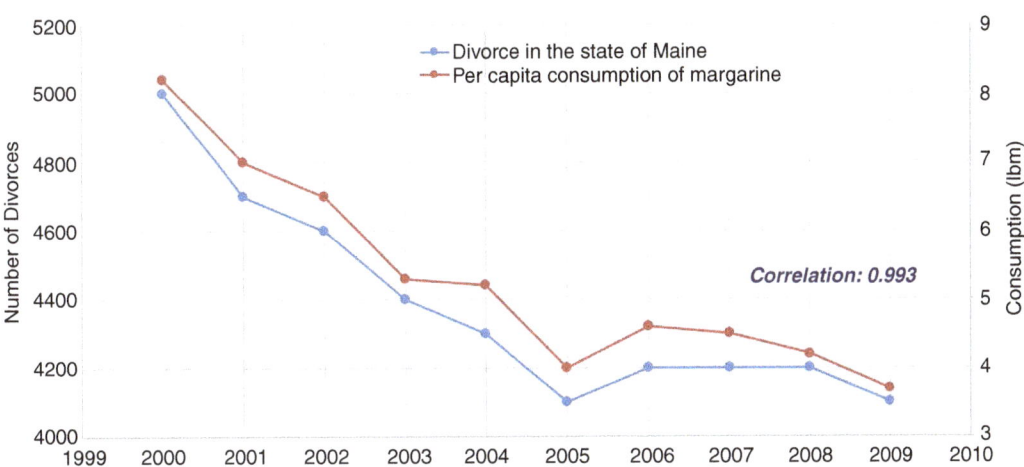

Fig. 18—Another example of lack of relationship between correlation and causation: Divorce rate in state of Maine highly correlates to per capita consumption of margarine in the US.

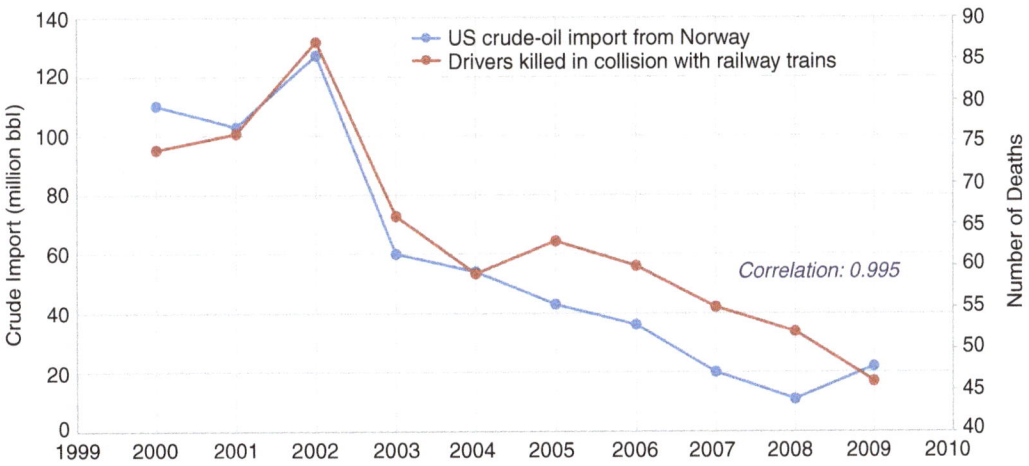

Fig. 19—Another example of lack of relationship between correlation and causation: US crude-oil imports from Norway highly correlate to number of drivers killed in collisions with railway trains.

Data presented in these figures are from public databases. Fig. 17 shows how US spending on science, space, and technology (in millions of dollars) correlates with the number of suicides by hanging, strangulation, and suffocations. The correlation is an impressive 0.992. However, there should be little doubt that these two phenomena have absolutely nothing to do with one another, and their correlation with one another is purely an accident. This is a clear example where correlation has nothing to do with causation.

Similarly, in Fig. 18, divorce rate in the state of Maine and per capita consumption of margarine in the US are plotted as a function of time. These two graphs show a correlation of 0.993, while having absolutely nothing to do with one another. In Fig. 19, it is demonstrated that US crude-oil imports from Norway have a correlation coefficient of 0.955 with drivers killed in collisions with railway trains. Another vivid example of lack of relationship between correlation and causation.

These examples emphasize the fact that when it comes to data-driven reservoir modeling, it is not enough to show correlations. Unlike many other problems and industries in which data analytics has thrived using mainly statistical approaches (such as social media and consumer relation management), the overwhelming number of problems related to the oil and gas industry are very much physics-based. Therefore, providing correlations without understanding and/or emphasizing the causation will result either in trivial conclusions or in conclusions that may not be useful to professionals in the industry.

A good example of such a situation recently occurred when a well-known international oil company hired an analytics vendor—with an impressive pedigree[42] and experience in application of statistics and analytics in social media and consumer relation management—to apply their sophisticated Big Data software applications to their oil-and-gas-related problems. This was an exercise spearheaded by the top management after they were exposed to the fascinating results that data-driven analytics can accomplish in other industries. After months of work and millions of dollars spent, the vendor's most important accomplishment was summarized in the findings that the data provided by the oil company reveal that higher porosity usually results in more oil. This is a good example of why physics-related domain expertise in highly physics-based industries, such as upstream oil and gas, plays such an important role in the acceptance and eventual implementation of this technology. In other words, a purely statistical approach will usually prove to be quite disappointing.

When addressing most of the problems in the oil and gas industry, the data-driven model must make physical and geological sense. Of course, the significance of physics and geology is only important when a good correlation can be achieved; otherwise, the entire case is moot. In other words, once we have a model that can make good predictions, then we can analyze its internal interaction between parameters (internal consistency) in order to see if it actually makes physical and geological sense.

This is how data-driven reservoir modeling is distinguished from its competitor empirical technologies that rely purely on statistics and mathematics without regard for physics and geology. Furthermore, when the data-driven model makes physical and geological sense, it addresses another important criticism that sometimes is made about data-driven technologies by those with only superficial understanding of the technology. Data-driven modeling has been referred to as black-box technology usually because of a lack of understanding (or a superficial understanding) of the machine learning technology.

If the term "black box" is used to emphasize the fact that there is not a deterministic mathematical formulation that can fully and comprehensively explain the behavior of a data-driven model, then this term is correct. However, if it means that the functionality of the model cannot be understood or verified (which many times is the reason that the critics use this terminology), then it is a misuse of the term. All interactions between different parameters in a trained data-driven reservoir model (and therefore in a top-down model) can be fully investigated in order to make sure that they make physical and geological sense. From this point of view, there is nothing in a data-driven reservoir model that makes it a black box.

7.5 Quality Control and Quality Assurance of the Data

We can readily acknowledge that real data are noisy. The only time you can expect clean data is when computer simulation models are used to generate them. Whenever real data (field measurements) are the source of information, one must expect to have noise. This fact must not deter us from using real data as the main source of information in order to build models. In the context of data-driven reservoir models, there are specific issues that need to be taken into account when data quality is being considered. For this reason, a serious data quality control (QC) and quality assurance (QA) process needs to be in place and implemented as an important part of the data-driven reservoir modeling.

There are a few facts that need to be considered when dealing with data-driven solutions in general, and in this specific case with data-driven reservoir modeling. It should be noted that usually more than 50% of a data-driven reservoir-modeling project's time (like any other data-driven

---

[42] A well-known outfit from the Silicon Valley.

solution) is spent on data QC/QA and data preparation. During this process, the modeler must spend considerable time to get to know the reservoir, the wells, and the data that are available for modeling.

How do you "get to know" your data? Well, you must familiarize yourself will all the details about the data that are available from each well. This may sound like an immense task, and it is. However, success of a data-driven reservoir-modeling project very much depends on how familiar you are with all aspects of production from the field that you are modeling. *There are no short cuts.* This is where the modeler's reservoir engineering expertise cannot be overemphasized as an uncompromising asset to the project. Make no mistakes: This is not a task that can be performed by a statistician or a "data scientist"[43] who does not have a reservoir engineering background.

Here are several preliminary items with which modelers should be very familiar. Please note that this list is by no means complete. Each project will have its own peculiarities and, therefore, must be comprehensively studied in close interaction with the reservoir and production engineers and geoscientists who have been working with the field at the operating company.

1. *Regarding the reservoir:* How large is the reservoir? When was it first discovered? When was the first well drilled? How many distinct geological formations are present in the field? Are there active aquifers present on the edges or at the bottom? Is there a gas cap? What is the drive mechanism of this reservoir?
2. *Regarding the wells:* How many wells are there? Are they vertical, slanted, or horizontal? How many are producing? How many were abandoned or plugged? When were they abandoned and/or plugged? Have any of the wells been converted to injection wells? When? What is being injected? Have there been any workovers? Or any stimulations?
3. *Regarding the completions:* Are the completed wells openhole, or have they been cased? Have there been any recompletions throughout the life of the wells? Any squeeze-offs? Have any downhole flow control valves been installed in any of the wells? Where in the oil column have the wells been completed?
4. *Regarding production:* Is the field in the primary- or the enhanced-recovery phase? Has water injection been started? If yes, since when? Is the reservoir producing any gas or water? Has water production become an issue? How is the oil production being measured? Is it being measured as a fraction of the total liquid rate? How is water cut being measured? What are the uncertainties associated with the measurements of water cut and liquid rates?
5. *Regarding the operational constraints and the surface facility:* What are the limits at the surface for handling liquid and gas? What have been the production strategies? Is there artificial lift installed in any of the wells? What kind? Since when? What are the operational constraints being imposed on the production?
6. *Regarding data availability:* Are well construction surveys available for all the wells? Are there well logs available for all the wells? What logs have been run? Are the available log data in digital format, or do they have to be digitized? Has any core analysis been performed? Has there been any work performed to correlate cores and logs? Has there been any rock-typing work performed using relative permeability curves and capillary pressure data? Are there completion data available? Have seismic surveys been performed—2D, 3D, or 4D seismic? What types of well tests have been performed, on how many wells and at what frequency? Have the well tests been interpreted by the same group of people? Have they used a

---

[43]When it comes to hard sciences and physics-based industries, "data science" must be addressed as a discipline-specific position. Therefore, as far as the upstream oil and gas industry is concerned, the term "data science" means very little, if anything. In order for the term to address the actual characteristics of the required position, the more proper term may be "petroleum data science." Such terminology will no longer be generic and will emphasize the undeniable fact that those wishing to be involved, and to become experts, in data-driven solutions in the exploration-and-production industry need to have a solid background in the related area in petroleum engineering (e.g., drilling, reservoir, production) as the foundation, and only after that does expertise in statistics, data mining, and machine learning become a necessity.

consistent software application? What is the production data resolution? Are wellhead and/ or bottomhole pressures available? Are the choke sizes available? What are the number of days of production per month, or the number of hours of production per day? And so on.

Performing TDM for a prolific mature field presents many challenges. The age of the field and the number of wells that have been completed in the field usually determine the amount of data that is available. Keep in mind that as the quantity of the data increases so does the probability of success in developing a top-down model. Also, as mentioned above, you must expect data to be noisy. Data are usually collected and recorded (especially in mature fields) by humans, and therefore noise and mistakes will be found in the data. The modeler must have the right tools to deal with noise. That said, one must know that the noise should not deter the modeler from taking maximum advantage of the data.

The author has encountered multiple situations where slight familiarity with artificial intelligence and data mining has resulted in conclusions that TDM (or any other data-driven modeling technology) cannot and should not be used because of the quality of the available data. In situations such as this, what is usually overlooked is the fact that any other technology that may be used for modeling and/or decision making will be using the same data. It is not the case that once you start using numerical modeling, or any other technology, the quality of the available data suddenly improves.

What technologies such as artificial intelligence and data mining bring to the task, when compared to other techniques, is the massive set of capabilities of taking maximum advantage of the existing information content of the available data. That includes data that are noisy. The alternative is to use technologies that will not incorporate the available data and most probably rely on no more than general knowledge or analogies. The utility of such technologies should be questioned.

The data usually are good enough to build at least some model. TDM is the best technology currently available to build a cohesive model from the available data from a mature field. One, of course, should conclude that the top-down model resulting from the available data from a mature field would be only as good as (1) the quality and quantity of the data that are available, (2) the expertise of the modeler who is engaged with the task of constructing the model, and (3) the modeling tool that is being used to construct the model. Please note that all these factors also apply when you are building a numerical reservoir simulation model; building a top-down model is no different in this regard.

7.5.1 Inspecting the Quality of the Data. Given the fact that TDM is a data-driven reservoir-modeling technology, it should be obvious that QC/QA of the data is of immense importance. The famous phrase "garbage in, garbage out" takes on new meaning during the TDM process because the foundation of the model is all about what we put in it (data).

However, there are misconceptions about QC/QA when it comes to data-driven analytics, specifically regarding its applications in reservoir modeling. In the context of TDM, QC/QA takes on an engineering meaning above and beyond the normal QC of the data. In data-driven reservoir modeling, the modeler is engaged in teaching reservoir engineering to a computer, with data as the only available tool. It is important to communicate reservoir engineering facts to the computer. A good example of this practice is communication of production behavior (oil, gas, and water production rates) to the computer, because it usually is one of the most important outputs of a reservoir model.

Let us use two examples in order to explain data QC/QA in the context of data-driven reservoir models. The first example has to do with formation thickness, while the second example is related to production values. In this context, we discuss the difference between "no data" (blank cell in a spreadsheet), and the value of "0" (zero). Unfortunately, some make the grave mistake of thinking these two are equivalent.

For example, when the parameter (variable) is formation thickness, the value of zero has a very specific meaning. Let us assume that we are developing a data-driven reservoir model for a field that is producing from two reservoirs R1 and R2. For each record in the database that refers to a month of production for a well in the field, we need to include two values for the formation thickness: one for each of the reservoirs—that is, one for R1 and one for R2 in ft. If for one of the formation thicknesses (say, for R1), we put the value of zero, we are simply stating a fact that the reservoir R1 is not present (has pinched out) at the location where this particular well has been completed. Therefore, for this particular well, all the production should be attributed (allocated) to reservoir R2.

However, if the value for the reservoir R1 is left blank (instead of giving the value of zero), this means that (for whatever reason) we do not know the formation thickness for this reservoir at the location of this well. Therefore, if there is no reason for us to believe that this reservoir is absent in this location, then we must identify a value for the formation thickness at this location. The value of zero is as likely to be true in this location as any other value (given the general formation thickness in this field). Therefore, the best solution in such a case would be to use geostatistics and populate the value of the formation thickness for this reservoir at the location of this particular well.

In the next example, we visit the data quality in the case of production. Since we are dealing with a real-world problem and not an academic one, the production profile from each well that is presented to the computer for training purposes is usually quite noisy. These production profiles from multiple wells are usually used as the target (output) for correlation. It is important to communicate the source of the observed noise to the computer in order to train the model on the types of noise that can be expected in production profiles. In other words, we need to teach the computer that if no disturbances are involved during production from a well, then the well will produce in a clean and well-behaved manner.

Good examples of such behavior are decline curves, or the production profile from a well generated by a numerical simulator. **Fig. 20** shows oil production from a well that includes no operational

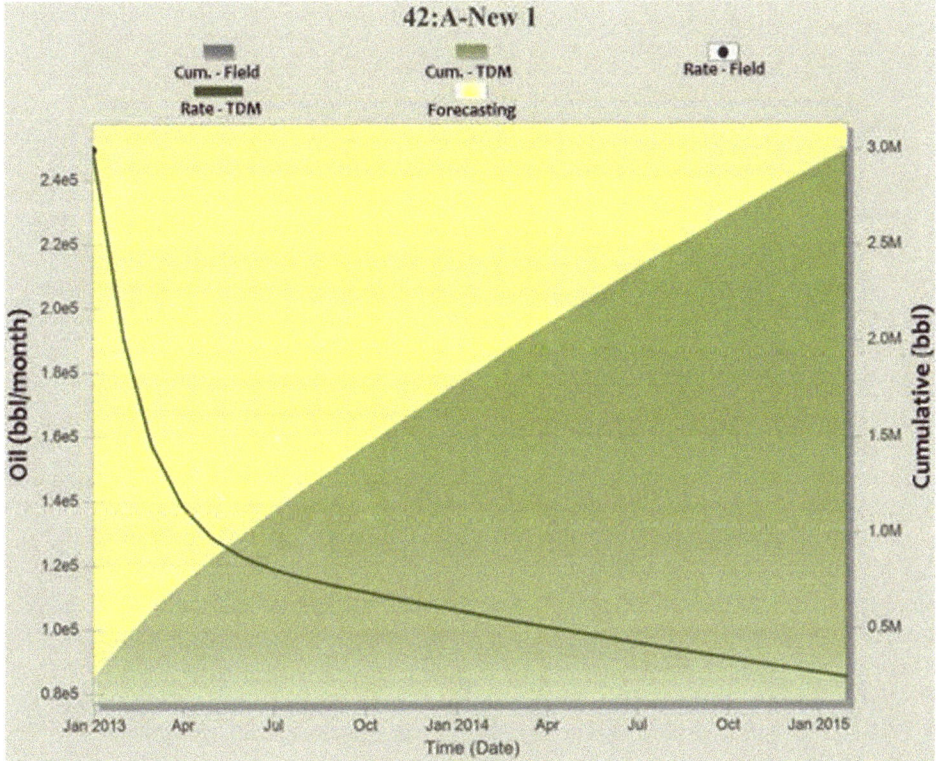

Fig. 20—Clean production behavior of a well when there are no disturbances (human involvement) from the surface. Reservoir characteristics are the only parameters responsible for the production behavior.

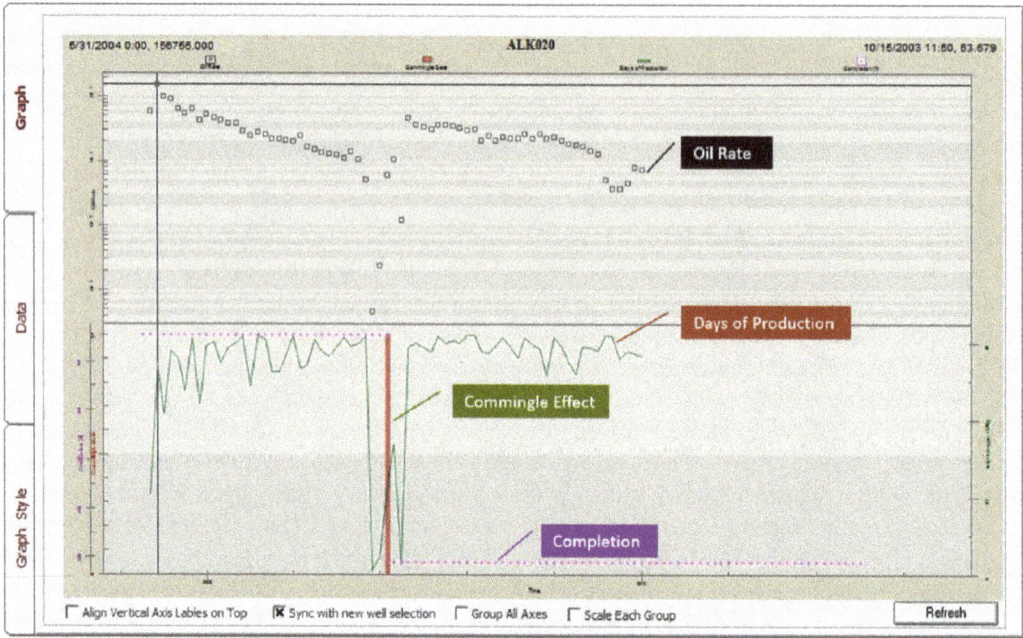

Fig. 21—Production behavior of a well completed in the Persian Gulf. The noise in production (barrels per month—the top graph) can be traced by the inconsistencies in operational constraints, such as wellhead pressure (choke size), number of days of production, and completion modifications.

disturbances, and therefore reservoir characteristics are the only parameters that are impacting production behavior. As can be seen from this figure, the production behavior includes no noise and is quite well-behaved. However, one will never see such behavior from a well producing from an actual reservoir.

Fig. 21 includes an actual oil production profile (in total barrels per month) from an offshore well in the Persian Gulf (top graph). The top graph in Fig. 21 is a good example of the noise that can be observed from actual production from a field. It must be noted that there are two types of noise that can be observed in this graph. The first type of noise is mainly white noise, which usually is the result of measurement inconsistencies. The result of such noise is a bit of up and down in the data, which does not actually disrupt the general trend in the production profile.

However, a second type of noise, which is the subject of this discussion, is the noise that causes a change in the trend of production. For example, in this figure, oil production during the second month is higher than the oil production during the first month. This jump in production (which is quite often observed in all wells) takes place during the first month, before a declining trend (which is expected as normal behavior) is started. Furthermore, halfway in the life of the well the production is disrupted to almost zero before starting an increasing trend that takes the production to a level even higher than when it was interrupted, before a new declining trend gets under way, and so forth.

The fact that this production behavior is not normal and is caused by human intervention (operational constraints or other parameters) must be communicated with the top-down model. This is done during the training of the data-driven model that is responsible for predicting the oil production behavior as a function of all other parameters. The bottom graph in Fig. 21 includes several profiles that may help explain the observed behavior of the oil production profile. In this graph, number of days of production per month and completion footage are plotted as a function of time (same x-axis of production).

This graph shows that during the first month of production the well was only producing for a few days (the well started production in the middle of the month), while starting with the second month the number of days became more consistent. This explains the increase in the total oil production from the first to the second month. Furthermore, it shows that in the middle of the profile, the well was shut in (total number of days of production per month goes to zero) and then when it was opened again, new parts of the formation were completed and are now contributing to production. This information contributes to understanding the behavior displayed in the oil production (top graph).

By providing these sorts of information (in the form of data in the spatio-temporal database) during the training of the reservoir model, we are assisting the deconvolution of the information. The oil production that is presented in the top graph, which is typical of all real-life cases, is convoluted by the impact of multiple classes of factors such as well trajectory characteristics, formation (reservoir) characteristics, completion characteristics, and, finally, production characteristics (operational issues and constraints).

By providing enough examples of a combination of all the above characteristics, we are helping (training) the data-driven model to distinguish between the contribution of each of the involved sets of parameters and, eventually, giving it the ability to deconvolve the information. This is the only way that the model will be able to perform reasonably in the future when it tries to perform production prediction.

Once the development of the top-down model has been completed and it is put to use, one of the exercises that is usually performed is to generate a production profile from a hypothetical well in a new location in the field, while leaving all operational constraints constant. If the top-down model has been able to successfully deconvolve the impact of the reservoir from the impact of the operational constraints, then the resulting production profile must be smooth and follow our understanding of fluid flow through porous media. In other words, the quality of the curve should not be different from one that has been generated by a numerical simulation model. Fig. 20 is such a figure. This figure was generated by the top-down model that was developed for the same offshore field in the Persian Gulf (Fig. 21).

7.5.2 QC of the Production Data. Top-down modelers must keep in mind that the information they are looking at (Fig. 21) is ultimately what is going to be used to train the top-down model. Therefore, chances are that if a certain obvious behavior in production of a well cannot be explained (in general terms) by a petroleum engineer, such data and behavior will confuse the top-down model as well. One example of such a case is shown in Fig. 21. Another example that clearly demonstrates this point is shown in **Fig. 22**. In this figure, approximately one-third into the life of the well, we notice an increase in production.

It is important to teach the top-down model that production generally decreases in a well if it is not interfered with. Therefore, if an increase in production is observed, there must be a reason. Looking at the FBHP, one can see a change in this parameter that most probably is the cause of the production increase. The modeler does not need to be able to write the equation for this change as long as the change makes logical sense. If the change in the production behavior has a physical, explainable reason, and is not the result of data being recorded wrongly, the machine-learning algorithm will be able to create the connection and draw its own conclusions.

When QC of data is approached from this point of view, and it requires more than some generic over-the-counter routines (mainly from statistical tools that are not specific to petroleum engineering), some critics have expressed concerns. These concerns may take many forms: for example, "Why is it necessary to make such detailed analysis and make sure that such data are present?" "Shouldn't the data-driven analytics (the smart algorithm) be able to figure this out on its own?" "What is the use of such an algorithm, after all, if everything has to be explained to it?"

These concerns are usually brought up either by those who are unfamiliar with the art and science of data mining and machine learning or by those who are unfamiliar with the main concepts of fluid

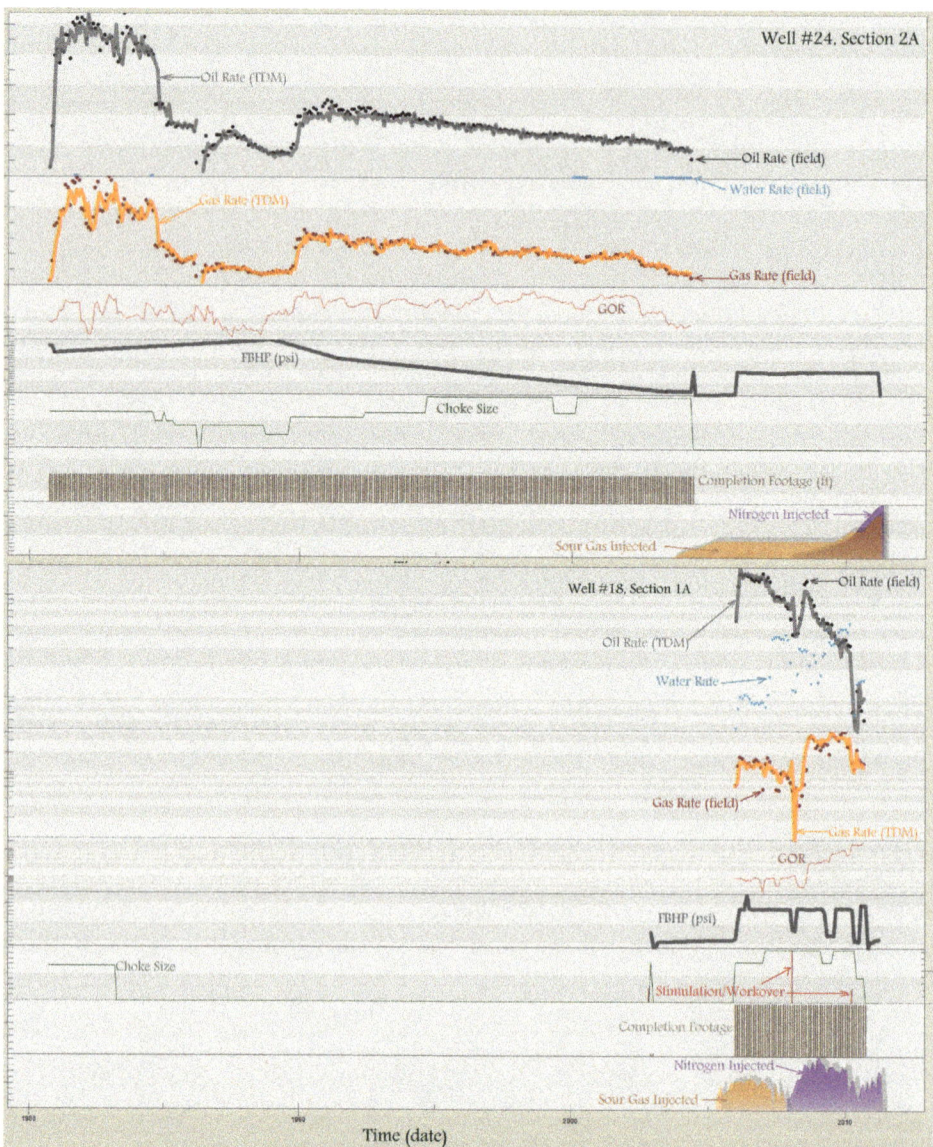

Fig. 22—Understanding the production behavior in two wells producing from the mature onshore field in Central America. FBHP, choke size, completion footage, and injection in the closest offset wells are plotted along with oil, gas, and water production to justify the production behavior. All this is taught to the top-down model through the spatio-temporal database.

flow through porous media and production engineering. It is interesting and important to examine these questions from two angles: first, if the question is asked by a "data scientist"[44] with little or no background in petroleum engineering, and second, if it is asked by petroleum engineers with no background in or understanding of data mining and machine learning.

---

[44] In this context, data science is nothing more than applied statistics. This fact further points to the issue mentioned earlier that being just a "data scientist" (statistician) is not enough to be a productive member of a data-driven analytics team in the upstream oil and gas industry.

When the question is asked from the point of view of a "data scientist" with little or no background in petroleum engineering, it demonstrates the degree of naivety and lack of understanding that there is a fundamental difference between applying machine-learning technology to nonphysics-based problems and applying them to physics-based problems.

When data mining and machine learning are applied to nonphysics-based problems,[45] the practitioner is hunting for "any" insight, whatsoever. "Anything" that can be learned from data may prove to be of value to the client. Such processes are usually too complex to be modeled by deterministic sets of equations, and that is the reason, in the first place, that data-driven analytics is being used. In such cases, not much can be revealed by looking at the raw data before processing it with data analytics. In such cases, data QC and QA take on a whole different meaning. We have seen many newcomers to the oil and gas industry try to overemphasize data quality, only from a generic point of view, not understanding that to a large extent this is very much a reservoir or production engineering problem. It is common for those who are new to data-driven analytics application in the oil and gas industry to make such beginner's mistakes.

On the other hand, petroleum engineers who are not familiar with data mining and machine learning sometimes have unreasonable expectations and look for magical results from this technology. It must be explained to them that there is no magic involved in this process. You can only expect the algorithm to learn what you try to teach it. Therefore, if intentionally or unintentionally you fool the algorithm by teaching it the wrong thing, it will get fooled and will generate unreasonable results. It is as simple as that.

So why use machine learning? It is not that hard to see why. Looking at Fig. 21 and Fig. 22, we can make sense of what happens to the production behavior of a well, given certain operational issues or human interventions. But in any given field, throughout its history, thousands and sometimes even hundreds of thousands of such incidents will take place. Furthermore, when one is trying to predict the behavior of a field into the future with hundreds of wells, it will become next to impossible for the human mind to keep track of all these variables and their details. Humans are very good at performing a small number of very complex tasks, and machines are impressive in performing a very large number of simple tasks at incredible speed. TDM tries to combine the complex problem solving of the human brain with the speed and vast reach of computers. This is the actual definition of smart problem solving.

---

[45]Applications to social sciences and social media that attempt to understand and model human behavior, consumer behavior in retailing, or even the pharmaceutical industry offer good examples of nonphysics-based industries.

Chapter 8

The Spatio-Temporal Database

The spatio-temporal database forms the backbone of the top-down model. This database is developed (assimilated/compiled) upon quality control of all the collected and gathered data. It includes two major data types: static data and dynamic data. As the phrase suggests, the static data include the field measurements that are not expected to change with time, while the dynamic data include parameters that are functions of time.

Furthermore, static data itself may be divided into two distinct classes. Truly static data that will not change as a function of time and dynamically modified static data. Dynamically modified static data are a series of parameters that represent averages of static characteristics calculated for some referenced reservoir volumes that change as a function of time. Static reservoir data such as average porosity associated with the drainage volume (where each well is producing from) is not a truly constant parameter. Because the drainage area that is accessible to each well changes as a function of time, as new wells are drilled in the reservoir, the average values of the static parameters representing the drainage volume, such as average porosity associated with the drainage area, will be subject to modification.

Inclusion of relevant (static and dynamic) data related to the offset production and/or injection wells in the spatio-temporal database was also mentioned briefly in previous sections. In this section, more details about this database, its different components, and how they should be arranged and managed are presented.

It can be argued that a top-down model is more about assimilation and compilation of the spatio-temporal database than anything else. A review of the literature shows that there have been attempts to build empirical reservoir models to substitute for full-field numerical simulation models. The capacitance/resistance model is an example of such attempts.

Using the principle that "simpler models are usually better than complex models" (especially when we do not fully understand the underlying physics), developers of empirical models have concentrated either on the "technology" or on the "data." To keep the models simple, those that have concentrated on the "technology" have used simple multivariate statistical techniques and sometimes even neural networks to build empirical models. Those that have focused on the "data" to keep models simple have usually used production data as the only source of information. A good example of a simple empirical model that uses "data" as the focus is the capacitance/resistance model (Sayarpour et al. 2009).

In many of these models, the simplification of building models goes as far as completely ignoring some of the basic facts and field measurements that are readily available, such as well and completion characteristics, well logs, core data, well tests, workovers, and sometimes seismic surveys. A closer inspection of these models reveals that the main reason for ignoring and not incorporating such a vast amount of readily available field measurements and information into the empirical model is not to keep the models simple; rather it seems to be the difficulty of incorporating these data into the models. Integration and incorporation of field measurements into the empirical model are not trivial, and leaving them out seems to be the simplest choice.

Some developers of empirical reservoir models (such as capacitance/resistance models) note that production and injection data that are being used in their models are proxies for all other information and have all the necessary information embedded in them. Consequently, they conclude that there is no need to explicitly include such information in the model. However, a closer inspection of some of the related literature points to their attempts at integrating and using as much of the field measurements in their models as possible. This clearly shows that the lack of integration of field measurements in their empirical models has more to do with not having the right technology to do it, rather than keeping the model simple. The fact is that integration of existing information into the model hardly contributes to the complexity of the model, while making the empirical model much more reliable, far more useful, and physically tractable.

The results generated by such simple models, which are usually the "production profile" at the well, end up not being conditioned (sensitive) to many measurements and constraints that play vital roles in well production. In other words, the production profiles generated by these models do not change if the user changes the operational constraints or reservoir characteristics. These are factors that will modify how a well produces, but almost all production profiles that are empirically generated are insensitive to these parameters.

The natural criticisms to these models are usually expressed in the form of statements such as "If operational constraints, or reservoir characteristics, or completion techniques, or well construction do not play any 'explicit' role in the model outcome, then how can the model be used in order to study the impact of these characteristics or to forecast the production in the presence of changes related to these characteristics in the future?"

One of the reasons that make integration of these data and field measurements (operational constraints, well tests, well logs, core analysis, seismic survey, completion techniques, or well construction details) into the empirical model so challenging is that they represent different scales in the reservoir. This nonuniformity in scale contributes to the complexity of incorporating them into these simple models. These realities point to the fact that although simplicity in modeling practices is a virtue, it is so much overemphasized that it compromises the reliability, utility, and practicality of a model. In other words, one can simplify a model until it is useless.

The ultimate in simple models (which are usually applicable to single wells and not to an entire field) are decline curves, in all their various versions. Decline curves only concentrate on the production profile and try to fit mathematical equations (represented through statistical curve-fitting procedures) through it, but they ignore almost all other aspects of well and reservoir functionalities.[46] Decline curves definitely have their place in the petroleum professional's toolbox, as long as their limitations and applicability are well understood.

When compared to decline curve analysis and capacitance/resistance modeling (CRM), top-down modeling (TDM) is a complex reservoir-modeling technology because it incorporates and integrates almost *all* the data, information, and field measurements that are available from a given reservoir into one comprehensive and cohesive, full-field reservoir model. When compared to numerical reservoir simulation and modeling, TDM is a simple reservoir-modeling technology, since it only uses the data and field measurements and information that are available from a given reservoir and refrains from any interpretations, biases, and extrapolations of the realities.

---

[46]This is quite understandable in cases where no other information or field measurements are available. But in cases in which large amounts of data are available on reservoir characteristics (e.g., well logs, well tests, seismic) and operational constraints (e.g., wellhead pressure, choke settings) relying only on decline curve analysis and ignoring all the field measurements is an unforgivable technical error, unless the objective of the analysis calls for only a quick screening and nondetailed results for specific purposes for which techniques such as decline curve analysis were developed in the first place.

The objective of TDM is to build a comprehensive, full-field, and empirical reservoir model so that its response is conditioned to all the facts, field measurements, and information that are available to the engineers and geoscientists, at any given period of time. Nothing that has been measured should be voluntarily ignored and left out of the model. The top-down model's spatio-temporal database is designed to provide the means of incorporating all available data (field measurements) into the empirical model. The mechanism through which this important task is accomplished is covered in this chapter.

It might also be useful to mention that although we use the term "database" when we refer to the spatio-temporal database, the shape of this database in its final form when presented to the machine-learning and pattern-recognition algorithms reflects a "flat file" or a matrix of rows and columns. A relational database may have to be developed in order to best accommodate the eventual assimilation and compilation of such a flat file. This important issue will become clearer as we cover the details that go into building the top-down model's spatio-temporal database.

In the context of the TDM, the rows in the matrix are referred to as "records," and the columns in the matrix are referred to as "variables," "features," or "parameters." Fig. 16 displays a general, high-level summary of the variables/parameters that are collected for each well in a given field.

The list presented in Fig. 16 is indeed summarized. The following considerations need to be mentioned regarding this list as far as the static (and dynamically modified static) parameters are concerned. Wells are usually completed in multiple formations. Therefore, static and dynamically modified static parameters must be compiled for every individual formation. In such cases, additional parameters are also included in the database to identify in which of the formations, and to what extent, each well has been completed. No data and information that can help articulate the details of the fluid flow in the reservoir should be intentionally (or by oversight) left out. They all must be communicated with the data-driven models that will form the top-down model.

Furthermore, when completions are squeezed off, or new parts of the well are completed, a new set of dynamic parameters is born. We must have the right set of parameters in the spatio-temporal database to manage the communication of such information with the machine learning algorithms. Included in the dynamic completion parameters should be information regarding the incorporation of inflow-control valves (ICVs) or any devices that would change the completion length that is the interface between the well and the reservoir. It is obvious that the length of this interface (completion) plays an important role in the production characteristics of a well. Details regarding the quality of the completion that are summarized in other data, including workovers and stimulation practices, should also be included in the database in the form of either static or dynamic parameters. The ways such information are included in the database are a function of the nature of these interventions.

Details of resolution in time and space are covered in a separate section. However, it will be briefly discussed here. In a top-down model, resolution in space is determined by the number of wells that are present in the field at any given time. Therefore, it has a dynamic nature. Resolution in time is determined by the data availability. If the production and injection volumes are available on a daily basis, the modeler will have more flexibility. In such cases, the time resolution can be daily, monthly, or annual—any time period equal to or larger than a day. On the other hand, if the production and injection volumes are available on a monthly or annual basis, then the modeler is limited to those time periods.

For simplicity, let us assume that we are attempting to build a top-down model for a field with 200 wells and each well has been producing for 10 years. Furthermore, let us assume that eight different static parameters and two dynamic parameters are available for each well. Production and injection volumes are available on a monthly basis for this field. In a case such as this, the data from each well occupy 120 rows. The number of rows occupied by each well is equal to the number of months of production multiplied by the number of years of production (because the time resolution for production is monthly), or 10 years × 12 month/year = 120 months (120 rows).

Because each well has eight different static parameters, these parameters will be repeated for all 120 rows. Furthermore, each well has two dynamic parameters: for example, number of days

62 Data-Driven Reservoir Modeling

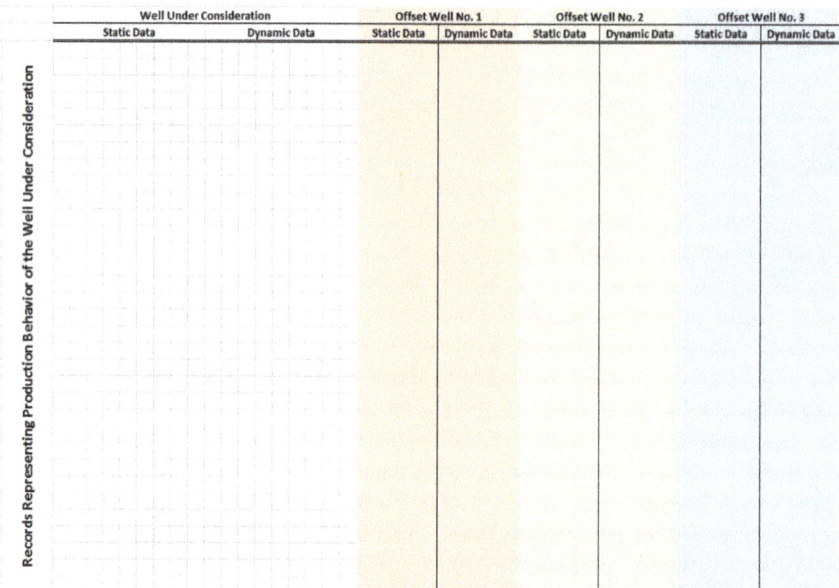

Fig. 23—Example schematic of a spatio-temporal database.

of production per month and the wellhead pressure. These two parameters will change for each of the rows or for each month of production. Therefore, data from one well will include 11 columns [8 static + 2 dynamic + production (output)] and 120 rows. Repeating this for all 200 wells, the final size of this particular matrix will be 24,000 (200 × 120) rows by 11 columns. However, this is *not* the "spatio-temporal" database. This is only the raw available data. These raw data will be used to assimilate the spatio-temporal database.

This field includes 200 wells. As reservoir engineers, we know that wells communicate and impact each other's behavior. In this field, each well has 199 offset wells. From a mathematical point of view, production from each of the 200 wells is impacted by all the other 199 wells.[47] However, from a practical point of view, the impact of wells on each other's production behavior has limitations. The limitation that we call practical communication is dictated by a combination of conductivity of the formations surrounding each well (permeability and thickness) and the duration of production. As the length of production time increases, or the conductivity of the reservoir increases, so too does the chance of interference between wells.

Needless to say, as the conductivity increases in a field so too does the number of offset wells that can impact production behavior of a given well. The same is true of the production time because these two parameters (conductivity and length of production time) determine the drainage area (volume) or the (practical) reach of the pressure transients caused by production from a given well. Therefore, when determining the number of offset wells that should be included in the final spatio-temporal database (in each record), the measure of the practical communication between wells must be taken into account. Let us assume that the practical communication in this particular field is limited to three offset wells. When considering three offset wells, this means that 3 × 11 = 33 more columns must be included in the original matrix (11 parameters for each offset well).

The final matrix is now 2,400 (rows) by 44 (columns). This is the spatio-temporal database for this particular field. The general shape of this spatio-temporal database is shown in **Fig. 23**.

---

[47]The diffusivity equation that governs fluid flow through porous media is a second-order, nonlinear, partial-differential equation (a parabolic equation); as such, the propagation of the dependent variable is instantaneous.

8.1 Static Data

The phrase "static data" means that the parameters that are of interest in this segment of the data-gathering process are those that will not change with time. One way to realize the importance of this set of parameters, and how they are incorporated in and are related to a reservoir model, is to consider the role of the geological models as the foundation of the numerical reservoir simulation models. Because the reservoir rock is the medium in which the hydrocarbon is residing before production, its characteristics are of importance to any type of reservoir modeling. Furthermore, it only makes sense that any serious reservoir model include a model of the container (the rock) where the hydrocarbon resides and inside of which it will move before it can appear in the wellbore for production. This container model is called the geological/static model.

The geological model concerns itself with the spatial variation of reservoir characteristics (Swan and Sandilands 1995). All reservoir rocks are heterogeneous and anisotropic. In the context of TDM, given the fact that different wells produce different amounts of fluid, the static or geological model is meant to play a distinguishing role between the wells and the drainage area they are in direct contact with and are producing from. The fact that reservoir rocks are heterogeneous and anisotropic actually is a good thing from a TDM point of view, because it assists the model in distinguishing between wells and their ability to produce fluid. Therefore, reservoir characteristics are one factor, out of several sets of characteristics, that control production.

The reservoir characteristics that are of interest to a reservoir engineer/reservoir modeler are those that control hydrocarbon storage and transport. Hydrocarbon storage is controlled by the reservoir characteristics that determine the hydrocarbon volume contained in the formation: in other words, the so-called hydrocarbon pore volume of the rock. This would include the top of the formation, the thickness of the formation, the porosity of the rock, and the initial water saturation. The overall shape of the rock (area multiplied by thickness) provides the bulk volume. Porosity lets the modeler calculate pore volume, and initial water saturation lets us determine the hydrocarbon pore volume.

$$Hydrocarbon\ Pore\ Volume = Ah\phi\,(1 - S_{wi}). \qquad(3)$$

Eq. 3 shows the formulation for calculating the hydrocarbon pore volume. Please note that unlike most reservoir engineering textbooks, no conversion factors are used in this formulation. The reason is that if this calculation is used as part of the spatio-temporal database, there would be no need for a conversion factor because this would represent a characteristic for each well (repeated for all wells in the field), and it would not be used in any formulation (equation) where it has to follow certain dimensional analysis and be expressed in some specific unit. As long as the same set of units is used for all wells, incorporation of conversion factors is not necessary (or it should be said that the use of conversion factors is optional).

Therefore, it becomes clear that in TDM, any data, measurement, and information that can provide knowledge about these characteristics will be useful to the model and are welcome. For example, formation top, formation thickness, porosity, and initial water saturation are among the parameters that would help the top-down model in learning about the hydrocarbon storage capacity of the reservoir, which will ultimately help the model in understanding the production characteristics of each well.

This is one reason that TDM is considered to be part of a new paradigm in advanced data-driven analytics that is called data-knowledge fusion. This particular paradigm distinguishes the application of data-driven analytics in disciplines that are heavily physics-based (such as the upstream oil and gas industry) from the use of data-driven analytics in other (quite popular) disciplines that are not physics-based, such as consumer relation management, social networks, and even pharmaceuticals. In these latter types of industries, no physics-based models exist that can be used as references to test the robustness and the integrity of the data-driven models. In other words, the data-driven models developed for a consumer relation management company cannot be tested against factual, well-known, physics-based models, but a data-driven reservoir model can (and should be) tested against physical facts (higher permeability usually results in higher production) to make sure that it understands and honors the known physics.

On the transport side, the fact is that not many data/measurements are usually available on permeability in a field. Furthermore, because rock/fluid characteristics such as relative permeability and capillary pressure are usually available on a regional basis and not on a per well basis, they may prove not to be very useful; however, if available, they can and should be incorporated in the top-down model.

When building a geological (static) model to be used as the foundation of the numerical reservoir simulators, deterministic or statistical models are used to determine the distribution of reservoir characteristics throughout the reservoir and to populate the geological model (Jensen et al. 2000; Davis 2002). These deterministic and/or statistical models include extensive amounts of interpretation that the modeler may or may not want to include in a top-down model. On the other hand, as was mentioned before, even in a top-down model, some sort of static model is required, since we must provide information regarding the storage and transport capacities of the reservoir. This information helps the top-down model to distinguish between wells and to learn and correlate them to the production characteristics of each well.

In TDM, information on the static parameters can be extracted from sophisticated geological models (if available) or by using simple and quick geostatistical or interpolative algorithms in order to populate the static model in a top-down model. As will be shown in more detail in the next few sections, in order to provide relevant information to the top-down model for learning, two types of grids are overlain on a field in order to characterize static information of a given field and to prepare it for the TDM.

The two types of grid systems are for two types of static characteristics. The finer grid system (Cartesian) is for the well-based static characteristics, while the coarser (polygon-based) grid is for dynamically modified, static characteristics that represent the average static characteristics of the drainage volume from which the well is producing. More about these grids is included in subsequent sections of this chapter.

Finally, as long as the modeler uses a consistent set of units for all the parameters that are involved, it really does not matter which specific set of units is used for calculation and/or storage of information in the spatio-temporal database.

8.2 Dynamic Data

Well logs, core analysis, and 3D seismic (any parameter or variable that does not change as a function of time) are among the static data that are used in the top-down model through the spatio-temporal database. Other parameters such as wellhead pressure, number of days of production in a given month (if the time resolution happens to be monthly), choke size, change in completion length (because of new perforations or squeezing off old perforations, use of ICVs, or other factors) are among the dynamic parameters.

Many of the dynamic parameters represent human intervention in production. Some of these interventions are intentional (such as changing the choke size or increasing the completion footage, or stimulating a well), and some are unintentional (such as changes in wellhead pressure because of surface facility limitations or changes to the surface facility in unrelated areas that impact the backpressure on the well). It is of utmost importance to teach the top-down model about the differences between reservoir behavior and human intervention.

The differences between the impacts of the reservoir characteristics and those of human intervention (operational issues) that are inherent in the production data need to be communicated to the top-down model. The only means to communicate such information with the top-down model is through data. Obviously, some of the observed production behavior results from reservoir characteristics (e.g., the amount of the fluid being produced and the extent of decline in the production), while other observed behavior results from the impact of operational issues (e.g., sudden changes in production behavior such as very sharp decline to zero production or a sharp increase in production).

The top-down model will be able to distinguish between the two sets of characteristics and deconvolve the related signals only after it has learned, through historical data, that there is a difference between signals coming from the reservoir and those that have been impacted by the operational constraints. The training of the top-down model is conducted through the collected records and parameters in the spatio-temporal database that carries such information (in a convoluted fashion). The spatio-temporal database is the only source of information that is used to educate the top-down model, whereupon it is expected to properly respond to the questions that are posed to it once it is trained.

It should be noted that the presentation of differences between the impacts related to reservoir characteristics and those related to operational constraints is performed implicitly, not explicitly. An explicit representation is usually in the form of a mathematical equation, while an implicit representation is through multiple, and sometimes redundant, data records. An explicit representation is easy to understand, detect, and digest, while deconvolution of an implicit representation is not very straightforward. Because the top-down model is a data-driven model and not a physics-based model, explicit mathematical equations for deconvolution are not used during their development. Furthermore, presentation of an explicit mathematical equation is an interpretation of our current understanding of the physics that we are intentionally staying away from while developing a top-down model.

Therefore, if discrepancies and unusual behavior in the production profile are observed but are not explained (through representative data) to the top-down model, the message that is being sent (what is taught to the top-down model) is that the reservoir can behave in these ways without any specific reasons or explanations. In other words, there are no explanations for the chaotic behavior that can be observed during the production process from a well that is producing hydrocarbon. Then, in return, the trained top-down model will behave irrationally and chaotically during the forecasting process. A top-down model that is being taught in this manner cannot be expected to provide reasonable and logical predictions in the future.

Fig. 24 is an example of the items mentioned above. In this figure, the fluctuations in production behavior are the result of operational issues and are not natural behavior related to the reservoir's characteristics. Once these operational issues are communicated to the top-down model in a proper manner (which will be covered in the next few sections), the top-down model usually does a good job of deconvoluting the signals that are associated with operational issues from those that are based on reservoir characteristics in order to achieve a good history match.

The gas production rate from a well in the North Sea, which is shown in Fig. 24, is a good example of both the general noise that is always associated with real data, and also of sudden changes in production behavior. In this figure, the top-down model has been able to history match the production rate behavior from a well with good accuracy, while the wellhead pressure (and not the bottomhole pressure) was used as the operational constraint.

8.3 Well Trajectory and Completion Data

One of the major misconceptions regarding TDM (data-driven reservoir modeling) is that because it involves a simple model (relatively speaking), the modeler may do away with some of the information that usually goes into a numerical reservoir simulation model. Those with such misconceptions mistakenly identify top-down models with simplistic empirical models such as decline curve analysis and CRM that incorporate minimal information in the construction of the model. As a result, their application becomes limited.

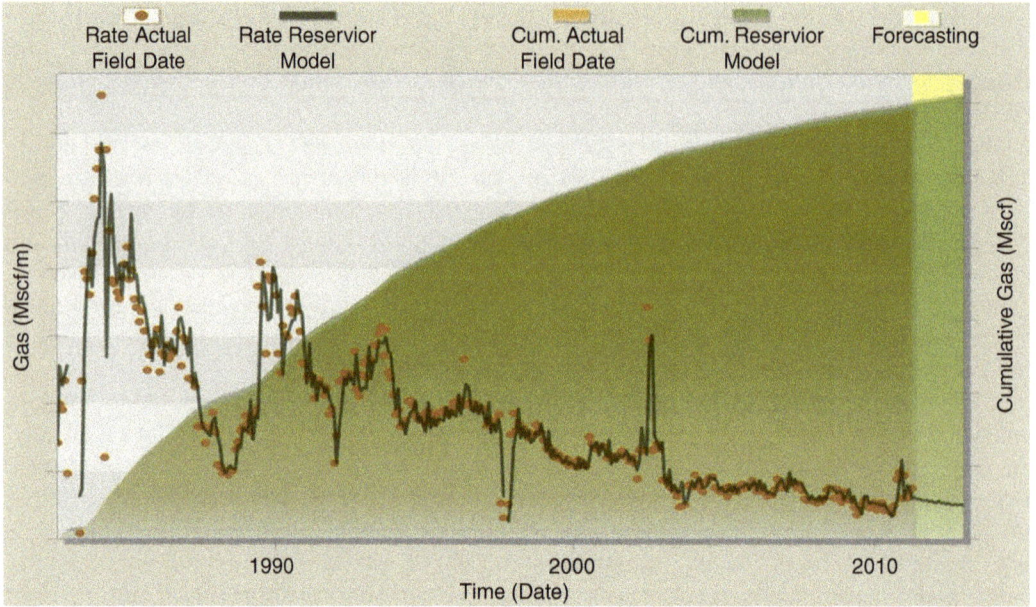

Fig. 24—Example of well behavior. The fluctuation in well behavior is caused not by reservoir characteristics but by operational issues. Once the operational data are communicated with the top-down model, it can perform good history matches.

The top-down model is a comprehensive reservoir model. As such, almost all the major components that are essential in the development of a traditional numerical reservoir simulation model will play similar roles in a top-down model. Inclusion of data and information regarding the well trajectory and completion is a good example.

Data and information regarding the well trajectory and completion define the interface between the wellbore and the reservoir. This interface determines the level and the extent of communication between the well and the reservoir, and to a large degree controls the fluid production by exposing the reservoir to pressure modifications that cause the flow. Furthermore, it is an important distinction between different wells and their production behavior. Therefore, information regarding the location and the trajectory of the wells is of utmost importance to the top-down model. Overlooking such information and failing to include it during the development of a top-down model are the equivalent of communicating the following message to the top-down model: "All wells in this field are drilled and completed in an identical manner, and there is no difference between them."

Well location, how much of it has stayed in formation (in case of horizontal wells), its azimuth and inclination, true vertical depth, measured depth, and whether it is updip or downdip are among the data that can and should be extracted and included in the spatio-temporal database. **Fig. 25** shows the form that includes some of these types of information and is available for almost all the wells in a field.

Completion data should be incorporated in the TDM with much care and with some creativity and innovation. The completion data, to a large extent, determine the versatility of a top-down model by identifying from which layers or through which perforations the fluid is being produced.

Fig. 26 is an example of inclusion of completion information for multiple wells that have been completed in the Marcellus Shale in southwestern Pennsylvania, USA. This figure shows that each well is completed in one or both of the formations (Upper and Lower Marcellus). When a well is completed in both formations, all parameters [porosity, net thickness (Net h), initial water saturation (S_{wi}) and total organic content (TOC)] in the table include real numbers, and the parameters

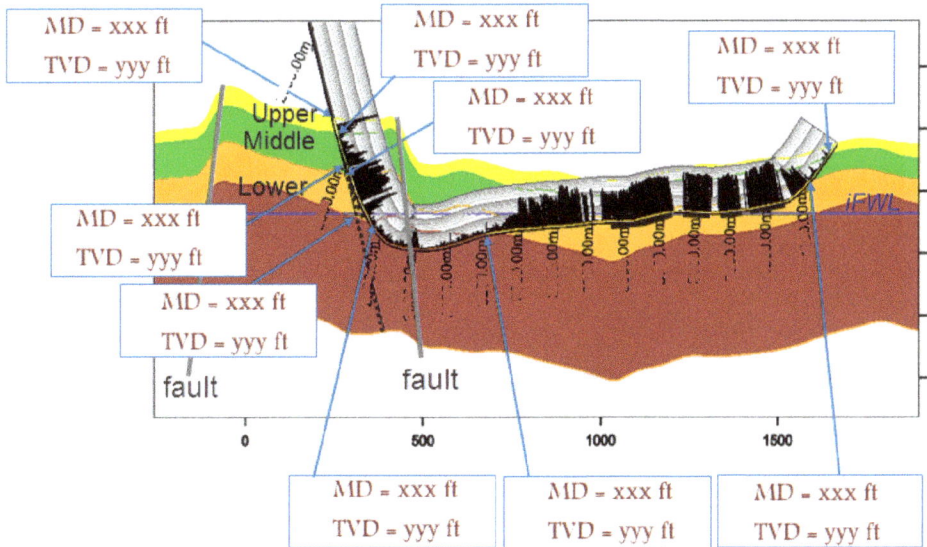

Fig. 25—Example of data usually available regarding well trajectory. MD = measured depth; TVD = true vertical depth.

	Upper Marcellus				Lower Marcellus				All Marcellus			
Well Name	Porosity	Net h	Swi	TOC	Porosity	Net h	Swi	TOC	Porosity	Net h	Swi	TOC
Well No. 1	xxx	yyy	zzz	kkk	xxx	yyy	zzz	kkk	XXX	YYY	ZZZ	KKK
Well No. 2	xxx	yyy	zzz	kkk	xxx	yyy	zzz	kkk	XXX	YYY	ZZZ	KKK
Well No. 3	xxx	yyy	zzz	kkk	xxx	yyy	zzz	kkk	XXX	YYY	ZZZ	KKK
Well No. 4	xxx	yyy	zzz	kkk	xxx	yyy	zzz	kkk	XXX	YYY	ZZZ	KKK
Well No. 5	xxx	yyy	zzz	kkk	xxx	yyy	zzz	kkk	XXX	YYY	ZZZ	KKK
Well No. 6	xxx	yyy	zzz	kkk	xxx	yyy	zzz	kkk	XXX	YYY	ZZZ	KKK
Well No. 7	xxx	yyy	zzz	kkk	xxx	yyy	zzz	kkk	XXX	YYY	ZZZ	KKK
Well No. 8	xxx	yyy	zzz	kkk	xxx	yyy	zzz	kkk	XXX	YYY	ZZZ	KKK
Well No. 9	xxx	yyy	zzz	kkk	xxx	yyy	zzz	kkk	XXX	YYY	ZZZ	KKK
Well No. 10	xxx	yyy	zzz	kkk	xxx	yyy	zzz	kkk	XXX	YYY	ZZZ	KKK
Well No. 11	xxx	yyy	zzz	kkk	xxx	yyy	zzz	kkk	XXX	YYY	ZZZ	KKK
Well No. 12	xxx	yyy	zzz	kkk	xxx	yyy	zzz	kkk	XXX	YYY	ZZZ	KKK

Fig. 26—Example of inclusion of completion data into the spatio-temporal database.

recorded under "All Marcellus" are the weighted average of Upper and Lower Marcellus. In cases where the well has been completed in only one of the two formations (e.g., in the Lower Marcellus), the only parameters that include real value are those of completed formation (Lower Marcellus in this case), and the parameters of the other formation (Upper Marcellus) are all equal to zero. In such cases, the parameter values of the "All Marcellus" will be the same as those for the formation that includes real values (Lower Marcellus in this case).

Please note that this is only one way of trying to educate the top-down model concerning the impact of the completion on production. There are other ways to accomplish the same objective, and the quality of the final product (model) will depend on how creative the modeler can get in presenting the information to the model for training.

8.3.1 Two-Dimensional vs. Three-Dimensional Reservoir Modeling.
A top-down model can be considered as a 2D reservoir model, because it treats the production coming to the well as a continuous slug from the entire reservoir. The preceding section demonstrated how the presence and the possible contribution of different distinct geological formations to the flow (production) can be accounted for in the spatio-temporal database. This is the information that is used during the training and history matching of the top-down model. Given the fact that TDM in essence is a 2D reservoir-modeling technology, it may be viewed as a weakness by reservoir modelers that are used to building 3D numerical reservoir simulation models. We need to point out some realities that sometimes go unnoticed (or are overlooked) by some who are relatively new to the reservoir-modeling community.

The fact that TDM models fluid flow in a hydrocarbon reservoir in two dimensions (rather than three dimensions) will come across as a relative weakness only to reservoir engineers and reservoir modelers who fail to realize that, in fact, all reservoir modeling (regardless of technology) is 2D in nature. The issue is that numerical reservoir simulation and modeling are only theoretically and mathematically 3D, not practically. In the discussion that will follow in the next few paragraphs, we attempt to clarify the fact that numerical reservoir simulation and modeling are actually and practically not so 3D after all.

If the premise for accepting the claims made by a technology is its validation against reality (field measurements), then numerical reservoir simulation will not pass as a 3D flow model. In other words, the 3D flow modeling of the numerical reservoir simulation can be validated only if it can be history matched against the flow in the third (vertical) dimension. This would mean that because, in numerical simulation, production of a given well is the result of the summation of production that is calculated at several gridblocks, the production that is modeled (calculated) at the gridblock level should actually be history matched at each completed gridblock. This would be the only acceptable confirmation for the numerical reservoir simulation as a true 3D modeling technology.

Here, we propose that if you are simply dividing the entire production or flow (what is measured as production at the wellhead) into multiple segments (gridblocks) and following the fluid in three dimensions without being able to validate the distribution of the flow vertically (in the third dimension), then this would qualify not as a field-validated 3D flow modeling but as a mathematically validated 3D flow modeling that may or may not have anything to do with the reality. This type of flow modeling does not necessarily reflect, or, at least, cannot be validated to represent, the reality of the fluid flow in three dimensions. It looks more like an interesting (and academic) mathematical exercise than a model of the reality. Just because we are able to calculate flow in three dimensions does not mean the calculations are reproducing what is really happening in the reservoir.

We propose that the only acceptable way to perform and validate 3D flow in a numerical reservoir simulation model is through access to continuous production logs, something that is not available in most wells today. The fact is that in most cases, production logs are not available to the engineer to see where exactly the produced fluid is coming from.[48] Even in the cases in which production logs are available, they only show snapshots in time. We know that flow behavior in any part of the well/reservoir interface (the completion) changes with time. Therefore, in order to obtain a realistic view of the fluid flow, what is needed is some sort of continuous production log.[49]

---

[48]This fact becomes even more prominent when modeling fluid production from shale wells. We know that some of the stages in a shale well do not contribute to production, but cannot model this using numerical reservoir simulations for exactly the same reasons that are being discussed in this section.

[49]New technologies called distributed temperature sensors and distributed acoustic sensors have been introduced and are gaining popularity. These sensors use fiber optics and are installed throughout the completed zone and transmit information regarding the temperature and acoustics that can be used to interpret entry of the fluid into the wellbore, and thus provide measurements (at least in a relative fashion) of the flow. Once the installation of such sensors is mastered and becomes commonplace, much can be achieved in modeling fluid flow in the reservoir in a more realistic fashion.

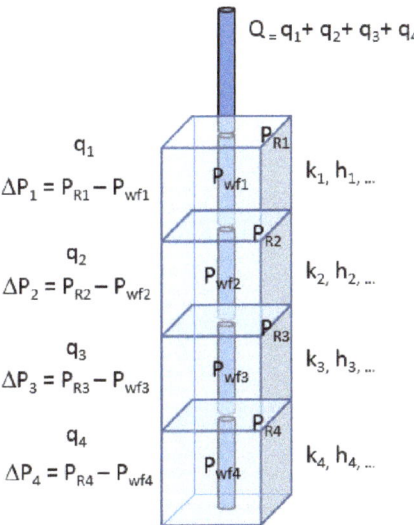

Fig. 27—Details of how 3D flow is calculated in a numerical reservoir simulation model.

In the absence of such information, most of the calculations that are currently made are mainly approximation of the reality.

Let us take a closer look at the modeling of fluid production in 3D numerical reservoir simulation models (see **Fig. 27**). Production from a given wellbore that is generated by the numerical model actually comes from production that is calculated at every gridblock that is penetrated by the wellbore and in which the wellbore has been completed. Therefore, by imposing the delta pressure [bottomhole pressure subtracted from the gridblock (reservoir) pressure] at every gridblock, flow (production) into the wellbore is calculated (as a function of reservoir characteristics). Then, by aggregating all the production rates from every completed wellbore section in every gridblock, the total production from the well is calculated. This is shown schematically in Fig. 27.

During the history-matching process, we are history matching a summation of productions from several gridblocks and not the production from each gridblock individually. Production from each segment of the well that is represented by the production from each gridblock contributes to the production from the well as a whole. Because we have no idea of where the actual production that we are trying to match is coming from (on a section-by-section basis), we are allowing the production (or lack of it) from different sections (gridblocks) to compensate for one another.

This is done routinely without ever knowing if we are modeling the correct amount of flow from each gridblock, which translates to production from different geological sections of the reservoir. Therefore, it can be claimed that the 3D modeling of the flow (production) in the numerical reservoir simulation is actually a 2D flow modeling that is being divided into multiple segments. This is what the author has chosen to call "the illusion of 3D modeling in the numerical reservoir simulation."

8.4 Resolution in Time and Space

The governing equation of the fluid flow through porous media is known as the diffusivity equation. The resolution in time and space in a top-down model, like all other characteristics of TDM, is determined on the basis of practical issues rather than mathematical factors. As a parabolic equation, the diffusivity equation is a second-order, nonlinear partial-differential equation. It defines changes in pressure (and saturation) as a function of time and space. Because time (t)

and space (x, y, z) are the independent variables, they need to be defined within the context of the discrete mathematics (in most cases finite-difference calculus) used for the numerical solution of the partial-differential equation.

$$\frac{\partial^2 p}{\partial x^2} + \frac{\partial^2 p}{\partial y^2} + \frac{\partial^2 p}{\partial z^2} = \eta \frac{\partial p}{\partial t}, \quad\quad\quad\quad\quad\quad\quad\quad\quad\quad\quad\quad\quad\quad\quad\quad\quad\quad\quad (4)$$

where p = pressure,
x, y, z = Cartesian coordinates in space,
t = time,
and η = hydraulic diffusivity.

The numerical solution of Eq. 4 (the diffusivity equation) usually includes discretization using finite-difference calculus. The number of gridblocks that are used to define the geological model for a midsized reservoir is usually measured in several millions. To prepare the geological model to be used as the foundation of the numerical reservoir simulation model, it is upscaled to several hundreds of thousands and sometimes several millions of gridblocks, which determines the spatial resolution of a numerical reservoir simulation model.

The time resolution is a function of several factors; however, it tends to be small at the start of the simulation when wells are producing in the transient flow regime and can be increased to month(s) or even year(s) once most of the wells in the model have reached the pseudosteady-state flow regime.[50] The reason behind small timesteps at the start of the simulation is the large changes in the dependent variable (pressure) near the wellbore. When an "automatic timestep" scheme is used in the simulation model, and given the fact that the resolution in space (the size of the gridblock) is fixed, the numerical solution must reduce the timestep to a value small enough for a stable solution (change in pressure) to be reached (converged) reliably. This is one of the reasons behind long simulation times in many cases.

Because no partial differential equations are solved (numerically or otherwise) during a TDM procedure, numerical convergence is not an issue, and therefore the requirement for multiple iterations for each timestep is eliminated. This contributes to fast-track solutions and the small computational footprint of the top-down model.

One of the first items that needs to be addressed in the development of the spatio-temporal database is the resolution in time and space. The ultimate size of the spatio-temporal database is a direct outcome of the decisions made regarding the space and time resolution. It should be noted that although some decisions need to be made, the size (number of wells) and the age of the field being modeled dictate, to a large extent, the space and the time resolutions in a top-down model.

The phrase "spatio-temporal database" indicates that this database is populated with data (records) that represent multiple aspects of the fluid flow behavior in the reservoir in both time and space. Therefore, the first step in explaining the characteristics of the spatio-temporal database requires an explanation of how time and space are discretized in a top-down model.

8.4.1 Resolution in Space. In TDM, the resolution in space is mainly a function of the number of wells in the field, while the resolution in time is a function of the age of the field; of course, in both cases the limitation is data availability dictates much of the choices that the TDM modeler has to make. Furthermore, the number of wells in a field determines how many records are generated in the spatio-temporal database at any given timestep. Essentially, every well generates one record

---

[50] An automatic timestep routine is usually built in the simulation model to monitor and regulate the timestep sizes in order to ensure convergence and also for optimum performance.

(a row in a flat file or matrix of data) per timestep. Therefore, one may expect that a mature field that includes 100 wells and has 10 years of production to include 100 × 10 = 1,000 records with a timestep that is equal to 1 year. If the timestep is decided to be 1 month (where monthly production data are available), then the total number of records will increase to 1,000 × 12 = 12,000.

This much about the size of the spatio-temporal data was covered in the previous sections as well. However, the explanation provided up to now on the size of the spatio-temporal database is quite superficial, and its objective was to provide a big picture of how a spatio-temporal database is populated with data. Once we get to the realities of developing a top-down model and actually try to assimilate a spatio-temporal database, we soon learn that the reality is usually more complex, and in order to provide adequate training to a top-down model, we need to be quite careful about two things:

1. *What we put in our spatio-temporal database.* In other words, what data are recorded in the spatio-temporal database for presentation to the learning algorithms.
2. *How we put it there.* Assimilation of the spatio-temporal database is much more than storing information and data in a data historian.

So far, we have written extensively about "what" goes into the spatio-temporal database, while we have only briefly talked about "how" this data and information is arranged. The reality is that the "how" is just as important as the "what" (maybe more important). We briefly touched on the "how" several pages ago and showed a summary schematic relating to the inclusion of the offset wells (please refer to Fig. 23). In this section, we will elaborate more on the techniques used in order to make sure that the machine-learning algorithms have enough information available to them and that they can make the most of the data that are presented to them. Although this realization stems from the understanding of how machines learn, nevertheless, as you will see in the next several pages, its implementation requires only (reservoir engineering) common sense.

As long as the top-down model is being trained to learn the reality, in order to be able to model and subsequently mimic it, we need to decipher the peculiarities and the nuances that are included in the reality and arrange them in a fashion that the top-down model can learn from. Here, we are referring to how a petroleum reservoir is usually developed.

The reality is that when we take time into account in our analyses, then the number of wells in a field becomes a dynamic variable. Oil fields are usually developed in phases. Therefore, not all the wells in a field are drilled at the same time. This fact must be represented in the data and be communicated to the top-down model during the training process. To accommodate this, static information in the top-down model is represented in more than one way. As was shown in Fig. 16, there is a class of static variables that are referred to as dynamically modified static parameters. If each well is assigned a drainage area (volume), and because the total size of the field (reservoir) will remain unchanged throughout the life of the operation, then as the number of wells operating in a field changes with time (new wells are drilled and some wells may be abandoned for one reason or another), the amount of drainage area (volume) that is assigned to each well will change. Therefore, the static properties that are assigned to a drainage area (for example, the average porosity that a well has access to) will change as a function of time.

To account for all these nuances that are an integrated part of the life of a petroleum reservoir, space in TDM is discretized using two interconnected grid systems. The first grid system is a 2D, comparatively fine Cartesian grid. The Cartesian grid system divides the field (reservoir) into relatively fine segments with square grids of approximately 1 acre. The thickness of each grid is the actual thickness of the formation, hence the grid system is referred to as a 2D grid system. The grid where the well is located will assume the static properties of the well, such as formation thickness, formation top, porosity, and initial water saturation. The total number of wells present at each phase of the development, represented with as many fine Cartesian grids, will be used as the known values, and all other grids are populated using geostatistics.

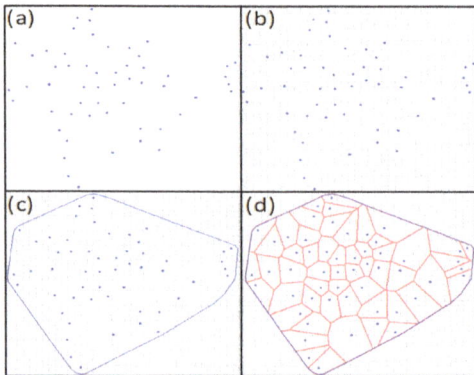

Fig. 28—Inclusion of overlapping fine-resolution Cartesian grid and coarse-resolution polygon Voronoi grids.

The second grid system used during the development of a top-down model is a 2D, comparatively coarse, polygon grid. Each polygon represents an ultimate drainage area accessible to a well during each phase of the development. Furthermore, each polygon is associated with a number of Cartesian grids, representing the well.

Fig. 28 demonstrates the four steps involved in the process of preparation and assignment of the static properties to be used in the spatio-temporal database to be presented to the machine-learning algorithms in the context of TDM.

1. Fig. 28a shows the relative locations of the wells in an oil field.
2. Fig. 28b shows the imposition of the Cartesian grids on the field.
3. Fig. 28c shows the reservoir boundaries that are uploaded (or drawn).
4. The Voronoi (Aurenhammer 1991) polygons are drawn and the field is delineated as shown in Fig. 28d.

As mentioned earlier, field development usually takes place in phases. Each phase includes a certain number of wells. **Figs. 29 through 31** demonstrate the change in the size of the Voronoi polygons (assigned drainage area, drainage volume) as more wells are drilled in a field. The increase in the number of wells during each phase of oilfield development constitutes a change in the spatial resolution.

Fig. 29 shows that during Phase One of the field development only three wells are placed; therefore, the corresponding Voronoi polygons for Phase One are identified and shown in this figure. The Cartesian grid used for this field is also shown in this figure. These three wells produce for the first 18 months, before new wells are drilled and put into production.

It can be seen clearly that each of Wells 1, 2, and 3 can reach (or hypothetically have access to) a large portion of the field identified by the polygons. In reality, each of these wells during Phase One of the production will not reach the hypothetical boundaries that are shown in Fig. 29. Nevertheless, for consistency purposes, these distinctions must be made.

During the 18 months of Phase One production, the spatial resolution for this field (the polygons) will remain constant as is shown in Fig. 29. For this period, the static properties of these three wells are used to populate the Cartesian grids. Each well will have two associated values for each static parameter, the well-based static property (that will remain constant throughout the life of the field) and the polygon-based static properties, also known as "dynamically modified static parameters" (which will be modified as new wells are drilled and put into production during the future phases

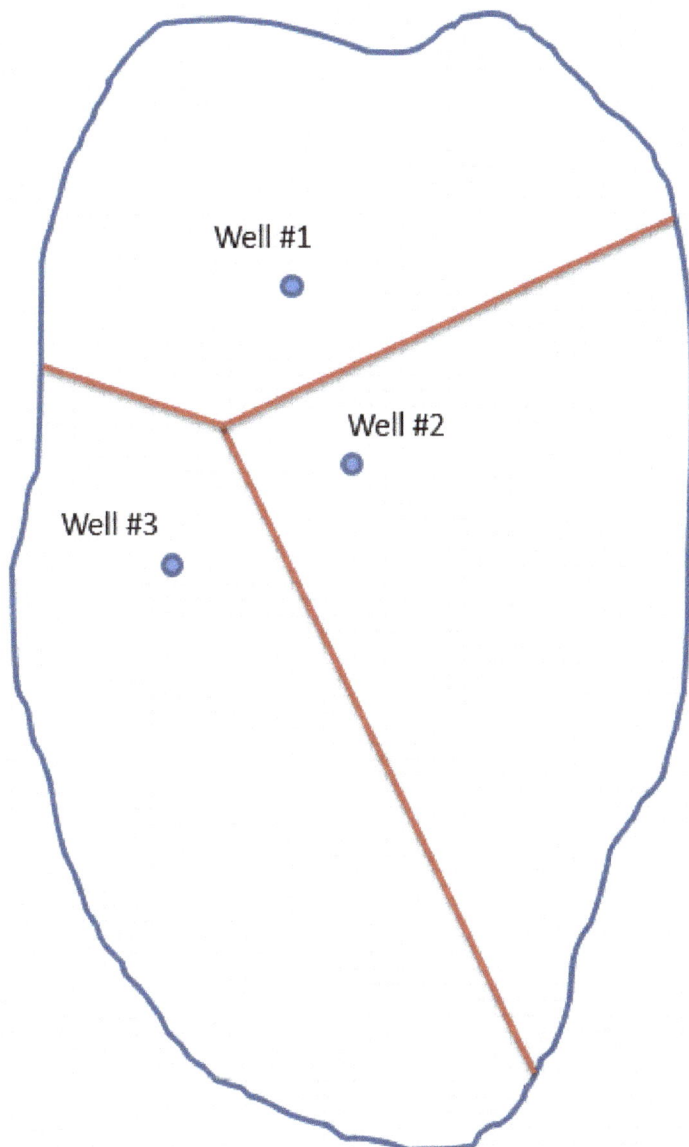

Fig. 29—"Phase One" of the field development where only three wells are drilled. These wells will produce for a certain amount of time before Phase Two wells are drilled.

of development). For example, there will be a porosity for this well (the well-based porosity) that is assigned to the Cartesian grid in which the well is located and is used in the spatio-temporal database. The value of the well-based porosity is the same as the one extracted from the field measurements (well logs).

The second value of the porosity, also used in the spatio-temporal database, is the polygon-based porosity (dynamically modified static parameters). Appropriate averaging techniques must be used to calculate the average static value for the polygon using the populated Cartesian grid values.

74 Data-Driven Reservoir Modeling

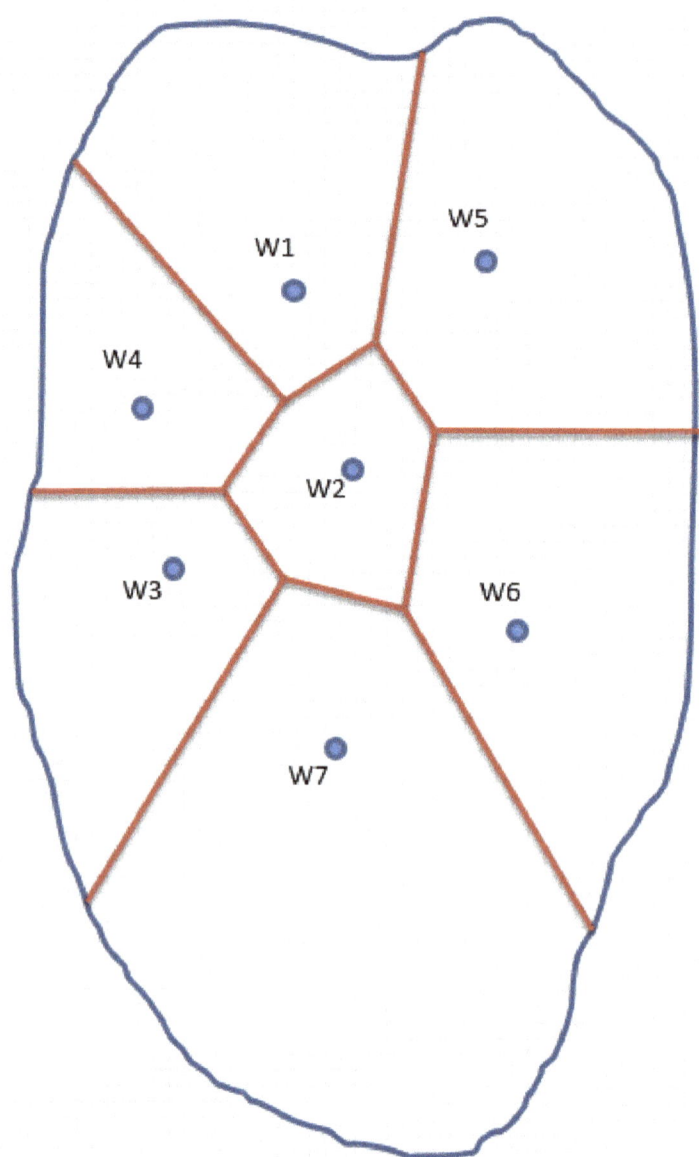

Fig. 30—Phase Two of the field development where only four more wells are drilled. These seven wells will produce for a certain amount of time before Phase Three wells are drilled.

The value of the polygon-based porosity is calculated as the arithmetic average porosity of all the Cartesian grids associated with that particular well in the specific polygon.

After 18 months of production, four new wells are drilled as Phase Two of development gets under way. Fig. 30 shows the spatial resolution (the Cartesian grids as well as the polygons) of the wells after the 18 months until the end of Phase Two. All wells (now seven wells) will produce during the next 48 months as Phase Two.

During Phase Two of production, as shown in Fig. 30, seven wells are actively in production. The same field (reservoir) is now divided into seven (instead of the original three in Fig. 29) segments, and the portions of the reservoir dedicated to the first three wells have changed in size.

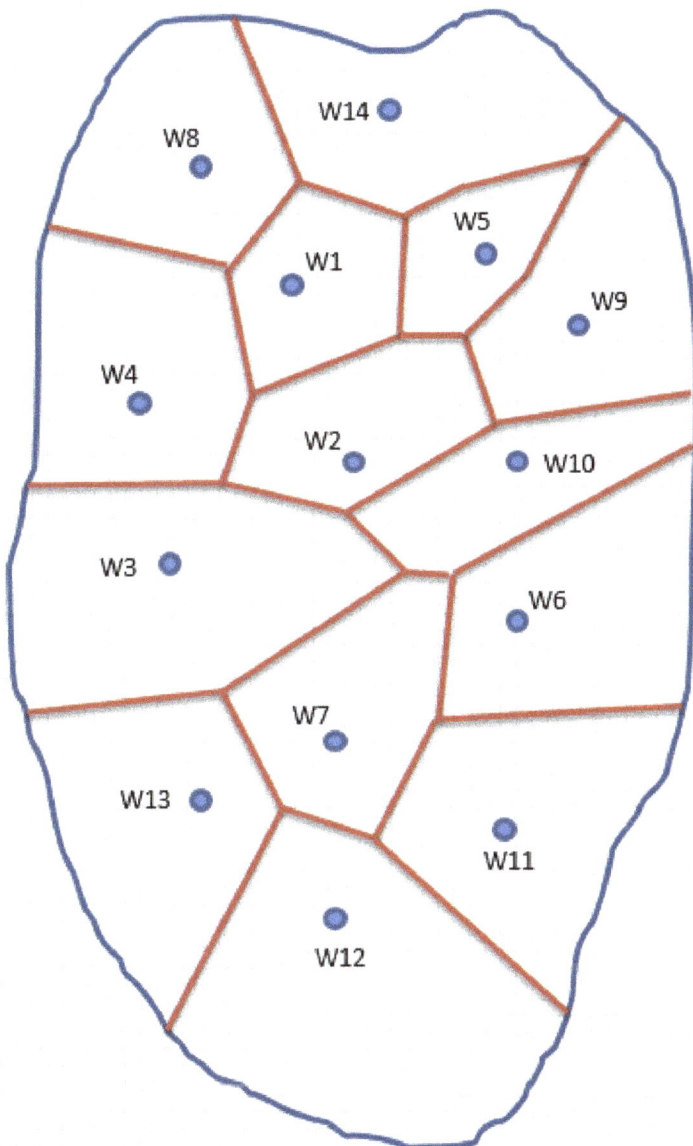

Fig. 31—Phase Three of the field development where seven more wells are drilled. These 14 wells will be producing up to the present time when the top-down model is being constructed.

This modification in the number of the wells creates substantial changes in the static model. The changes take place on two fronts:

1. Now that there are seven actual measurements for each static property, a new geostatistic calculation is performed (this time with seven wells as anchor/known values, instead of three wells) as the starting point, and the values of the static properties for all the Cartesian gridblocks are modified.
2. As for the polygons, the field is now divided between seven wells instead of three; therefore, a smaller volume is dedicated to each well.

Therefore, the static property values in the Cartesian gridblocks and the change in the size of the polygons associated with each well create new averages and new polygon-based static property values for each well. These new values will be in place throughout Phase Two of the production until new wells are introduced in Phase Three.

At the end of the 66 that is (18 + 48) months of production (Phase Two) by these seven (3 + 4 =) wells, another seven wells are drilled as Phase Three of development is implemented. These seven new wells produce for the next 30 months. The resolution in space for this field during the final 30 months is shown in Fig. 31. When the spatio-temporal database is being constructed, the static information associated with each well, and the polygon that they represent, will acquire a dynamic nature. Examining the volume that is represented by Well No. 1 in Figs. 29, 30, and 31 clearly shows the dynamic nature of the static parameters such as formation thickness and porosity.

Such information is extracted and consequently recorded (in proper form as will be shown in subsequent sections) in the spatio-temporal database. While the polygons in the top-down model represent the average of the static parameters for each well, the finer Cartesian grids represent the static parameters at the well that are usually acquired through well logs and sometimes core analysis. Conventional geostatistical techniques, such as Kriging and nearest-neighbor weighting, are used to populate the fine Cartesian grids, and then the collection of the given reservoir characteristics of the fine grids that are contained in a polygon are averaged in order to calculate the average parameter for the polygon.

8.4.2 Resolution in Time. The number of records in the spatio-temporal database is determined by the combination of the total number of wells in the field and the length of their production. The decision made regarding the time resolution (daily vs. monthly or annually) controls the number of records that each well contributes to the spatio-temporal database. For example, for the field that has been discussed in the preceding section and is shown in Figs. 29 through 31, the resolution in time can be either in days or in months.

To show this a bit more clearly, the details are shown in **Fig. 32 and Fig. 33**. In these figures, we calculate the number of records when the time resolution is in "months" (Fig. 32) and when the time resolution is in "days" (Fig. 33). As can be seen, the total number of records in the spatio-temporal database is 810 when the time resolution is monthly and will increase to 24,300 when the time resolution is changed to daily. The large difference between these two numbers shows the sensitivity of TDM to time resolution.

Phases of Development	No. of Wells (Phase)	No. of Wells Cumulative	No. of Months	No. of Months Cumulative	Total No. Months Produced/Well	Total No. Records in the Data Set (Cum.)
Phase 1	3	3	18	18	96	288
Phase 2	4	7	48	66	78	600
Phase 3	7	14	30	96	30	810

Fig. 32—Calculating the number of records from the three phases of development in the field used in the example, using "month" as the time resolution.

Phases of Development	No. of Wells (Phase)	No. of Wells Cumulative	No. of Days	No. of Days Cumulative	Total No. Days Produced/Well	Total No. Records in the Data Set (Cum.)
Phase 1	3	3	540	540	2880	8640
Phase 2	4	7	1440	1980	2340	18000
Phase 3	7	14	900	2880	900	24300

Fig. 33—Calculating the number of records from the three phases of development in the field used in the example, using "day" as the time resolution.

In Fig. 32, the first column (Phases of Development) includes the names of different phases of file development. The second column [No. of Wells (Phase)] shows the number of wells drilled in each phase of the development, while the third column (No. of Wells Cumulative) shows the cumulative number of wells in the field by the end of each phase. Column four (No. of Months) is the number of months that each well in each phase is producing. The fifth column (No. of Months Cumulative) includes the cumulative number of months that the entire field is in operation. Column six (Total No. of Months Produced/Well) shows the length of time the wells in each phase are in production. For example, as is shown in column six, the three wells that were producing from the start will end up having 96 months of production, while the four wells that started production in Phase Two have produced for 78 that is (96 − 18) months. By the same token, the seven wells that have started production in Phase Three have only produced for 30 that is (96 − 66) months.

Finally in the last (seventh) column [Total No. of Records in the Data Set (Cum.)], the total number of records that is generated in the spatio-temporal database, as a function of the number of phases, wells, and number of months of production, are shown. As we mentioned earlier, each record in the spatio-temporal database is generated by a single unit in space and time. The unit in space is determined by the resolution in space (well), and the unit in time is determined by resolution in time, which in the case of Fig. 32 is "month." Because the three wells in Phase One have produced for a total of 96 months, they will generate a total of 288 that is (3 × 96) records. In Phase Two, four wells have produced for a total of 78 months; therefore, they generate a total of 312 that is (4 × 78) records that when added to the previous records generate a total of 600 that is (312 + 288) records. Similarly, in Phase Three, seven wells have produced for a total of 30 months; therefore, they generate a total of 210 that is (7 × 30) records that when added to the previous records generate a total of 810 that is (210 + 600) records. So it is easy to see how quickly the numbers add up. Furthermore, if the time resolution is reduced to days instead of months, this field will generate a spatio-temporal database with 24,300 records, as shown in Fig. 33.

8.5 Role of Offset Wells

One of the fundamental principles of reservoir engineering that is clearly reflected in the numerical solution to the diffusivity equation (the governing equation of fluid flow through porous media) is that wells in a field are in contact with one another. Therefore, when a full-field reservoir model is being developed, the impact and influence of production and injection from offset wells must be taken into account. When production from a given well is being modeled, the data set must include the impact (or lack thereof) of the offset wells. Just like the influence of static and dynamic parameters on the production of a well, the impact of the offset wells also can be divided into static and dynamic parameters.

The degree of the influence of the offset wells on each other is a function of their distance from one another. The distance between two wells in a reservoir is not summarized only in the Euclidian distance, but also in other reservoir characteristics. It may be better to call this distance "the reservoir conductivity distance" in order to emphasize the role of reservoir characteristics such as permeability and formation thickness.[51] Therefore, because the degree of the impact of the offset wells on each other is a function of the degree of communication between the wells (the reservoir conductivity distance), the static parameters such as porosity, formation thickness, and permeability for the polygons that encompass each of the wells must be identified and included in the spatio-temporal database.

This inclusion of (dynamically modified static parameters) polygon-based reservoir characteristics in the spatio-temporal database and their possible inclusion during the training and history

---

[51]Throughout the development of the top-down model, we often need information and data, such as permeability, that may not be available. It is important to be aware that, in such cases, we have little option but to use whatever data and information are available to us as proxies. Using production and/or porosity as a proxy for permeability is an example of such cases.

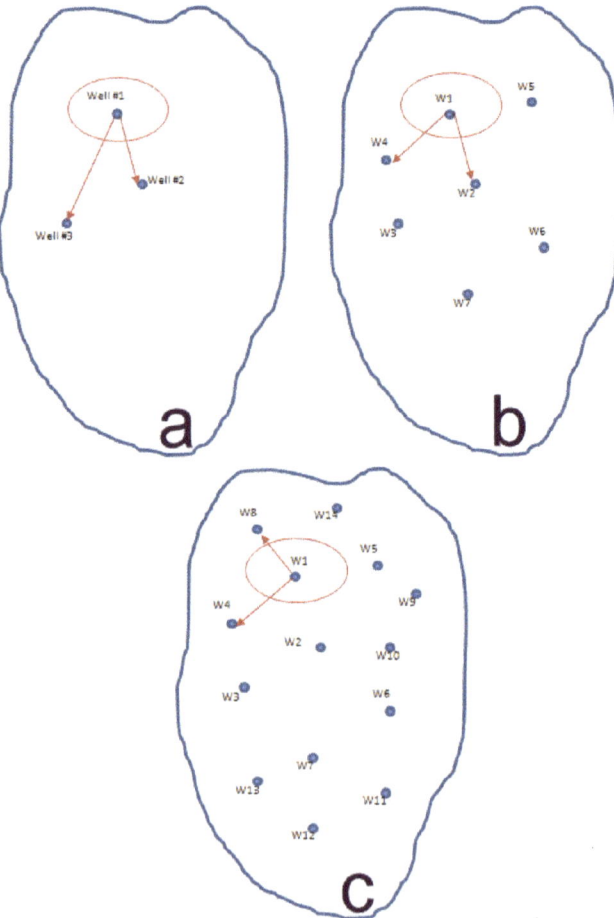

Fig. 34—Impact of offset wells is a time-dependent variable that will change as new wells are drilled in a reservoir. In this figure, the field goes through three phases of development. During each phase, the two closest offset wells to Well No. 1 change.

matching[52] will assist the top-down model in determining the geologic (reservoir) characteristics between each pair of wells. It can help determine if there is a barrier between the wells, or if there is a high-permeability streak in the path between them, as well as any other possible flow path scenario between the two extremes. This is how the geology of the reservoir is incorporated into the model and how production of the two wells can help us determine the nature of their communication. This becomes evident when one realizes that the entire historical production (one timestep at a time) is included in the spatio-temporal database so that the top-down model can learn from it.

It must be noted that the impact of the offset wells on production of any given well is dynamic in nature. This dynamic behavior has to do with the fact that wells in a field are drilled and put on production in phases and at different times. Therefore, this fact must be incorporated into the assimilation of the spatio-temporal database. **Fig. 34** clarifies the time dependency of the offset wells during the multiple phases of field development and their impact in the assimilation of the spatio-temporal database. This figure summarizes the dynamic nature of the inclusion of

---

[52]The training and history-matching process is covered in the next sections.

information from the offset wells in the spatio-temporal database using the three phases of field development previously shown in Figs. 29 through 31.

Let us assume that for the development of the top-down model for this field, which includes the process of modeling the production from each well, we are interested in including the impact of the two closest offset wells. During the first phase of the development, only three wells are drilled and produced, for 18 months (as explained in the preceding section). The closest offset wells to Well No. 1 are identified as Wells No. 2 and No. 3, as shown in Fig. 34a.

When Wells No. 4 through No. 7 (four new wells) are drilled during Phase Two of the development, the picture of the closest offset wells changes. Now for the next 48 months (duration of the production in Phase Two before Phase Three starts), starting on Month 19, the two closest offset wells to Well No. 1 are no longer Wells No. 2 and No. 3.

Fig. 34b clearly shows that the two closest offset wells (to Well No. 1) from Month 19 to Month 66 (48 months of Phase Two production) are Wells No. 4 and No. 2. Furthermore, when Wells No. 8 through No. 13 (seven new wells) are drilled during Phase Three of the development, and produce for the next 30 months, starting on Month 67 (the first month after the start of Phase Three), the two closest offset wells to Well No. 1 are no longer Wells No. 4 and No. 2. Fig. 34c shows that during Phase Three of production, the two closest offset wells (to Well No. 1) from Month 67 to Month 96 are Wells No. 8 and No. 4. Therefore, during the construction of the spatio-temporal database, the changes to the closest offset wells (their static and dynamic parameters) must be incorporated, accordingly.

One more thing that needs to be taken into account and incorporated in the spatio-temporal database is the nature of the offset wells. Depending on the type of operation that is being conducted in the field (primary production vs. enhanced recovery), the offset wells are either production wells or injection wells, or both. Furthermore, the injection well can be injecting water, gas, or other fluids (e.g., chemicals or polymers). Also, it should be noted that in some operations, production wells are inverted into injection wells, and sometimes the nature of the fluid being injected changes as a function of time. All these operational issues must be incorporated into the spatio-temporal database, in much the same manner that was covered in the preceding two sections. The structure of the inclusion of the information regarding the offset wells is shown in Fig. 23.

8.6 Structure of the Spatio-Temporal Database

Top-down models are appropriate only for mature fields. These are fields with a reasonable amount of production history to learn from. In TDM, the concentration is on individual wells and their closest offset wells. When this process is repeated for all the wells in a field, eventually all wells get involved multiple times: once for being the individual well that is the center of the modeling focus, and several times as offset to other wells. This redundancy of focusing on a well from multiple angles provides the means for fully understanding the fluid flow around each well.

Therefore, TDM may be thought of as a network of multiple sector models that focus on each individual well with all its offsets. These sector models are connected to one another through the interaction in space and time. **Fig. 35** is a graphical representation of how the interaction between wells and sector models is modeled in a top-down model.

While completely different from its predecessors, TDM has indeed learned from and enacts several fundamental characteristics of traditional reservoir-modeling technologies, such as numerical reservoir simulation and streamline simulation. Since the general approach of TDM to reservoir modeling is to model fluid flow in porous media by focusing on individual wells and the interaction between wells, it can be visualized as a network of connected wells in a porous medium. Looking at Fig. 35, one can see that top-down models have similarities with streamline simulation (Datta-Gupta and King 2007).

From a general philosophical point of view, this statement may be valid; however, the formulation and modeling paradigm of streamline simulation and TDM are completely different.

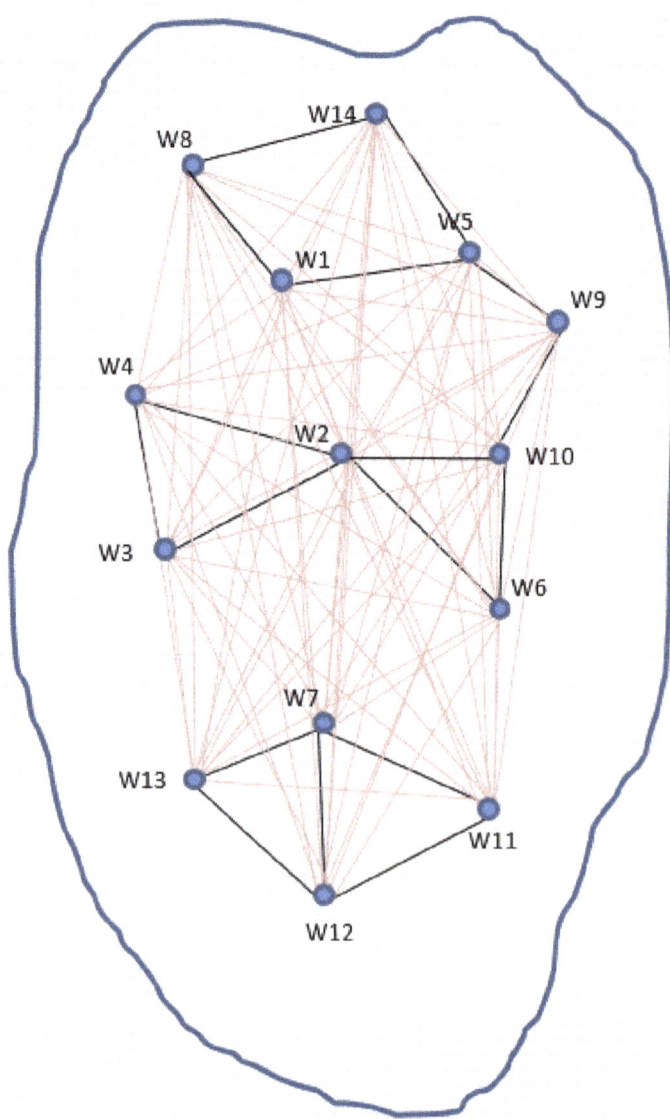

Fig. 35—TDM may be considered a connected network of individual wells. The darker connections indicate direct modeling, while the lighter connections indicate indirect modeling between well connections.

In streamline simulation, like other traditional modeling techniques, a specific and deterministic formulation that reflects our current understanding of fluid flow in porous media—and therefore remains constant and never changes—is used to define interaction between wells. In TDM, every case is different. Each reservoir (field) imposes its own unique characteristics on the model. The difference between reservoirs (fields) that is being mentioned here goes beyond just reservoir characteristics, and includes the nature of the fluid flow in the reservoir as well as parameters such as well construction and trajectories and operational constraints. Top-down models also include the overall understanding of fluid flow behavior in each specific reservoir, including all its faults, barriers, thief zones, and geologic nuances that differentiate one hydrocarbon-producing reservoir from another.

As mentioned in previous paragraphs, the TDM approach seems to be similar to that of sector models. This is true, as long as one realizes that the top-down model represents the interaction of a collection of several sector models (as many as there are wells—in a mature field) that have been integrated into a comprehensive and seamless entity—that work well with one another. One may ask, "How many sector models does it take to build a top-down model?" The answer is "As many as there are wells in the field." Therefore, one may consider the top-down model as a tight and interactive integration of multiple sector models.

A general structure for the spatio-temporal database was presented in Fig. 23. The single most important item that needs to be mentioned regarding the structure of the spatio-temporal database, as the foundation of the top-down model, is that each of its records consists of data from a single well. Each record includes one instance of production from one well as the output, and all the parameters that are responsible for that specific production value as the inputs. This would serve as a snapshot in time and space that represents the fluid flow in the specific porous media being modeled. The input parameters, as discussed in the previous subsections, include static parameters, dynamic parameters, and all relevant information from the offset wells.

The number of offset wells that should be included is not a set number and is controlled by reservoir engineering principles. For example, for a field with high permeability that has been producing for a long period of time, it is expected that the number of offset wells should be higher than for a tight formation with a short period of production life. The reason for this should be quite clear to any reservoir engineer. High permeability readily accommodates interaction between more wells in a reservoir, while in tight formations this may not be true, unless wells are stimulated. Furthermore, length of production history also provides the opportunity for interaction between wells in close connection with the conductivity of the reservoir, which is controlled by permeability and net formation thickness.

Here, we explain the process of preparing the spatio-temporal database to be used as the source of information to train, calibrate, and eventually validate a top-down model. To make the explanation easier to understand, we use an actual case study for a mature field.

As mentioned in the previous sections, the first step is to overlay a Cartesian grid on the reservoir and then divide the reservoir into polygons, based on Voronoi graph theory. **Fig. 36** shows the polygons for each well in an onshore field in the Middle East.

Next, the field is divided into sectors. There will be as many sectors as there are wells. Each sector has one well as the focal point and multiple offset or neighbor wells. This results in sectors with different volumes and areas. **Figs. 37 and 38** show multiple examples of the sectors as applied to the mature field in the Middle East. Each sector generates a number of records. A sector includes a well that is the focal point of the sector and all its offset wells. Records generated by a sector share the following elements:

1. Well construction and trajectory characteristics, if wellhead pressure and choke sizes are being used as operational constraints, it might be necessary to use well design characteristics (e.g., casing and tubing sizes) as input. This will allow an internal estimation of the flowing bottomhole pressure by the top-down model. If wells in the field are generally similar in design and construction, this step may be overlooked. Other inputs will include well location (latitude and longitude) whether it is a vertical, slanted, or horizontal well; inclination and azimuth; true vertical depth, and measured depth.
2. Static parameters that refer to reservoir characteristics measured at the well location for the well that is the focal point of the sector.
3. Polygon-based static parameters for the well that is the focal point of the sector.
4. Polygon-based static parameters for the wells that are offset to the focal well. Please note that this may end up being a dynamic parameter (see Section 8.5 Role of Offset Wells) if new wells are drilled in the field during the life of the focal well.
5. Completion characteristics, if they are not changing with time.

While the above parameters will be constant for all the records that are generated by one sector, several parameters will have new values for each record. The number of records generated by a sector is a function of two numbers related to the production of the focal well: (1) the life of the well, identifying how long the well was in operation, and (2) the time resolution, or the timestep. The dynamic parameters that are included in each record are

1. The time.
2. Operational constraints on the well (this can be flowing bottomhole pressure, or wellhead pressure, and or the choke size, at time t).
3. Operational constraints of the offset wells at time $t-1$.
4. Production rates of the offset wells at time $t-1$.
5. Injection volumes of the injector wells at time t.
6. Any changes in completion at time t.
7. Number of days of production during time t (if the timestep is a month or a year, this value will be in days; if the timestep is in days, this value will be in hours).

Inclusion of the above parameters will generate a series of records for each sector. The total number of records generated by each sector will define the final size of the spatio-temporal database.

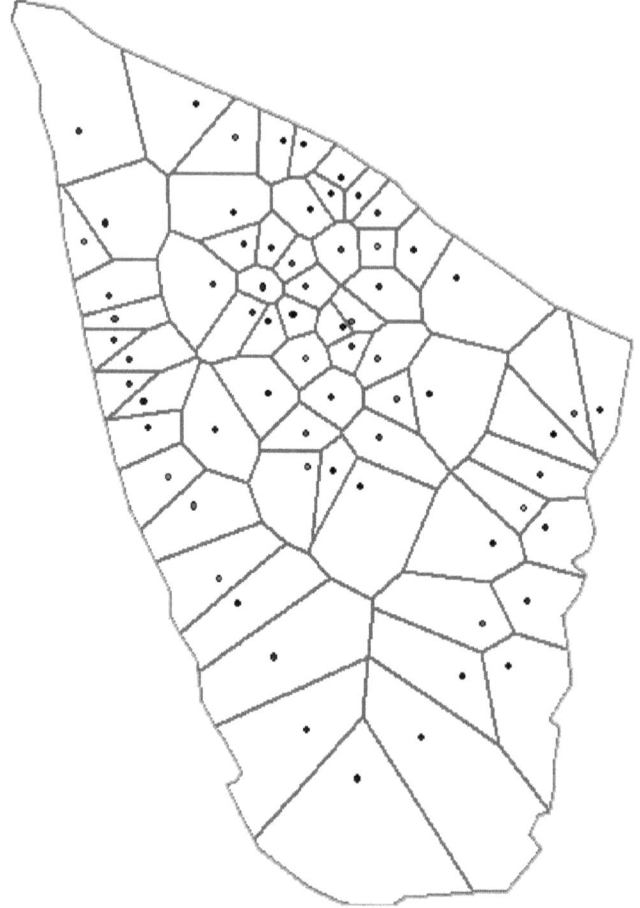

Fig. 36—Voronoi polygons have been generated for a mature asset.

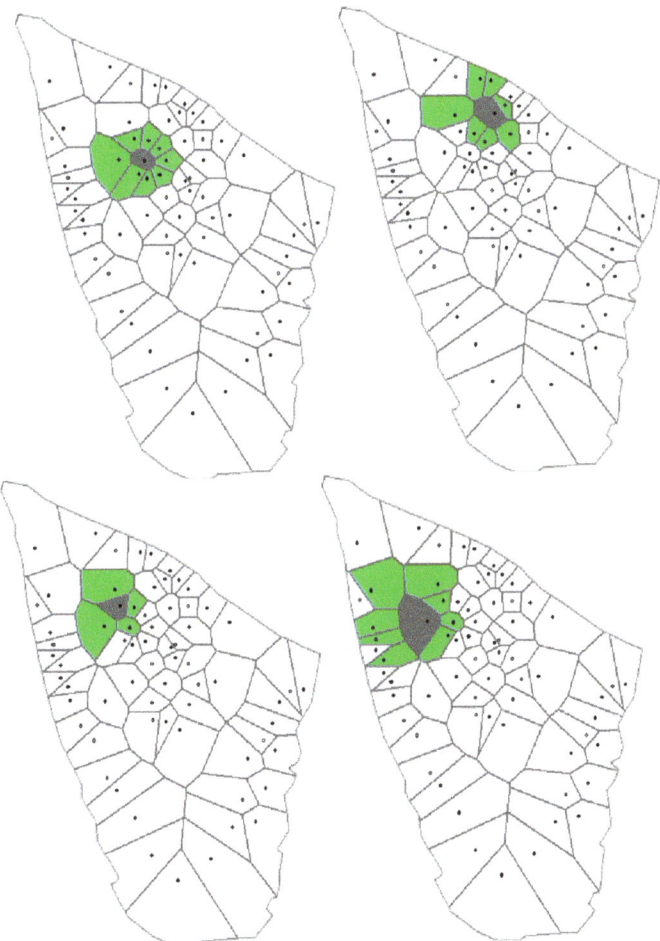

Fig. 37—Closest offset wells (in green areas) play a role in production behavior of the well that is being modeled (in gray areas).

Figs. 37 and 38 include multiple examples of the sectors being modeled in the top-down-model development for this field. Each sector model in these figures is identified by the nonwhite background. In each sector, the well that is the focal point of the modeling is identified with a gray background while the wells that are included in the sector model and are the offset wells are identified with a green background.

Furthermore, it is interesting to note that the number of offset wells in each of the sector models is different. This number is a function of the shape of the polygon that is used to delineate the area (volume) that is accessible to the focal well at the timestep that the calculations are being made. In TDM, there are no restrictions that force the spatial (volumetric) size of the sector models. These sizes are imposed by the number of wells and how the field has been developed.

8.7 Required Quantity and Quality of Data

One of the most common questions that is posed when the top-down model is presented is "How many wells do we need to be able to build a top-down model?" Because the top-down model is a data-driven reservoir model, its accuracy, robustness, and dependability are directly related to the amount of data that is available from a field. The answer to the above question is not a simple

84 Data-Driven Reservoir Modeling

Fig. 38—Each combination of the gray and green areas generates the static and dynamic information for sector models.

number of wells. The answer involves a combination of multiple parameters. In order to decide whether there are enough data to warrant the development of a top-down model, the following issues should be considered:

1. *The complexity of the reservoir.* As the amount of nuances associated with the geological characteristics of a reservoir increases, more data will be needed to learn about all or most of such nuances.
2. *The number of wells.* Obviously, the larger the number of wells the better will be the chances of developing a successful top-down model. However, the minimum number of wells that is required for the development of a top-down model is a function of age and frequency of the production data or the time resolution.
3. *The time resolutions.* If data are available on a daily basis, then we might be able to develop a successful top-down model with approximately 20 wells that have been producing for 2 to 3 years. Because it all comes down to the number of records that are extracted from the available data to train the top-down model, as was shown in the previous sections, 20 wells producing for 3 years will generate a spatio-temporal database with 21,900 that is $(20 \times 3 \times 365)$ records.

As a rule of thumb, as long as there are more than 15,000 records, one should be able to build a top-down model. Of course, as the number of wells, the age, and the time resolution of a field increase, so does the probability of success in developing an acceptable, robust, and high-quality top-down model.

However, it should be noted that if the production from all the wells in the field only represents the early (transient) flow regime in the field, it cannot be expected that the top-down model will be able to provide reasonable predictions for the boundary-dominated flow regimes. In other words, reservoir engineering common sense should never be abandoned during the development of a top-down model.

As for the quality of the data, the author's firsthand experience with a reasonable number of cases studies suggests that the quality of the data that are usually available in most operators' databases is good enough for the development of the top-down model. It is impossible to get 100% clean data in the situations where people are involved in the data collection and curation. Machine-learning algorithms are known to have a certain tolerance for noisy data. As long as data make sense to you as a reservoir engineer, they should be good enough for the development of the top-down model.

Chapter 9

History Matching the Top-Down Model

When it comes to reservoir models, the logic goes like this: "Would you believe a model's forecast of the reservoir's behavior in the future if it fails to match the production history of the reservoir in the past?" Answering this question should be quite easy: "No." If a reservoir model fails to match the production history, it will enjoy little or no credibility in forecasting production into the future. However, the opposite is not necessarily a "Yes." That is, if the question is posed as "Would you believe a model's forecast of the reservoir's behavior in the future if it is able to match the behavior of the reservoir in the past?," then the answer should be "It depends" or "Yes, but only to a certain degree."

Therefore, when it comes to reservoir models, history matching is necessary but not sufficient. This stems from the fact that reservoir models do not offer unique solutions. One of the major reasons for the rise of stochastic reservoir modeling is this nonuniqueness of the reservoir models. Top-down models are no different. Even after achieving satisfactory history matching results generated by a top-down model, it is a nonunique solution. What is achieved by history matching, in cases of both numerical and data-driven reservoir modeling, is the internal consistency[53] of the model. In both cases, to develop more confidence in the model's results and its forecast of future reservoir behavior, more (than just history matching) needs to be done.[54] Nevertheless, the history-matching process must be performed, and the result must be acceptable before any other step can be taken.

In numerical simulation and modeling, the functional relationships used in Eq. 1 consist of the law of conservation of mass, Darcy's law (Fick's law of diffusion in the cases that such formulation is required), thermodynamics and energy conservation (if modeling thermal recovery), and so on. These functional relationships are deterministic and are believed to be true and unchangeable. Therefore, if the production that results from numerical simulation and modeling does not match the observations (measurements) from the field, the conclusion is made that the reservoir characteristics (the static model) may not have been accurately measured and interpreted, and therefore must be modified in order to achieve a match.

This is the conventional approach and has been the common practice during the past several decades. Here, our objective is not to comment on the validity and/or the application of this technology. However, it should be pointed out that the functional relationships that are used to model fluid flow through porous media, and are represented in specific formulations, have evolved from simple relationships in the early days of reservoir simulation (single-phase, Darcy's law) to a much more

---

[53]Here is a definition for internal consistency: In statistics and research, internal consistency is typically a measure based on the correlations between different items on the same test. It measures whether several items that propose to measure the same general construct produce similar scores.

[54]In the context of data-driven reservoir models, we introduce and will practice a new idea that we call blind history matching to address this specific issue.

complex set of relationships in today's commercial or academic models. This is the very definition of the research-and-development efforts in the many institutes (universities and research centers) that have developed state-of-the-art numerical reservoir simulation models.

These functional relationships enable modeling of more complexities in reservoir behavior (e.g., multiphase flow, dual-porosity formulation, pressure-sensitive permeability formulation, compositional formulation, coupling with geomechanics and surface facilities) and are bound to evolve even further as our knowledge of these physical phenomena deepens.

Therefore, during the history matching of a numerical reservoir simulation model, because the functional relationships are constant and unchangeable (assuming that our current understanding of the physical phenomena is good enough that we do not need modification, no matter which reservoir we are modeling) the engineers (reservoir modelers) concentrate on altering the reservoir characterization parameters (such as permeability) in order to reach a reasonable match. Since the reservoir characterization is represented by a geocellular (static) model, developed by a group of geoscientists (geologists, geophysicists, and petrophysicists), and consists of interpretations and uncertain values, engineers feel comfortable changing these numbers in order to match the production history, using their numerical simulation models. Please note that this approach is not being criticized but merely explained in order to emphasize the differences between the technologies used to model a hydrocarbon reservoir.

In top-down modeling (TDM), some of the assumptions that are made in the conventional numerical modeling are modified. Instead of holding the functional relationship constant, these relationships are allowed to change in addition to the possibility of modifying the reservoir characteristics. In other words, during the history matching of a top-down model, constant, deterministic, and nonflexible functional relationships between production and reservoir characteristics are avoided. The functional relationship that generates the observed production data from the reservoir using the set of measured reservoir characteristics is sought through machine-learning and pattern-recognition technologies, not modification of a geological (static) model.

In addition, reservoir characteristics can also be modified, if one set of reservoir characteristics (measurements) is believed to be better than the one being used. Once a set of reservoir characteristics that geoscientists are reasonably comfortable with is identified, they are not modified during the history-matching process. Instead, the functional relationships are modified until a match is attained. This idea is displayed in **Fig. 39**.

	Numerical Model	Top-Down Model
Reservoir Charactersistics	*Uncertain:* • Measurements • Interpretations (subject to modification during history matching)	*Uncertain:* • Measurements • Interpretations (subject to modification during history matching)
Functional Relationships	*Certain:* • Conservation of mass • Darcy's law (unchanged during history matching)	*Uncertain:* • Relationship between reservoir characteristics and production (subject to modification during history matching)

Fig. 39—Differences between history matching numerical reservoir models and top-down models.

During the history matching of a top-down model, the relationship between input parameters (usually a combination of several static and dynamic parameters as explained in previous sections) and the reservoir output (oil, gas, and water production from wells and, sometimes, static reservoir pressure and water saturation) is determined. Given the fact that machine learning is used in order to determine these relationships, the outcome is usually a matrix of coefficients. To understand this process better, one needs to develop a good understanding of how neural networks are trained and calibrated. This process was covered in Section 4.3 Artificial Neural Networks. It is also recommended that the references provided in Section 4.3 be thoroughly examined.

Once the neural network (or an ensemble of neural networks; please refer to Figs. 13 and 14 for clarification of the number of neural networks that is needed to construct a top-down model) is trained and calibrated in a satisfactory manner, the results are evaluated against the field measurements in order to see if the top-down model is able to match the production history for all the wells in a the field (history matching).

Fig. 40 shows the history-matching results for several individual wells from a top-down model developed for a mature field in southern Mexico. As displayed in this figure, in many cases

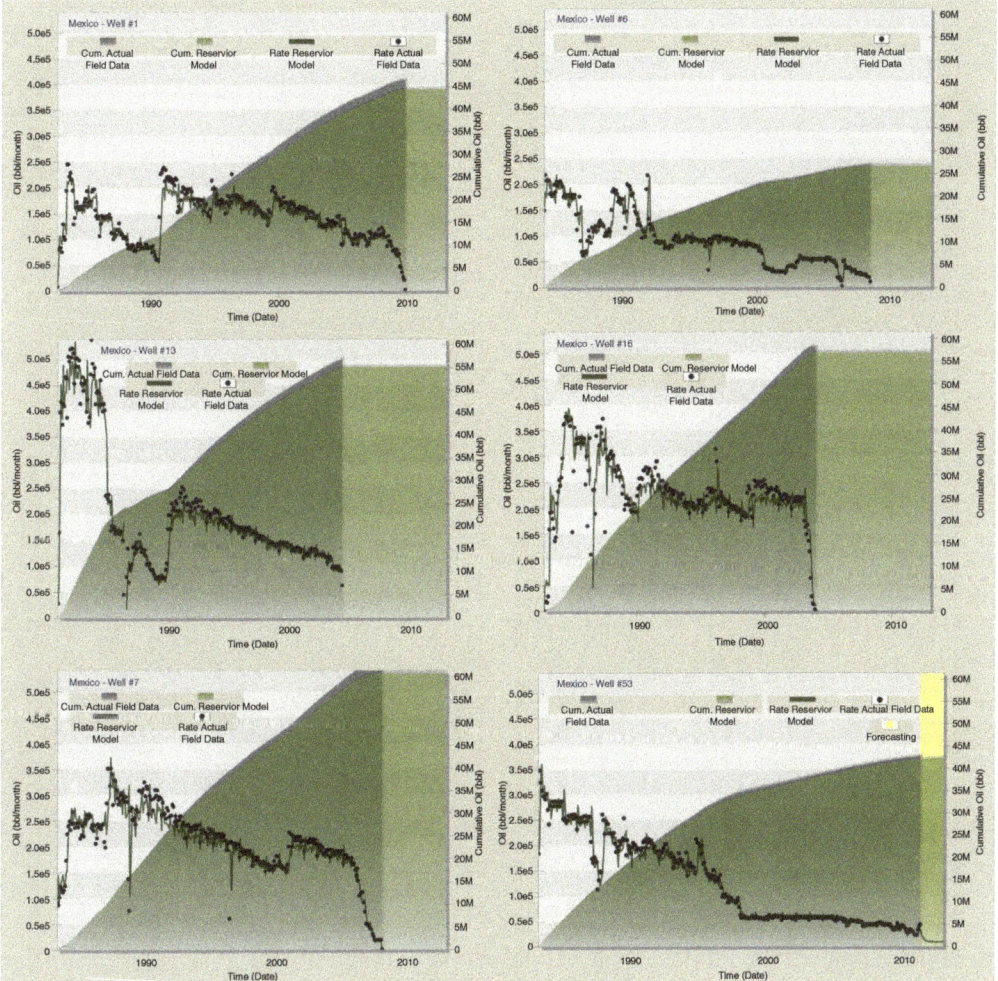

Fig. 40—Examples of a top-down model's history match. These are six out of more than 100 wells that were history matched during the development of a top-down model for a mature field in southern Mexico.

top-down models converge to impressive history matches even for cases for which it is very hard to get a history match using the traditional numerical reservoir simulation models. By not restricting the reservoir model to modifications from the geological model and by allowing the functional relationship between the reservoir characteristics and the production from the wells also to be the subject of modification (as mentioned in Fig. 39), exciting results can be achieved, as shown in Fig. 40. More results are shown in **Fig. 41**, representing both oil and gas history matches for two example wells during the top-down-model development for a mature offshore field in the North Sea.

In the context of reservoir modeling, the training and calibration of the ensemble of artificial neural networks (as shown in Figs. 13 and 14) that together form the main engine of the top-down model is referred to as "history matching." Figs. 40 and 41 clearly demonstrate the capability of the TDM process in understanding the nuances of oil and gas production when reservoir characteristics are combined with complex operational constraints to reproduce the ups and downs of the production operation.

During the training process, the top-down model learns from the information content of the spatiotemporal database and becomes able to deconvolve the production signals and distinguish between the impacts of the operational constraints and those of the reservoir characteristics. To demonstrate this particular capability of the top-down model, it is interesting to see the well production behavior shown in **Fig. 42** and compare it with graphs in Fig. 41.

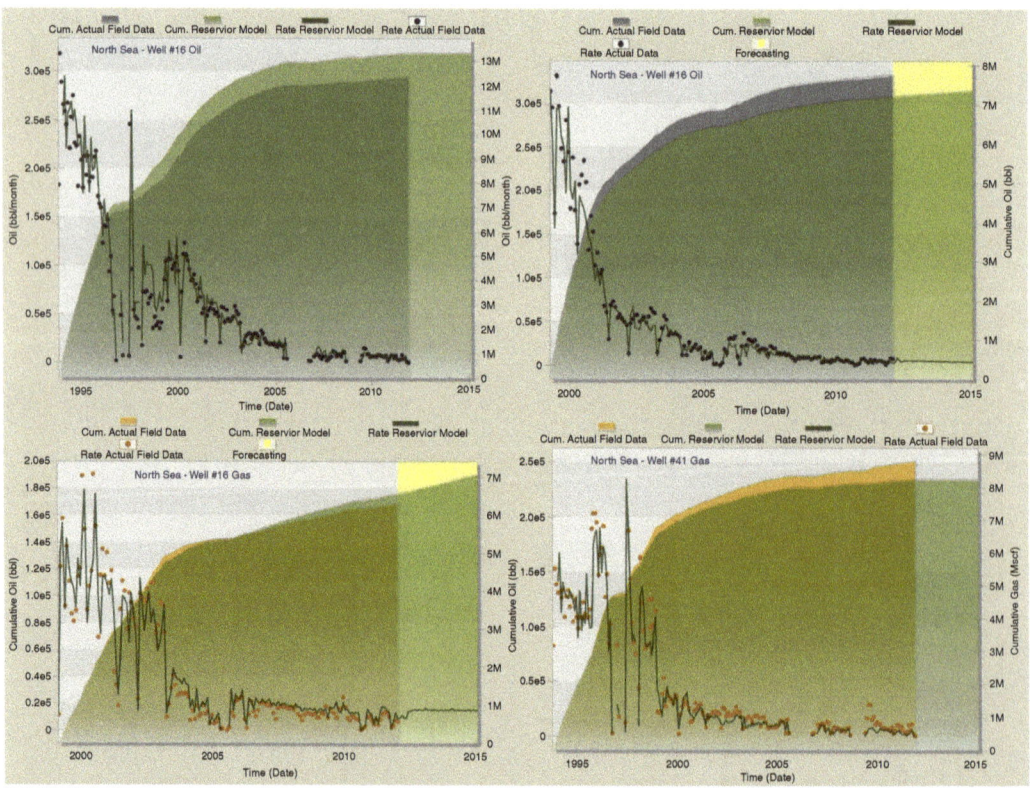

Fig. 41—Examples of a top-down model's history match. These are oil (top graphs) and gas (bottom graphs) history matches for two of many wells during the development of a top-down model for a mature offshore field in the North Sea.

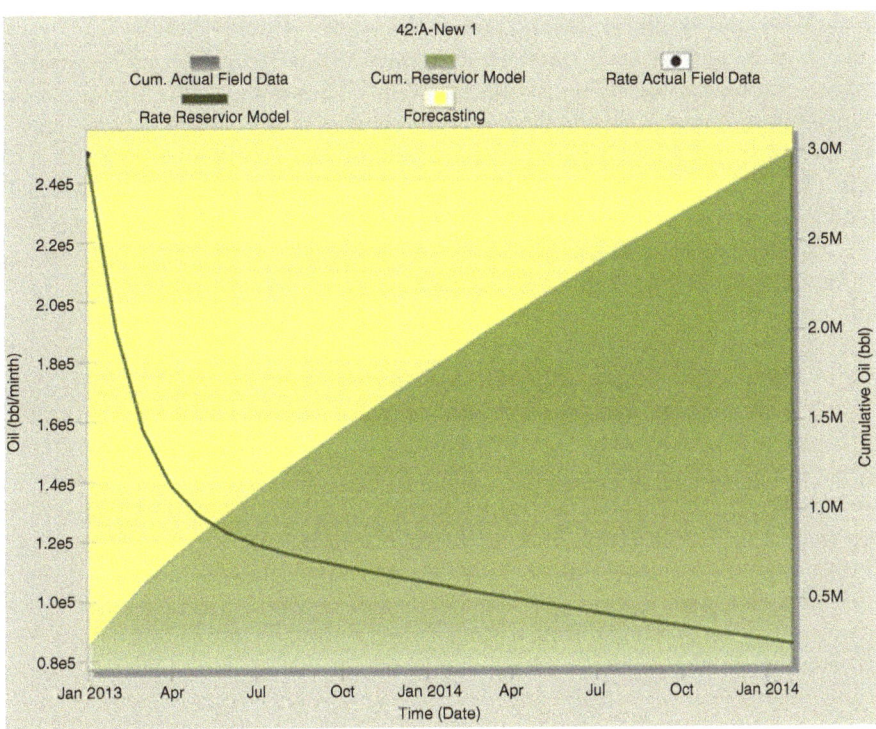

Fig. 42—Production from a new well in the offshore asset in the North Sea as forecast by the top-down model.

Both of these figures are generated by the same top-down model. However, the graph of the production vs. time shown in Fig. 42 is for a new well in a new location in the field, but because the operational constraints are kept constant (no changes in wellhead pressure or choke setting, with the well producing every day in a month) during the deployment of the top-down model, the production behavior is smooth and without any ups and downs as observed in the historical production, as shown in Fig. 41. In other words, just like the response from a numerical reservoir simulation, when reservoir characteristics are the only set of parameters that are controlling production, the production profile is smooth, just as shown in Fig. 42.

This type of well-behaved production profile is confidently expected to be generated by a numerical reservoir simulation model because it solves a well-behaved partial-differential equation (the diffusivity equation) to generate such production behavior. However, in the case of a top-down model, no differential equation (or any other type of mathematical equation for that matter) was solved. The results produced by a top-down model is what it has learned from being trained on the spatio-temporal database. Please note that none of the production profiles that were used to train the top-down model has the type of behavior that is shown in Fig. 42. The top-down model is trained using actual field data that are full of noise, as shown in Figs. 40 and 41. But once the training is completed, the top-down model is capable of generating production profiles (such as the one shown in Fig. 42) that include no noise or disruptions resulting from operational issues.

Fig. 42 may be considered testimony to the fact that the top-down model has learned the underlying physics of the fluid flow through porous media, with reasonable accuracy, and can successfully mimic the reservoir behavior. After all, teaching a computer reservoir engineering with the help of data *is* the definition of data-driven reservoir modeling.

9.1 Practical Considerations During the Training of a Neural Network

Details regarding the artificial neural networks can be found in a large number of books and articles, some of which were cited in Section 4.3 Artificial Neural Networks. As you might have already learned and noted in your readings on the subject or by some of your own practices, there is a substantial amount of art that is involved in the training of a neural network. In this section of the book, the objective is to share some personal experiences that have been gained throughout many years of developing data-driven models for oil-and-gas-related problems. These are mainly practical considerations, and they may or may not agree with similar practices in other industries, but they have worked very well for the author in the past 2 decades.

It was shown in Figs. 13 and 14 that data-driven models are an integral part, and maybe even the central and main engine, of top-down models. Therefore, to successfully build a top-down model, one should be able to develop (train, calibrate, and validate) data-driven models. Data-driven models are developed using machine-learning algorithms. Artificial neural networks have been used as the machine-learning technology of choice to develop data-driven models for the top-down model.

During the history matching of a top-down model, the neural networks that form the top-down model are trained using the data records that have been assimilated in the spatio-temporal database, so it is necessary for a data-driven reservoir modeler, or a top-down modeler, to be familiar with the ins and outs of training a neural network. Understanding how machines learn is not complicated. The mathematics associated with neural networks, including how they are built and trained, is not really complex (Haykin 2009) (1). It includes vector calculus and differentiation of some simple functions. While being a good reservoir engineer and a capable reservoir modeler is essential for building and effectively implimenting a top-down model, it is not a requirement to have degrees in mathematics, statistics, or machine learning.

For developing a functional top-down model, one does not need to be an expert in machine learning or artificial neural networks. What is required, though, is the ability to understand the fundamentals of these technologies and eventually to become an effective user and practitioner of them. Although such skills are not taught as part of any petroleum engineering curriculum in the universities, acquiring such skills is not a far-reaching task, and any petroleum engineer with a bachelor's degree should be able to master them with some training and effort. It is important to understand and subscribe to the philosophy of machine learning. This means that although as an engineer you have learned to solve problems in a particular way, you need to understand and accept that there is more than one way to solve engineering-related problems.

The technique that engineers have been using to solve problems follows a well-defined path of identifying the parameters involved and then constructing the relationships between the parameters (using mathematics) to build a model. The philosophy of solving a problem using machine learning is completely different. Given the fact that in machine-learning algorithms, such as artificial neural networks, models are built using data, the path to follow in order to solve an engineering problem changes from what you have learned as a petroleum engineer. To solve problems using data, you have to be able to teach a computer algorithm about the problem and its solutions. This process is called supervised learning. You have to create a large number of records (examples) that include the inputs (parameters involved) and the outputs (the solution you are trying to solve for). During training, these records (the coupled input/output pairs) are presented to the machine-learning algorithm and by repetition (and some learning algorithms) the machine will eventually learn how the problem is solved. The algorithm does this by building an internal representation of the mapping between inputs and outputs.

In Section 4.3 Artificial Neural Networks of this book, fundamentals of this technology were covered. In this section, some practical aspects of this technology will be briefly discussed. These practical aspects will help a top-down modeler to train useful neural networks that will be the heart and the engine of the top-down model. The neural network training includes several steps that will be covered in this section.

9.1.1 Selection of Input Parameters. Because all models are wrong, the scientist cannot obtain a "correct" one by excessive elaboration. On the contrary, following William of Ockham,[55] the scientist should seek an economical description of natural phenomena. "Just as the ability to devise simple but evocative models is the signature of the great scientist, so overelaboration and overparameterization are often the marks of mediocrity" (Box 1976). In order not to overparameterize our neural network model, we need to use a fraction of the total number of variables that have been collected in the spatio-temporal database.

Selection of the input parameters that are going to be used to train a neural network from among the large number of variables (potential inputs) that have been assimilated in the spatio-temporal database is not a trivial procedure. This topic was touched upon in Section 7.3 Curse of Dimensionality. The spatio-temporal database includes a very large number of parameters, all of which are potential input parameters to the neural networks that are going to be trained for the top-down model. They include static parameters, dynamically modified static parameters, and dynamic parameters as well as similar parameters for several offset wells. This was covered in detail in previous sections. These parameters are designated as columns in the flat file that is eventually used to train data-driven models (neural networks).

Not all of the parameters that are included in the spatio-temporal database are used to train the neural networks (top-down model). Actually, on the basis of the quotation from Box (1976) that was used at the beginning of this section, it is highly recommended that the number of parameters that are used to build (train, calibrate, and validate) the neural network be limited. This limitation of the input parameters should not be interpreted as implying that other parameters do not play any role in forming or calculating the output of the model (for example, production rate).

Elimination of some of the parameters and use of some others to build the data-driven model simply means that a subset of the parameters plays such an important role in the determination of the model output that they overshadow (or sometimes implicitly represent) the impact of other parameters, such that a model can be developed using only these parameters and safely ignoring others. Therefore, only a subset of these parameters should be selected and used as the input to the data-driven models that eventually would form the top-down model. Experience with developing successful top-down models has shown that the process of selecting the parameters that must be used as input to the model needs to satisfy the following three criteria:

1. The impact (influence) of all the existing parameters (in the spatio-temporal database) on the model output (in this case production from a well at time t) should be identified and ranked. Then, the top $X\%$ of these ranked parameters should be used as input in the model. This is easier said than done. There are many techniques that can be used to help top-down modelers in identifying the influence of parameters on a selected output. These techniques can be as simple as linear regression and as complex as fuzzy pattern recognition.[56] Some have used principal-component analysis (Jolliffe 2002) to accomplish this task.
2. In the list of input parameters that are identified to be used in the training of the neural network, there must exist parameters that can validate the physics and/or the geology of the model. Such parameters might already be among the highly ranked parameters in the previous step; if not, the top-down modeler must see to it that they are included in the model. Being able to verify that the top-down model has understood the physics, and honors it, is an important part of TDM.

---

[55]Ockham's Razor is a problem-solving principle devised by William of Ockham (c. 1287–1347). The principle states that among competing hypotheses, the one with the fewest assumptions should be selected. In the absence of certainty, the fewer assumptions that are made, the better.

[56]This is a proprietary algorithm developed by Intelligent Solutions Incorporated and used in their TDM software application, IMagine™ (www.IntelligentSolutionsInc.com).

3. In many cases, the top-down model is developed in order to optimize production. Identification of optimized choke setting during production is a good example of such a situation. In such cases, parameters that are needed in order to optimize production should be included in the set of input parameters. The optimization parameters might already be among the highly ranked parameters in the previous step; if not, the top-down modeler must see to it that they are included in the model.

Machine-learning literature includes many techniques for this purpose. In this literature, the technology is referred to as Feature Selection.

9.1.2 Partitioning the Data Set. Data in the spatio-temporal database is transferred into a flat file once a subset of the parameters is selected to be used in the training of the neural networks. The data in the flat file need to be partitioned into three segments: training, calibration, and validation. As will be discussed in the next section, the way these segments are treated determines the essence of the history-matching process (the TDM history-matching scheme). In this section, the characteristics of each of these data segments and their use and purpose are briefly discussed.

In general, the largest of the three segments is the training data set. These data are used to train the neural network and create the relationships between the input parameters and the output parameter. Everything that one wishes to teach a top-down model must be included in the training data set. One must realize that the range of the parameters as they appear in the training set determines the range of the applicability of the top-down model. For example, if the range of permeability in the training set is between 2 and 200 md, one should not expect the top-down model to perform reasonably well for a data record with permeability values less than 2 md and higher than 200 md. This is because of the well-known fact that most machine-learning algorithms, neural networks included, demonstrate great interpolative capabilities, even if the relationship between the input parameters and the output(s) is highly nonlinear. However, machine-learning algorithms are not known for their extrapolative capabilities.

As we mentioned in Section 4.3.1 Structure of a Neural Network, the input parameters are connected to the output parameter through a set of hidden neurons. The strength of the connections between neurons (between input neurons and hidden neurons, between hidden neurons with one another if such connections exist, and between hidden neurons and output neurons) is determined by the weight associated with each connection. During the training process, the optimum weight of each connection is determined through an iterative learning process.

During the training process, the weights between the neurons (also known as synaptic connections) in a neural network find their optimal value. The collection of these optimal values forms the coefficient matrices that are used to calculate the output parameter. Therefore, the role of the training data set is to help the modeler to determine the strength between the neurons in a neural network. Convergence of a network to a desirable set of weights that will translate to a well-trained and smart neural network model depends on the information content of the training data set. When the neural networks are being trained for TDM purposes, the size of the training data set may be as high as 80% or as low as 40% of the entire data set. This percentage is a function of the number of records in the spatio-temporal database.

The calibration data set is not used directly during the training process, and it actually plays no role in changing the weights of the connections between the neurons. The calibration data set is a blind data set that is used after every epoch of training[57] in order to test the quality and the goodness of the trained neural network. In many circles, this is also called the "test" set. The calibration data

---

[57] An epoch of training is completed each time that all the data records in the training set have been passed through the neural network and the error between neural network output and the actual field measurements has been calculated.

set is essentially a watchdog that observes the training process and decides when to stop the training process, since the network is only as good as its prediction of the calibration data set (a randomly selected data set that is actually a blind data set).

Therefore, after every epoch of training (when the network gets to see all the records in the training data set once) the weights are saved, and the network is tested against the calibration data set to see if there has been any improvement of the network predictive performance against this blind data set. This test of network predictive capabilities is performed after every epoch to monitor its generalization capabilities. Usually, one or more metrics, such as the R^2, the correlation coefficient, or the mean square error (MSE), is used to calculate the network's generalization capabilities. These metrics are used to determine how closely the set of synaptic connection weights will enable the calculation of the outputs as a function of the input parameters by comparing the output values computed by the neural networks against those measured in the field (the actual or real outputs) and used to train the neural network.

As long as this metric is improving for the calibration data set, the training can continue, and the network is still learning. When the neural networks are being trained for TDM purposes, the size of the calibration data set is usually between 10 and 30% of the entire data set, depending on the size and the life of the field being modeled.

The last, but arguably the most important, data set (segment) is the validation or verification data set. This data set plays no role during the training or calibration of the neural network. It has been selected and put aside from the very beginning to be used as a blind data set. It literally sits on the sidelines and does nothing until the training process is over. This blind data set validates the generalization capabilities of the trained neural network.

While having no role to play during the training and calibration of the neural network, this data set validates the robustness of the predictive capabilities of the neural network. The top-down model that will result from the combination of all the neural networks that are being trained is as good a reservoir model as the outcome of the validation or verification data set. When the neural networks are being trained for TDM purposes, the size of the validation (verification) data set is usually between 10 and 30% of the entire data set, depending on the size and the life of the field being modeled.

Since the spatio-temporal database is being partitioned into three data sets, it is important to make sure that the information content of these data sets is comparable to one another. If they differ, and many times they will, then it would be best that the training set have the largest, most comprehensive information content of the three data sets. This will ensure healthy training behavior and will increase the possibility of training a good and robust neural network. Information content and its relationship with entropy within the context of information theory is an interesting subject that those involved with data-driven analytics and machine learning should understand (Shannon 1948).

9.1.3 Structure and Topology. The structure and the topology of a neural network are determined by several factors, and hypothetically can have an infinite number of possible forms. However, almost all of them include a combination of factors such as the number of hidden layers, the number of hidden neurons in each hidden layer, the combination of the activation functions, and the nature of the connections between the neurons. In this section, the objective is to briefly discuss some of the most popular structures, specifically those that have shown success when used in the development of top-down models. In other words, the intention is not to turn this into a neural network tutorial, but rather to present practices that have proved successful during the development of data-driven reservoir models in the past and can be used as rules of thumb for those who will be entering the world of TDM.

As far as the connection between neurons is concerned, the structures that have been used most successfully in top-down models are fully connected neural networks. When every input neuron is

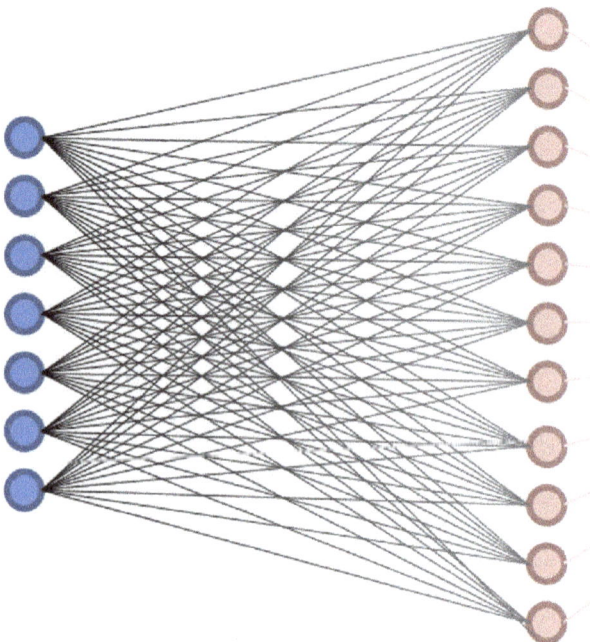

Fig. 43—A fully connected neural network with one hidden layer that includes 11 hidden neurons, seven input neurons, and one output neuron.

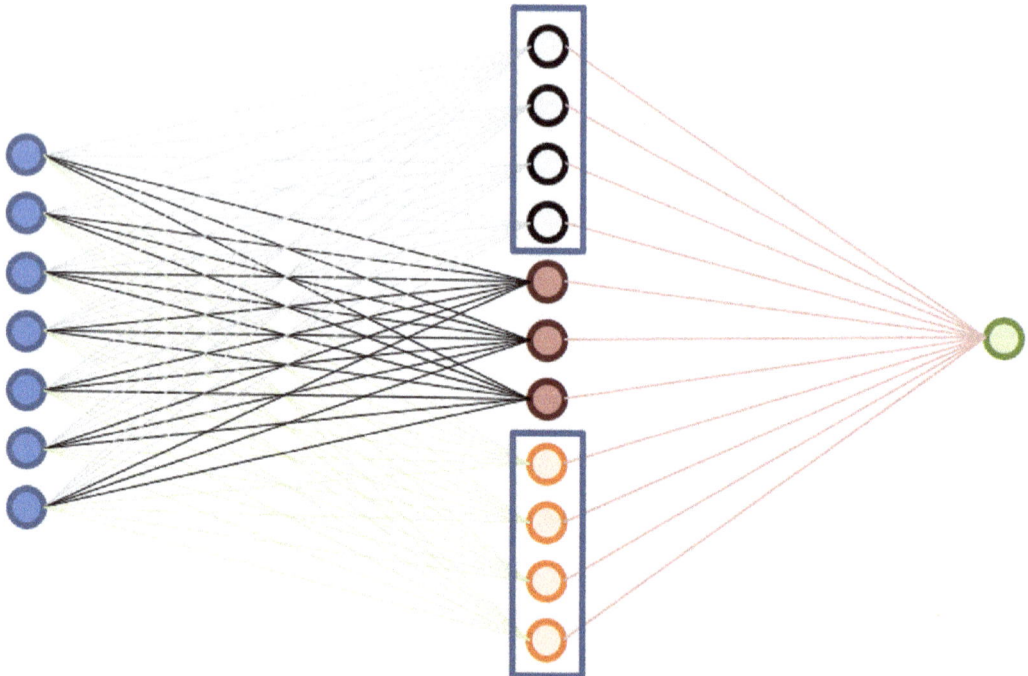

Fig. 44—A fully connected neural network with one hidden layer that includes three different sets of activation functions along its 11 hidden neurons, seven input neurons, and one output neuron.

connected to every hidden neuron, and every hidden neuron is connected to the output neuron, the network is called a fully connected network, as shown in **Figs. 43 through 45**.

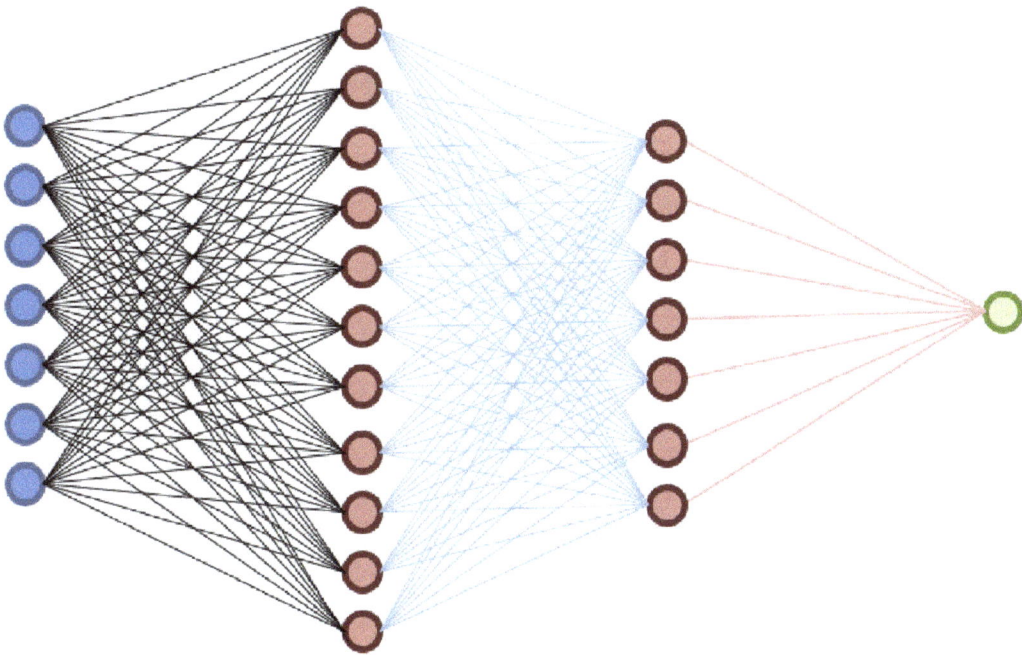

Fig. 45—A fully connected neural network with two hidden layers that includes 11 and seven hidden neurons, respectively, as well as seven input neurons and one output neuron.

Fig. 43 shows the simplest and most-used type of neural network for the development of data-driven models that form the main engines of the top-down model. This is a simple, three-layer, fully connected neural network. The three layers are the input layer, the hidden layer, and the output layer. Furthermore, while the number of output neurons in the output layer can be more than one, our experience with the top-down model has shown that, except in some specific situations, a single output neuron in the output layer performs best.

Furthermore, after experiencing a large variety of network structures, our experience has shown that if you are not able to train a good network[58] using the simple structure shown in Fig. 43, your chances of obtaining a good network with any other structure will be slim. In other words, it is not the structure of the network that will make or break your top-down model, rather it is the quality and the information content of the spatio-temporal database that determine your chances of being successful in developing a network and by the same token a top-down model. If you see persistent issues in developing the top-down model (the networks cannot be trained properly or do not have good predictive capabilities), you need to re-examine your spatio-temporal database rather than manipulating the structure and the topology of your neural network.

In the author's opinion, when the practitioners of machine learning (specifically in the upstream oil and gas industry) start talking about the neural network structure and how it can be modified in order to control the training of the model, one must take that as an indication of naivety and not an indication of expertise. You will find that an expert in the art and science of machine learning will concentrate mostly on the information content and details of the data set being used

---

[58] A good network is a network that can be trained and calibrated and validated. It can learn well and has robust predictive capabilities. The rest is very problem-dependent.

to train the neural network, as long as very basic issues (e.g., the number of hidden layers and hidden neurons, the learning rate and momentum) in the structure of the neural network have been reasonably determined to be solid. The details regarding the structure and the topology of a neural network can have enhancing impact on the results, but they will not make or break your data-driven model.

Sometimes, changing some of the activation functions can help in fine-tuning the neural network's performance, as shown in Fig. 44. In this figure, the hidden neurons are divided into three parts, and each set of hidden neurons can be assigned a different activation function. Some details about activation functions were covered in Section 4.3.1 Structure of a Neural Network. The author does not recommend that the initial structure of a neural network model be designed as shown in Fig. 44; rather, if necessary, the structure in Figs. 44 and 45 may be used to enhance the performance of a good network.

Once the structure of the neural network has been determined, it is time to decide upon the learning algorithm. By far the most popular learning (training) algorithm is "error backpropagation" (Haykin 2009) (1) or simply "backpropagation." In this learning algorithm, the network calculates a series of outputs on the basis of the current values of the weights (strength of the connections between neurons—synaptic connections) and compares its calculated outputs for all the records with actual (measured) outputs (what it is trying to match).

The calculated errors between the network output and the measured values are then backpropagated throughout the network structure with the aim of modifying the connection weight between neurons as a function of the magnitude of the calculated errors. This process is continued until the backpropagation of the error and modification of the connection weights no longer enhance the network performance.

Several parameters are involved and can be modified during this training process, which can impact the progression of the network training. These parameters include the network's learning rate and momentum for the weights between each set of neurons (layers) as well as the nature of the activation function. However, as mentioned before, none of these factors will make or break a neural network; rather, they can be instrumental in fine tuning the result of a neural network. The information content of the spatio-temporal database (which is essentially domain expertise related to reservoir engineering and reservoir modeling) is the most important factor in the success or failure of a top-down model.

9.1.4 The Training Process. Because neural networks are known to be universal function approximators, hypothetically speaking, they are capable of complete replication (reproduction) of the training data set. In other words, given enough time and a large enough number of hidden neurons, a neural network should be able to reproduce the outputs of the training set from all the inputs with 100% accuracy. This is something that one expects from a statistical or mathematical spline curve-fitting process. Such a resulting form of a neural network is highly *undesirable*. This is because a neural network that is so accurate on the training set has literally memorized all the training records and has close to no predictive value.

This is the process that is usually referred to as overtraining or overfitting and in the artificial intelligence jargon is referred to as "*memorization*" and must be avoided. An overtrained neural network memorizes the data in the training set and can reproduce the output values, almost identically, but does not learn from the training set. Therefore, it cannot generalize and will not be able to predict the outcome of new data records. Such a model (if it can actually be called a model) is merely a statistical curve-fitting, and has no value, whatsoever. One of the roles of the calibration data set is to prevent overtraining. It is a good practice to observe the network behavior during the training process. There is much that can be learned from this observation. A simple plot of MSE vs. number of training epochs displays the neural network's training and convergence behavior. Furthermore, if the MSE is plotted for both the training data set and the calibration data set (after every training epoch), much can be learned from their side-by-side behavior. Several examples of such plots are shown in **Figs. 46 and 47**.

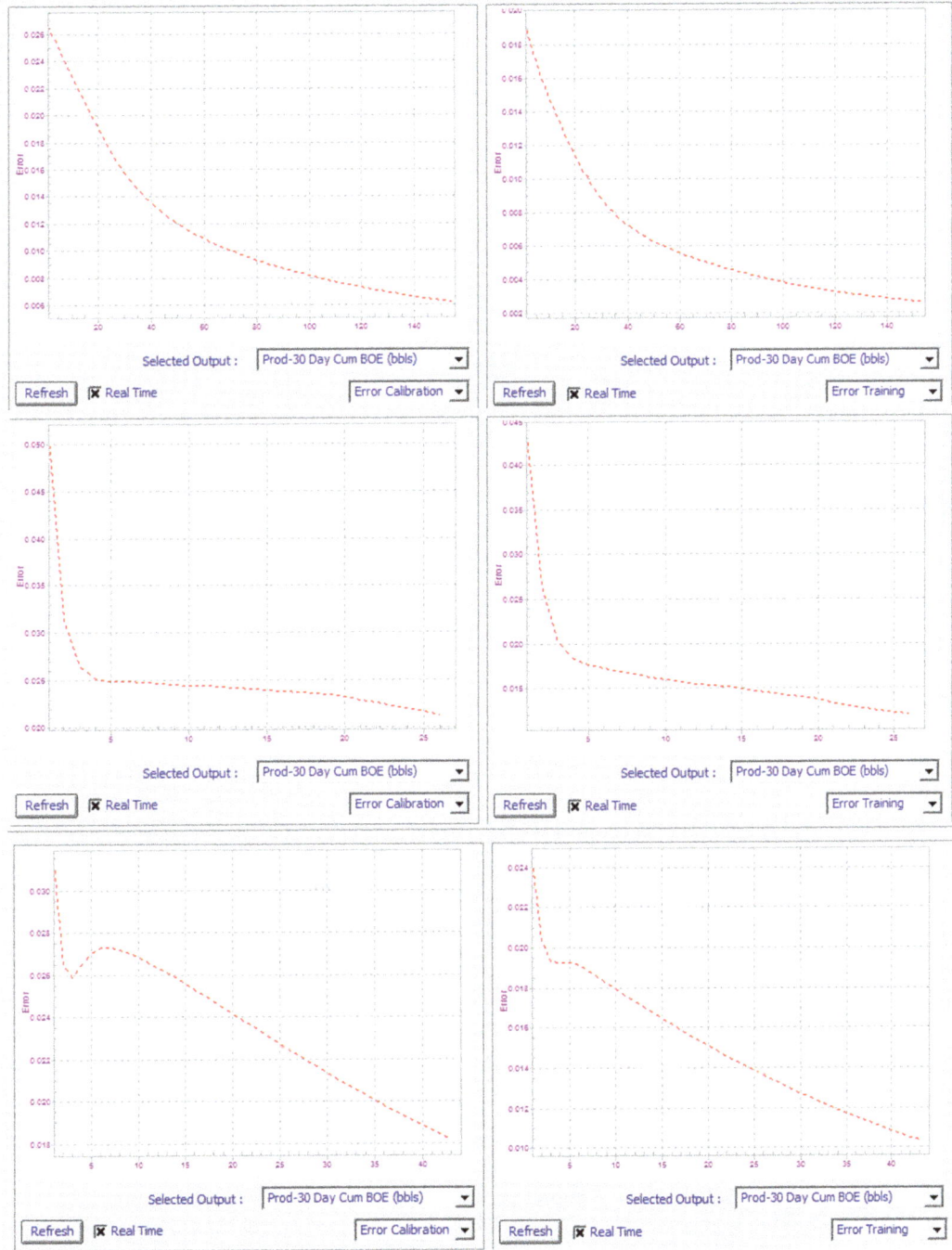

Fig. 46—Plot of MSE as a function of number of training epochs. The plot on the left shows the error for the calibration data set, and the plot on the right shows the error for the training data set. Three examples of a training process that is progressing in a satisfactory manner are shown, where the behavior of the errors is mirroring.

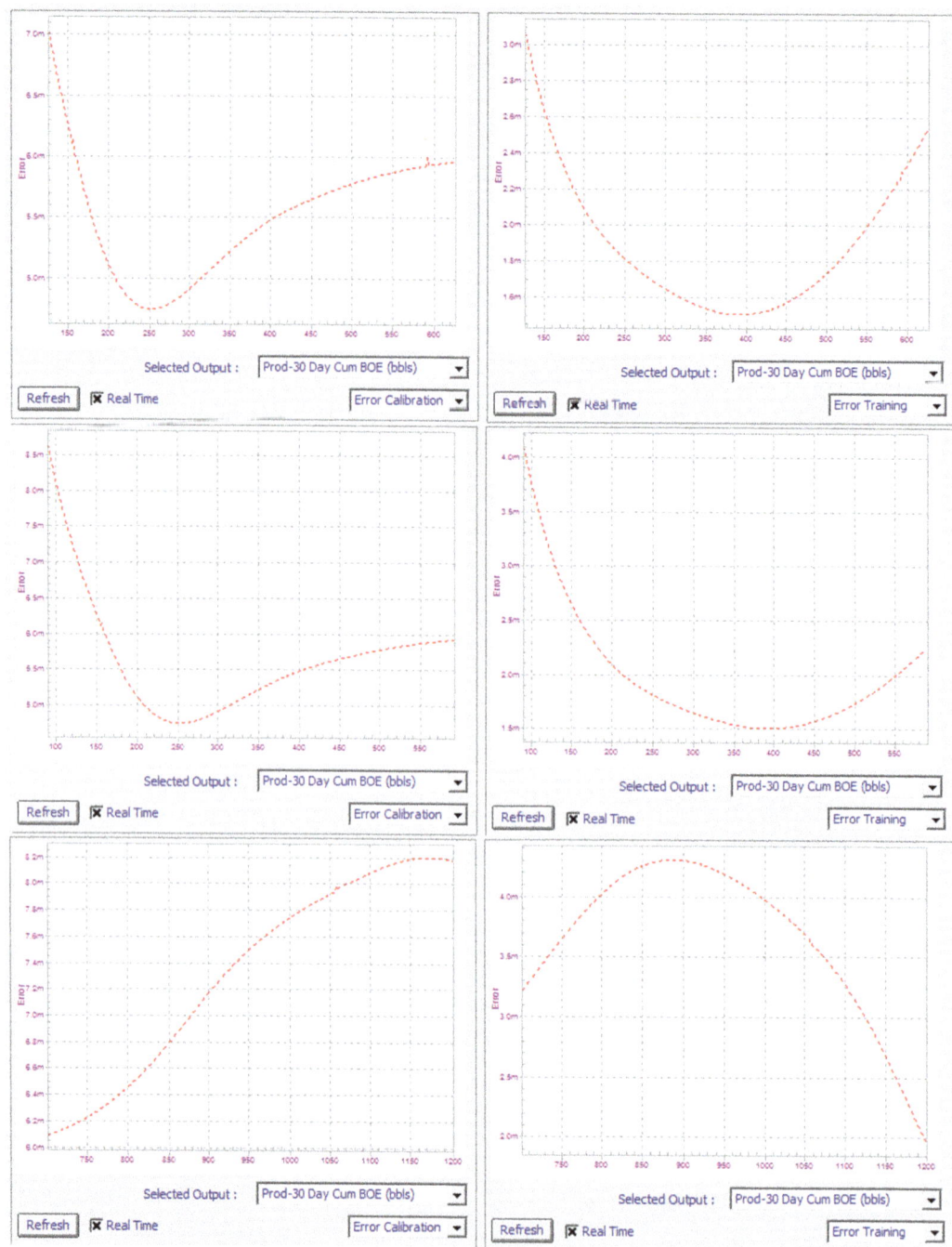

Fig. 47—Plot of MSE as a function of number of training epochs. The plot on the left shows the error for the calibration data set, while the plot on the right shows the error for the training data set. Three examples of a training process that is NOT progressing in a satisfactory manner are shown, where the behavior of the errors is different and exhibits opposite slopes.

During a healthy training process, the error in the calibration data set (2D graphs on the left side of Figs. 46 and 47) that is playing no role in changing the weights in a neural network is expected to behave quite similarly to the error in the training data set (2D graphs on the right side of Figs. 46 and 47). Several examples of a healthy training process are shown in Fig. 46. In the plots shown in Fig. 46, the MSE is plotted vs. the number of training epochs. There are two graphs. The ones on the left show the MSE vs. number of epochs for the calibration data set, while the ones on the right show the MSE vs. number of epochs for the training data set. Each pair of graphs in Fig. 46 represents the training process of one neural network. Fig. 46 includes three examples.

The graph in Fig. 46 represents plots that are being updated in real time, so that the modeler can observe the error behavior of the training progress in real time and decide whether it should continue or should be stopped so that modifications can be made to the network structure or the data sets. Actions such as this may be necessary once it is decided that the training process has entered a potential dead-end and that there will be no further learning.

A healthy training process is defined as one where continuous, effective learning is taking place and the network is getting better in each epoch of training. One of the indications of such a healthy training process is the similarity of the behavior between the two plots, as shown in Fig. 46. In the three examples shown in this figure, errors in both calibration and training sets have similar slope and behavior. This is important because the calibration data set is blind and independent of the training set, and such similarities in the error behavior indicate an effective partitioning of the data sets.

On the other hand, an unhealthy training process is one in which the behaviors of error in the training and calibration data sets are different and sometimes start moving in the opposite direction. Fig. 47 shows three examples of unhealthy error behavior, when error behavior of the calibration data set is compared with that of the training data set. That said, it also should be mentioned that given how gradient-descent algorithms such as backpropagation work, it is expected that from time to time you may see a difference in the error behavior between these two data sets, but it would be temporary. In such cases, if you give the algorithm enough time, it will correct itself, and the behavior of error will start getting healthier. This is, of course, a function of the data set and must be carefully observed and judged by the modeler.

At this point in time, a legitimate question arises: What would make a training behavior unhealthy, and how can it be overcome? For example, if the best network that is saved is the one with the best (highest) R^2 and/or lowest value of MSE for the calibration data set, how can we try to avoid an early convergence? A premature convergence is defined as a situation in which the error in the training data set is decreasing while the opposite trend is observed in the error of calibration data set, as shown in Fig. 47. The answer to this question depends on the information content of the training, the calibration, and the validation data sets, as mentioned previously. In other words, one of the reasons such phenomena can happen is the way the spatio-temporal database has been partitioned. To clarify this point, an example is provided. The example is demonstrated in **Figs. 48 through 50**.

In these three figures, you can see that the largest value of the field measurement for the output (30 days' cumulative production in BOE) in the training data set is 3,850 bbl (Fig. 48) while the largest value of the field measurement for the output in the validation data set is 4,550 bbl (Fig. 50). Clearly, the model is not being trained on any field measurements with values larger than 3,850 bbl. Therefore, the model is not learning what set of conditions can be the reason for such a large value for 30 days' cumulative production. This is a clear consequence of inconsistency of the information content of the training, the calibration, and the validation data sets, which needs to be avoided.[59]

---

[59]The author is not aware of any software applications for the training of neural networks that provides means for addressing such issues. The software application that has been mentioned in footnote 56 (page 93) is the only software application that includes the means to detect and rectify such issues. This is because of identifying and then addressing the practical issues that can be encountered when data-driven models are built to address upstream exploration and production problems.

Fig. 48—Crossplot of observed (measured) output vs. neural network prediction for the training data set. The largest field measurement is 3,850 bbl.

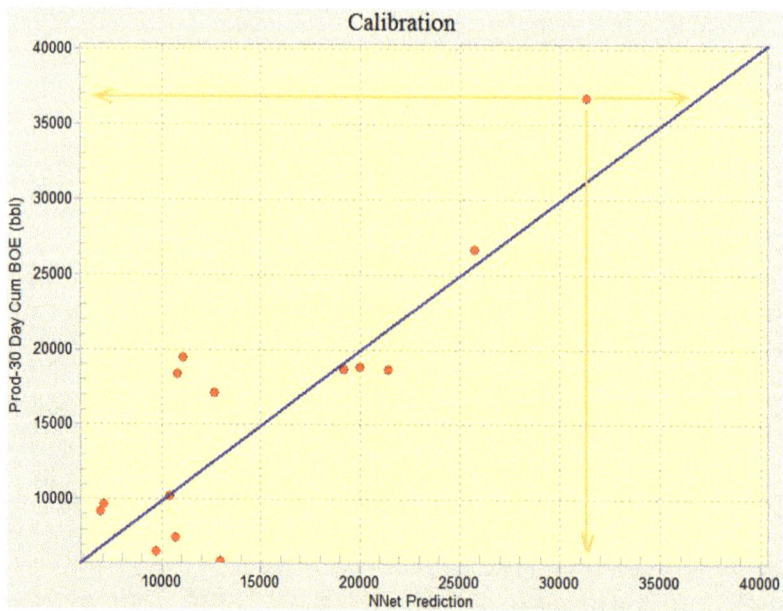

Fig. 49—Crossplot of observed (measured) output vs. neural network prediction for the calibration data set. The largest field measurement is 3,700 bbl.

9.1.5 Convergence. In the context of data-driven models, convergence is the point at which the modeler or the software's intelligent agent that oversees the training process decides that a better network cannot be trained and therefore the training process must end. As you may note, this is a bit different from the way convergence is defined in mathematically iterative procedures. Here, it is not

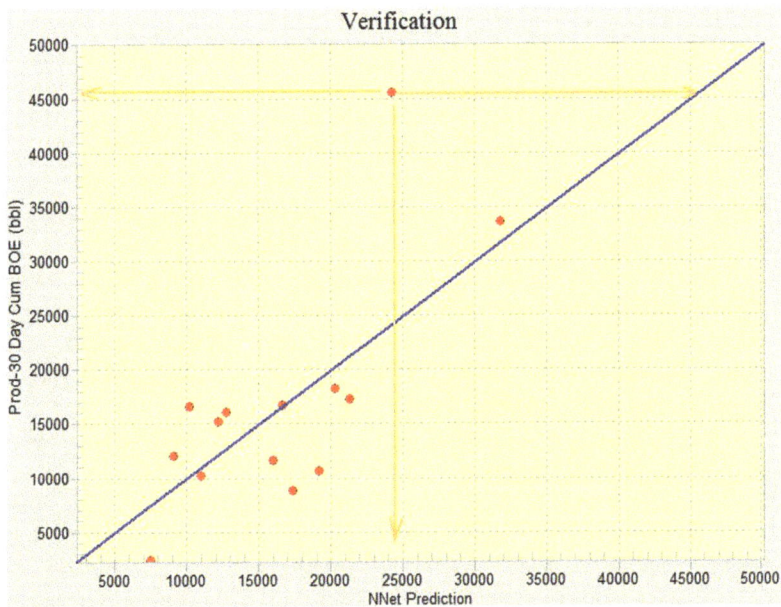

Fig. 50—Crossplot of observed (measured) output vs. neural network prediction for the validation data set. The largest field measurement is 4,550 bbl.

advisable to identify a small enough delta error for the convergence because such an error value may never be achieved. The acceptable error in data-driven models is very much problem-dependent.

In data-driven models, the best type of convergence criteria are the highest R^2 or the lowest MSE for the calibration data set. It is important to note that in many cases, these values can be somewhat misleading (although they remain the best measure), and it is recommended to visually inspect the history matches of all the wells in the field individually before making a decision about whether the training should stop or the search for a better data-driven model should continue.

9.2 History-Matching Schemes in TDM

History matching of a top-down model is a process during which the top-down model learns all that there is to learn regarding the production behavior of a given reservoir. Upon successful completion of the history-matching process, the trained and completed top-down model should be able to

1. Match the production history (oil rate, gas/oil ratio, and water cut) of every individual well in the field with acceptable accuracy.
2. Generate a production forecast of the existing wells such that it responds logically to changes in operational constraints.
3. Generate a production profile for new wells in any location in the field, such that it responds logically to changes in reservoir characteristics and operational constraints.
4. Generate reservoir pressure distribution throughout the field as a function of time, if and when historical data of such measurements are developed through well tests.
5. Generate saturation distribution throughout the field as a function of time, if and when historical data of such measurements are developed (for example, pulsed neutron logs).
6. Do all the above such that they all make physical and geological sense.

History matching of the top-down model can take several forms. The type of history matching is an indication of the robustness of the final model. In other words, some top-down-model history-matching techniques result in better models than others. As we discuss the details of the history-matching process and its variants in this section, the reason for this statement will become more evident. Different types of top-down-model history matching are functions of how the sequence of timesteps during the convergence process is treated. One may find some similarities between these types of approaches to top-down-model history matching and the mathematical solutions that are used in numerical solution of the partial-differential equations in the traditional numerical reservoir simulation models.[60]

As mentioned in previous sections, the dynamic data that are included in the spatio-temporal database represent the timestep (daily, monthly, or annual production) in the TDM. For example, if the output of the model is oil-, gas-, or water-production rates at timestep t, then it would be advisable to include other dynamic parameters (operational constraints) at the same timestep t in the data record. For example, dynamic parameters such as flowing bottomhole pressure, wellhead pressure, choke setting, or number of days of production (referred to as operational constraints), as well as injection volumes in the injection wells, are among the dynamic parameters that need to be present in the data record at the same timestep t as the production data.

This is because when the top-down model is deployed in the forecast mode, one or more of these aforementioned dynamic parameters should be available in order to control the value of the production. However, other dynamic parameters such as production rate of the well being analyzed and the production rates of the offset wells are presented at one timestep behind ($t-1$). This is because such values will only be available to the modeler at one timestep behind when the top-down model is being deployed in forecast mode in order to predict the reservoir and well performance.

Furthermore, as already discussed, the structure of the spatio-temporal database includes production from each well in a sequence that starts from the day it was put into production until the day it was abandoned (shut in) or converted to an injector, or until today if it is still producing. The spatio-temporal database has a structure that honors the sequence of time during the life of the field.

For example, monthly production for the focal well (the well that is the focal point during each record of the database) and one of its offset wells will (and should) appear in the database, as shown in **Fig. 51**. In this figure, when the timestep t is February 1999, then the tubing pressure and production for the focal well (the well under consideration) are recorded at the same timestep of February 1999, while the production for the offset well is recorded one timestep behind and for January 1999, and so forth. This sequence of events should be honored throughout the spatio-temporal database. Treatment of the sequential structure of the spatio-temporal database during the process of history matching determines the type of history-matching technique that is being implemented.

Once all the above characteristics are decided upon, the most important criterion that decides the nature of the history-matching technique in a top-down model is the partitioning of the spatio-temporal database. There are three types of history-matching techniques that can be performed in TDM:

1. Sequential history matching
2. Random history matching
3. Mixed history matching

9.2.1 Sequential History Matching. During the sequential history matching, data records in the spatio-temporal data set are presented to the neural networks for training in the exact sequence in which they appear in the spatio-temporal database. The partitioning of the data is carried out according to the date. The makeup of the training data set would include the largest portion (the lion's share) of the data set that will also be the earliest part of the production. The calibration and the validation data sets will follow in the same manner, each honoring the sequence of the data.

---

[60]Implicit vs. explicit solutions.

	Well Under Consideration			Offset Well No. 1		
Static Data	Dynamic Data			Static Data	Dynamic Data	
	Time t	P (tubing)	Prod.		$(t-1)$	Prod.
	2/1/1999	p1	$q_{1,1}$		1/1/1999	$q_{2,0}$
	3/1/1999	p2	$q_{1,2}$		2/1/1999	$q_{2,1}$
	4/1/1999	p3	$q_{1,3}$		3/1/1999	$q_{2,2}$
	5/1/1999	p4	$q_{1,4}$		4/1/1999	$q_{2,3}$
	6/1/1999	p5	$q_{1,5}$		5/1/1999	$q_{2,4}$
	7/1/1999	p6	$q_{1,6}$		6/1/1999	$q_{2,5}$
	8/1/1999	p7	$q_{1,7}$		7/1/1999	$q_{2,6}$
	9/1/1999	p8	$q_{1,8}$		8/1/1999	$q_{2,7}$
	10/1/1999	p9	$q_{1,9}$		9/1/1999	$q_{2,8}$
	11/1/1999	p10	$q_{1,10}$		10/1/1999	$q_{2,9}$
	12/1/1999	p11	$q_{1,11}$		11/1/1999	$q_{2,10}$
	1/1/2000	p12	$q_{1,12}$		12/1/1999	$q_{2,11}$
	2/1/2000	p13	$q_{1,13}$		1/1/2000	$q_{2,12}$
	3/1/2000	p14	$q_{1,14}$		2/1/2000	$q_{2,13}$
	4/1/2000	p15	$q_{1,15}$		3/1/2000	$q_{2,14}$
	5/1/2000	p16	$q_{1,16}$		4/1/2000	$q_{2,15}$
	6/1/2000	p17	$q_{1,17}$		5/1/2000	$q_{2,16}$
	7/1/2000	p18	$q_{1,18}$		6/1/2000	$q_{2,17}$
	8/1/2000	p19	$q_{1,19}$		7/1/2000	$q_{2,18}$
	9/1/2000	p20	$q_{1,20}$		8/1/2000	$q_{2,19}$
	10/1/2000	p21	$q_{1,21}$		9/1/2000	$q_{2,20}$
	11/1/2000	p22	$q_{1,22}$		10/1/2000	$q_{2,21}$
	12/1/2000	p23	$q_{1,23}$		11/1/2000	$q_{2,22}$

Records Representing Production Behavior of the Well Under Consideration

Fig. 51—Sequence of arranging dynamic data in the spatio-temporal database.

As shown in **Fig. 52**, this history-matching scheme provides for the largest data set for blind history matching and therefore is the most robust model from the history-matching standpoint. Blind history matching is a process in which the history matching is performed when the top-down model is deployed in the forecast mode. In such cases, the top-down model is actually predicting (forecasting) production on the basis of combinations of reservoir characteristics and operational constraints that it has never been exposed to (or seen) during the training process. Therefore, it is using its own generalization and predictive capabilities to estimate the production from the wells in completely new sets of circumstances. However, because the top-down model is performing these estimations for events that have already taken place, we as the modeler know the answer and can measure the goodness of the top-down model's predictions against actual production values. The top-down model that results from this process is the most robust that can be trained.

Sequential history matching is the best and the most robust technique for history matching a top-down model. This is the recommended type of history matching for data-driven reservoir models. This must be the default type of history matching. Other types of history matching should be considered only if and when sequential history matching fails to converge to a good solution.[61] Sequential history matching will succeed if there is enough data (for the definition of "enough data." Please refer to Section 8.7 Required Quantity and Quality of Data).

---

[61] We will discuss the definition of "convergence to a good solution" in the next section. The goodness of a top-down model is judged by its performance in predictive mode. This will be determined during the blind history-matching process that will be covered in the Validation section.

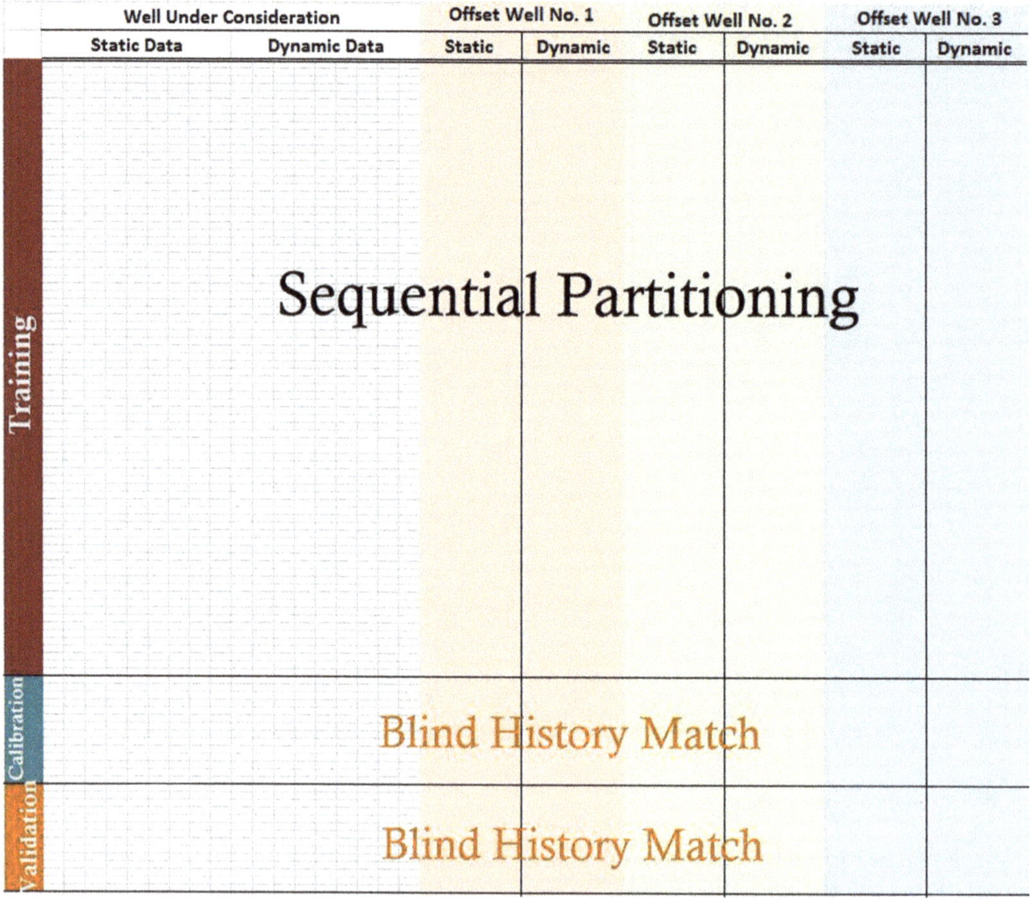

	Well Under Consideration		Offset Well No. 1		Offset Well No. 2		Offset Well No. 3	
	Static Data	Dynamic Data	Static	Dynamic	Static	Dynamic	Static	Dynamic
Training				Sequential Partitioning				
Calibration				Blind History Match				
Validation				Blind History Match				

Fig. 52—Partitioning of the spatio-temporal data set during a sequential history-matching process. This scheme has the largest blind history-matching segment and results in the most robust top-down model.

If the sequential history matching fails to converge to a satisfactory solution, it is usually an indication that the spatio-temporal database has room for improvement, and updating the top-down model is highly recommended as soon as new data become available.

Sequential history-matching schemes usually work well when the spatio-temporal database covers a reasonably healthy number of static and dynamic parameters and when there are enough wells in the field to satisfactorily train, calibrate, and validate all the neural networks that are involved in the formation of a top-down model. As displayed in Fig. 52, in this technique the training and the calibration data sets are selected and presented to the model in a sequential manner. In other words, the time sequence in presentation of the data records is honored.

The robustness of the sequential history-matching scheme stems from the fact that only the first data record in the calibration data set gets its dynamic data of timestep $t-1$ from actual measurements, and starting from the second data record in the calibration data set (all the way through the validation data set and then to forecasting) all the dynamic data of timestep $t-1$ are actually the output of the top-down model. In other words, the sequential history-matching scheme results in a completely independent and self-reliant dynamic model.

9.2.2 Random History Matching. In a completely random history-matching scheme, the training, calibration, and validation data sets are selected and presented to the model in a completely random manner. In other words, the time sequence in presentation of the data records is not honored. Although the calibration and validation data sets are still blind, they are not considered to be a blind history match. The blind history match is defined to include the sequence of time where the output (such as oil-flow rate) is estimated back to back for a sustainable time sequence rather than being a collection of disjointed rates within a period of time. In other words, in a blind history match all the dynamic data that are provided to the model at timestep ($t-1$) are actually outputs of the same model. In this random history-matching scheme, all the dynamic data that are provided to the model at timestep ($t-1$) are actual values from the history and are not outputs of the model. This compromises the robustness of the top-down model.

A schematic of the random history-matching scheme is presented in **Fig. 53**. In this figure, the calibration data records (identified with a blue record heading) and the validation data records (identified with an orange record heading) are scattered throughout the training data records (identified with dark red record heading). The random history-matching scheme usually produces the least-robust type of top-down model.

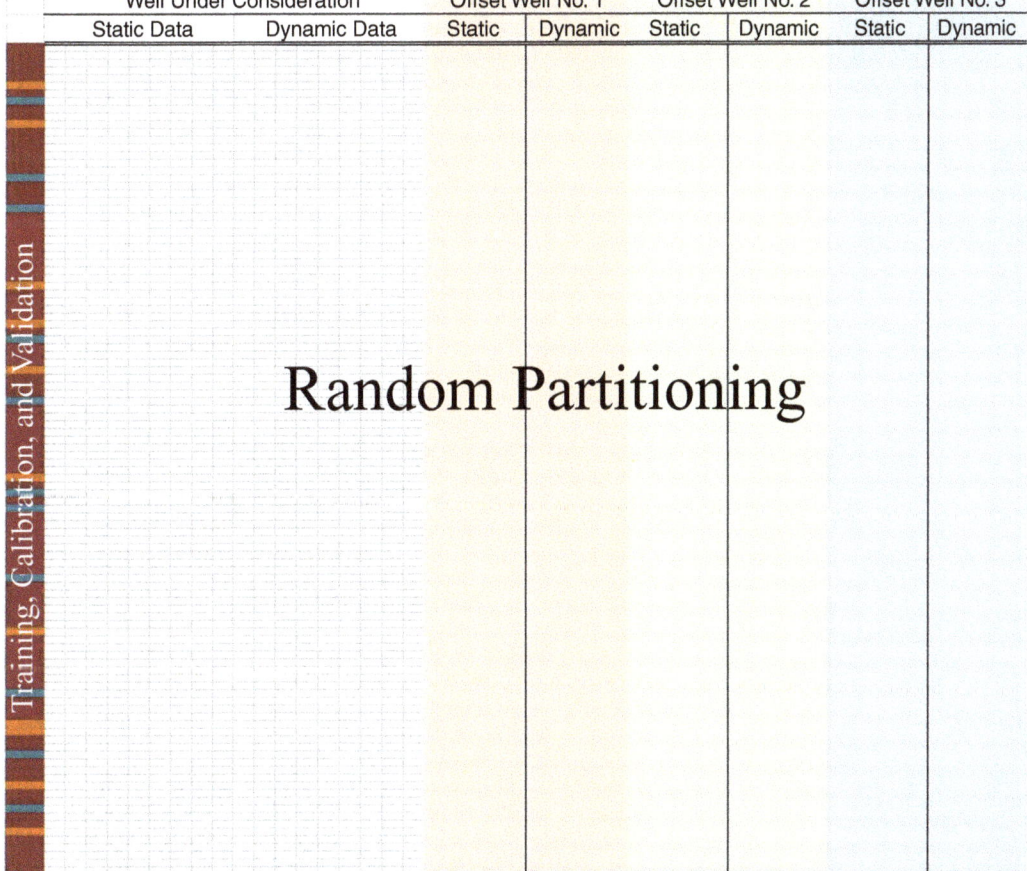

Fig. 53—Partitioning of the spatio-temporal data set during a random history-matching process. This scheme has no blind history-matching segment and results in the least-robust top-down model. In this figure, calibration data record s are identified with a blue record heading and validation data records are identified with an orange record heading.

The reason for this should be clear. Because the output at timestep $t-1$ is an input to the data-driven model and because the top-down model has been trained, calibrated, and validated by measured values of the output at timestep $t-1$ (rather than predicted values by the data-driven model), the top-down model has never been tested to see how it will perform if it receives its own output as input. This means that the robustness and predictive capabilities of this top-down model actually have never been tested. This lack of testing of the robustness of the top-down model reduces the amount of confidence that the reservoir modeler can have in the developed top-down model.

It should be noted that sometimes, because of insufficient data (number of wells or number of years/months of production history), the modeler is forced to use this scheme to develop a top-down model. In such cases, the top-down model should be updated regularly as new data become available (more wells are drilled or the production history is extended), and other history-matching schemes should be incorporated and substituted for the random history matching as soon as the data availability permits.

9.2.3 Mixed History Matching. The mixed history-matching scheme is a compromise between the sequential and the completely random history-matching schemes. In this scheme, as depicted in **Fig. 54**, the training and calibration data records are selected randomly in a fashion that is very much like the random history-matching technique, while a sequential set of records, usually at the end of the time domain, are selected and put aside as the validation data set.

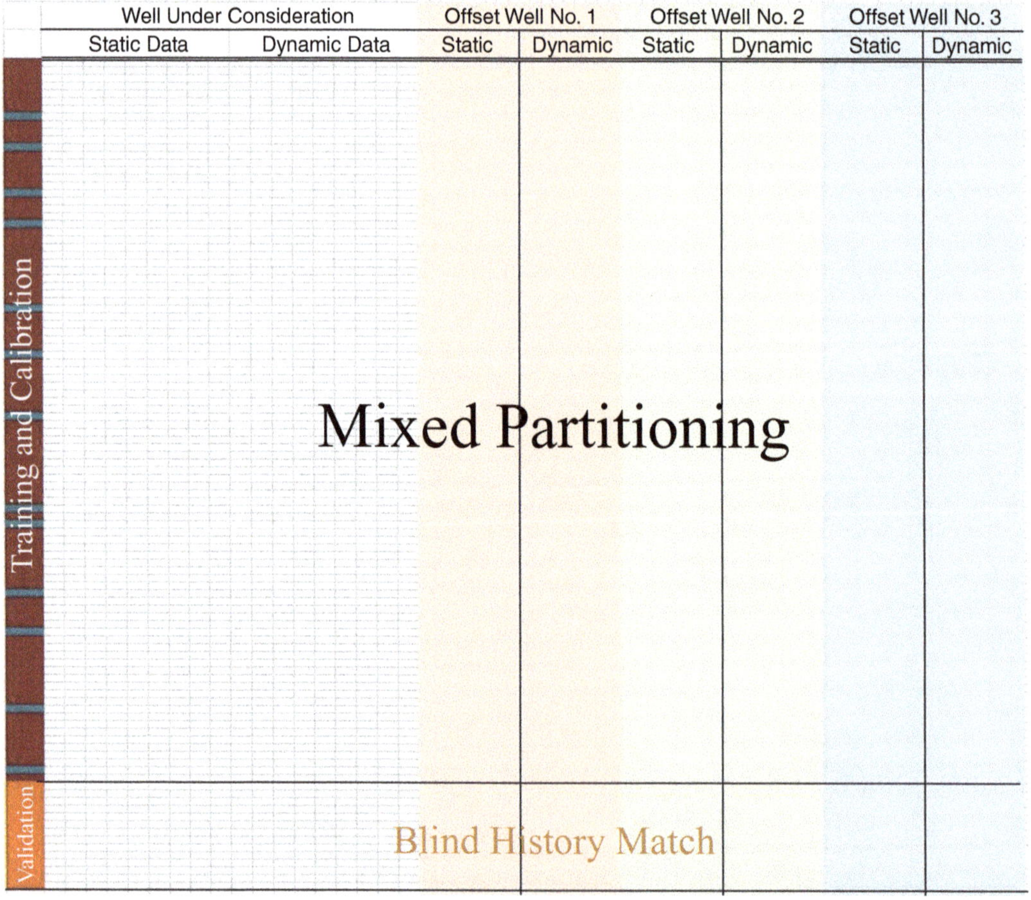

Fig. 54—Partitioning of the spatio-temporal data set during a mixed history-matching process. This scheme has a smaller blind history-matching segment and results in a good and reliable top-down model.

Since the training and calibration are performed using randomly selected records, the output at timestep ($t-1$) is an input parameter to the data-driven model. Therefore, this particular input [the output at timestep ($t-1$)] will always have the real (measured) value, causing a higher probability of convergence. However, the validation data set would be using the model output at timestep ($t-1$). This scheme allows the modeler to evaluate the robustness and predictive capabilities of the data-driven model before deciding whether it is ready to be deployed in the forecast mode. This scheme provides more information regarding the degree of confidence that should be associated with the top-down-model forecasts.

9.3 Validation of the Top-Down Model

Validation of the top-down model is very much aligned with the history-matching scheme used during the development of the data-driven models. The history-matching scheme is mainly concerned with each of the data-driven models, separately, while the overall validation of the top-down model concerns itself with the top-down model as a whole, which usually includes multiple data-driven models and a set of intelligent agents, as covered in Section 7.1 and in Figs. 13 through 15.

It is of utmost importance that a top-down modeler be mindful of the following two facts:

1. A top-down model is only as good as its validation results.
2. A top-down model must be internally consistent.

The first item is self-explanatory. It is not advisable to expect a top-down model to perform well in the forecast mode if it is not performing well during the validation tests. As mentioned previously, the validation of the top-down model is concerned with blind history matching of the production data that are already available to the modeler but have not been shown to (have been hidden from) the top-down model during training. Once the top-down model performs acceptably against the blind data (has acceptable predictive capabilities when presented with input data it has not seen before), then it is ready to be tested for Item 2 above.

The top-down model should be internally consistent, or be able to produce physically meaningful results as the input parameters take on different values. For example, in the forecast mode, when the modeler changes the choke size (a dynamic parameter), the result should make sense in terms of increase or decrease of production. Or when static parameters change, such as porosity, thickness, or permeability, the impact on the model output should be physically justifiable or understandable.

During the validation of the top-down model, the modeler must make sure that the top-down model is evaluated properly. The proper evaluation for validation purposes must include (dynamic) inputs to the top-down model that have been generated by the model itself. This means that the modeler must make sure that the top-down model can generate results (outputs) that make physical sense when dynamic parameters (those included in the input space and used as input parameters in the data-driven models) are generated by itself at one (or more) timesteps behind. In other words, when the operating constraints that are not real field measurements are used as input (for testing purposes), the results generated by the top-down model must be sensible and make physical sense. This is usually called internal consistency.

Internal consistency must be honored, because when the top-down model is deployed in the forecast mode, such data (the dynamic parameters) are available to the model only at one (or more) timestep(s) behind. In other words, the top-down model will be operating in a mode that is completely independent of the historical measurements of the dynamic parameters.

9.3.1 Material Balance Check. One of the items that is commonly brought up when a top-down model is presented and is discussed with reservoir engineers, specifically reservoir modelers, is the validity of the material balance throughout the TDM process. The reason for such questions from a traditional reservoir modeling point of view is quite clear. When reservoir engineers and reservoir modelers build a reservoir model, they are engaged in a bottom-up approach during which a container (the rock) is first designed and defined according to the static data that are collected from the field. This container is the reservoir rock where the fluids that are the target of production, as well as water, reside. The reservoir rock has a structure and boundaries that define the bulk volume. The porosity measurements that are made at the well locations are used to populate the entire reservoir in order to calculate the pore volume. Then, with the aid of water saturation initialization throughout the reservoir, a hydrocarbon pore volume is calculated. This is the amount of hydrocarbon that is in the container and is the ultimate production target. By knowing the reservoir depth and, consequently, its pressure (preferably through some measurements and/or well tests), an original oil in place (original hydrocarbon in place) is calculated.

During the traditional reservoir-modeling process, the structure is discretized by imposition of a grid system on the reservoir, and so the original hydrocarbon in place can be, and usually is, calculated on a grid-by-grid basis. The summation of the fluid volume in these grids determines the original hydrocarbon in place. As the wells are placed in the reservoir, fluid-flow equations are applied, and the reservoir starts producing through its wells, the idea of a material balance check takes on primary importance in order to make sure that the model is internally consistent. In other words, the law of conservation of mass is honored. In this check, the total amount of the fluid that is produced, when added to the total amount of fluid that still remains in the reservoir, should result in the original hydrocarbon in place. This internal check makes sure that the formulation of the model is correct and that all the "t's" are crossed and all the "i's" are dotted. In other words, in a deterministic reservoir-modeling approach, modelers use this technique to make sure that they are being consistent and have not missed anything, or in reservoir-modeling parlance, that the reservoir is not leaking and new fluid is not being created from thin air.

Given the above facts, once the top-down model is presented, it is only natural for a reservoir engineer or reservoir modeler to ask if the material balance check has been performed (honored). However, one must note that such a material balance check is not a necessary calculation in TDM. Why? Because in TDM, we do not start with a container with the assumption that we know (or are capable of accurately calculating) how much hydrocarbon is originally in place.[62] One may even argue that in a TDM approach original hydrocarbon in place (a version of it that would be the producible hydrocarbon) is an outcome of the modeling process and the real number that would represent it is estimated, and more confidence is attached to this estimate as a function of time as more data are collected and the top-down model gets better at predicting the reservoir behavior.

Nevertheless, it is indeed possible to calculate an initial-hydrocarbon-in-place value when performing TDM. This will be presented in case studies in the next chapters. The original-hydrocarbon-in-place value in the context of TDM is generally a volumetric calculation and is calculated as a function of the polygons that are associated with each well. Therefore, hypothetically speaking, even with a single well, one can calculate ("estimate" would be a better word here) an original-hydrocarbon-in-place value.

As the number of wells that are drilled and completed in the field increases, more data are gathered regarding the parameters (such as formation top, thickness, net-to-gross ratio, porosity, and initial water saturation) that are needed to calculate a better, more-accurate original-hydrocarbon-in-place value. These volumetric calculations, when cross-referenced with the production (and estimation of a recovery factor), can help the modeler in tracking the fluid volume and checking for material balance. It goes without saying that better measurements of reservoir pressure will play an important role in the accuracy of these calculations.

The internal consistency of a top-down model consists of other factors that were mentioned in earlier paragraphs in this section.

---

[62]It is well-understood that from an economic point of view estimating such a number is of value to the company and one must strive toward a reasonable estimation of original hydrocarbon in place. One of the problems associated with the traditional approach is that modelers have historically been reluctant to change this number, and all history-matching procedures try to honor the originally calculated value of original hydrocarbon in place for as long as they possibly can, while showing little reluctance with changing other reservoir characteristics to achieve a history match.

Chapter 10

Post-Modeling Analysis of the Top-Down Model

Post-modeling analysis is the main reason that reservoir models are developed in the first place. Post-modeling analyses help to answer questions that concern reservoir engineers, reservoir managers, and reservoir modelers. The objective of building reservoir models is to, for example, forecast production performance of existing wells, with the aim of optimizing production or making economic calculations. Reservoir models can help engineers to identify the best location to drill new wells, or to characterize the reservoir for many other purposes.

Once a top-down model is developed, history matched, and validated, it can be used to perform a large number of analyses. Almost every type of analysis that is performed with a completed and history-matched numerical reservoir simulation model can also be performed with a completed and history-matched top-down model. Project objectives, but mostly data availability, determine the limitations of a top-down model and what can be expected to be the model's output. In some cases, data limitations force the model output to be only the oil rate (gas rate). In other cases, gas/oil ratio (GOR) and water cut (WC), in addition to the oil rate, can be expected as the top-down-model output. Furthermore, as will be demonstrated in one of the case studies (Case Study No. 3: Mature Onshore Field in the Middle East), parameters such as static reservoir pressure and water saturation may be incorporated into a top-down model and be expected to appear as model output.

The objective of the post-modeling analysis is to showcase the utility of top-down modeling (TDM) as a reservoir management tool—a tool that is capable of generating accurate responses in a short period of time. In this section, a few examples of post-modeling analyses are presented. It also needs to be mentioned that almost all of the post-modeling routines that are mentioned here can be (and some already are) programmed to be performed automatically within a TDM environment in a computationally efficient manner.[63]

10.1 Forecasting Oil Production, GOR, and WC

During the development of a top-down model, all the wells in the field need to be examined in detail in order to extract maximum information and data from them. Furthermore, every well must be history matched. This includes the wells that are currently active and producing during the time when the top-down model is being developed and wells that are currently inactive (either abandoned or temporarily shut-in). Upon completion of the top-down model, it can be deployed in the forecast mode in order to estimate the future production of oil, gas, and water production (as well as GOR and WC). **Fig. 55** shows the oil production forecast for one of the wells in an offshore mature field in the Persian Gulf.

---

[63]Some of these post-modeling analyses are already part of one software application (IMagine) that has been created for the development of top-down models.

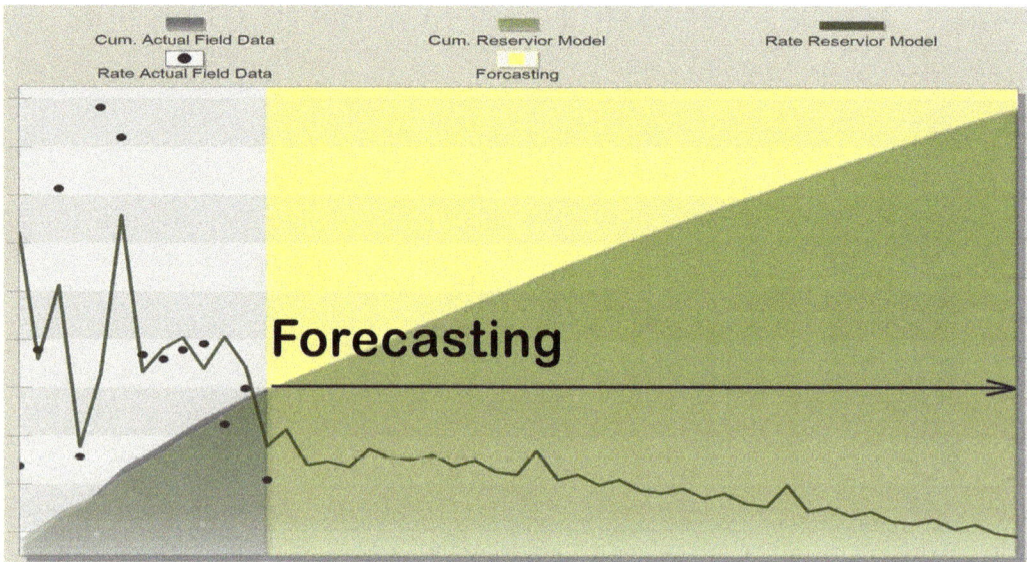

Fig. 55—Oil production forecasting from a recently developed top-down model—an offshore field in the Pesian Gulf.

A question that usually comes up when TDM and its predictive capabilities are presented concerns the length of time for which the forecasts of a top-down model are valid. Answering such a question for top-down models and for any other predictive modeling technology is not simple and straightforward. Theoretically speaking, there should be no limit, and there are always uncertainties that are associated with any predictions. In numerical modeling, modelers sometimes forecast production of wells until abandonment in order to get an estimate of well life; in some cases, this is done with little regard for the predictive capabilities of the model and the degree of uncertainty associated with predictions. This (production prediction of a well far into the future) is a common practice when decline curve analysis is used to analyze the production performance of almost any type of well in the upstream oil and gas industry. One may say that when it comes to the long-term production forecast by a top-down model, it can be at least as trustworthy as decline curve analysis. However, since the author has been trying to present the extensive differences between TDM and decline curve analysis, he will refrain from making such claims.

The author believes that in TDM, the modeler must impose certain practical limitations to the forecasts made by the model. The time (duration) of a forecast should be a function of the availability of historical data. In the cases of mature fields, it is not recommended to extend the forecast period above the number of months/years of historical production.

As will be discussed in later sections of this chapter, the top-down model should be treated as an evergreen model and should be updated on a regular basis. In such cases, the confidence level of its early production forecast is high, although the confidence level decreases as the time for forecast extends in the future. Any reservoir modeler will tell you that the same is true with numerical reservoir simulation models.

10.2 Production Optimization

In many cases, including the field mentioned in the previous section (Fig. 55), multiple wells are connected to a single gathering system, and the surface facility limitations force certain constraints on the production process. Furthermore, the ability of wells to produce liquids and the ratio between oil, gas, and water production make it difficult (sometimes close to impossible) to get the best possible production from a well if the choke setting on the surface is not optimized. Identifying the best mode of operation in order to maximize oil production and minimize gas and water production is a well-known production-optimization practice.

The optimization of the production from multiple wells in a field is a tricky problem that requires multiple tools that are integrated and are working in concert. First and foremost, a subsurface model (the reservoir model) must be constructed and validated, and then it should be connected to (coupled with) a wellbore model that simulates the fluid movement in the wellbore from the interface with the reservoir (the bottom of the hole) to the surface, where it is controlled by valves and chokes that will restrict the flow into the surface facility. Usually, the surface facility has a certain capacity that must be honored in order to optimize the process. The optimization problem usually becomes quite complicated because it is usually difficult to find a single integrated model (system model) that can efficiently handle all the moving parts.

Even if such a tool is constructed, it will have such a large computational footprint that the optimization process (that is usually the result of an exhaustive search process) becomes impractical. Two reasons make top-down models ideal tools to represent either the subsurface component or coupled subsurface and well model component for such optimization problems (in the context of a system model):

1. Top-down models are by nature an integrated wellbore/reservoir model, and therefore can serve as more than one component of such an integrated system model.
2. Top-down models have small computational footprints. A single run of a top-down model (when optimization is the objective) is performed in a few seconds.

Therefore, a history-matched top-down model can easily be integrated into a system model and represent a subsurface model and in some cases a coupled subsurface-and-wellbore model. Because the top-down model can be easily and even automatically updated on a regular basis with actual data from the field, it can serve as a viable tool for system modeling and optimization.

10.2.1 Choke-Setting Optimization. In situations when wellhead pressure and choke settings are part of the historical data that have been used to train a top-down model, and as long as these parameters are used as input to the top-down model, the model, upon training and validation, can be used to optimize choke settings for the future production from the well. As mentioned in Section 9.1.1 Selection of Input Parameters once it is determined that one of the objectives of the top-down model is production optimization by manipulation of the choke settings, the modeler will of course include the data associated with the choke setting to be part of the input parameters, even if they are not selected as the very top input parameters. However, chances are that if choke settings are part of the field measurements and have been reported and are available to the modeler, they will become top input parameters included in the operational constraints.

Once the choke-setting data are included in the input, upon completion of the top-down model (training and validation), the inverse problem is solved in order to identify the choke setting for a given well to find the best combination of operational constraints at any given timestep that will increase oil production and decrease GOR and WC.

10.2.2 Artificial-Lift Optimization. When artificial lift is incorporated during the operation of wells, it is important that all relevant data associated with the specific lift mechanism be collected and used during the training, calibration, and validation of the top-down model. Once production from wells in a field has been conditioned to the parameters involved with the specific lift mechanism, the rest of the modeling and optimization operation is very much like those explained in the previous case. In other words, any design parameter that is used as input during the development of the top-down model can ultimately be used as an operational constraint that can be optimized.

10.2.3 Water-Injection Optimization. Since a large number of mature fields have experienced waterflooding operations, one of the common applications of TDM concerns mature fields that have been subjected to water injection. Water injection serves multiple purposes. It can serve as a pressure maintenance method, while it can also work to sweep the oil toward the production wells.

Once water-injection volumes and the associated injection wells are incorporated into a top-down model as input and have been used to condition the production from all production wells, they become an integrated part of the top-down model. In such cases, water-injection optimization can become another post-modeling analysis. **Fig. 56** is an example in which the top-down model is used to optimize the water-injection scheduling in a mature field. This figure represents the historical analysis of water injection in a mature field in the Middle East. Once the historical analysis of water injection is completed, it can be extended into the future in order to identify the optimal water-injection schedule for maximum oil production.

In Fig. 56, it is shown that oil production in this field has indeed benefited from water injection. This is evident from the differences between the two shaded areas. The dark-shaded area represents the volume of historical annual oil production from the field that has enjoyed the historical amount of water that has been injected. This historical amount of water injection is called the 100% water-injection case. Then, the top-down model is deployed again, and this time all the water injections are eliminated, and all the wells produce again with no water injection. The result is shown in the lighter (brown) shades. The difference is the incremental oil production that can be attributed to water injection in this field. This demonstrates that water injection had a positive impact on oil production.

However, the question that can be raised is whether it was necessary to inject all the water that was actually injected, or maybe even more water should have been injected to get more oil. This question can be answered in the following manner. If by reducing the amount of injected water the amount of incremental oil is reduced, then one may conclude that (a) it was good that we injected all the water that had historically been injected, and (b) it would even be possible to get more oil if we had injected more water—something that we would never know since we did not inject more water. On the other hand, if as we decrease the amount of injected water the amount of incremental oil does not change or even increases, we may conclude that too much water was injected and a smaller volume of water should have been injected.

Fig. 56 shows that both scenarios are taking place in this field in different years. For example, during 2003–2007, the amount of incremental oil production (different blue-color lines pointing to the

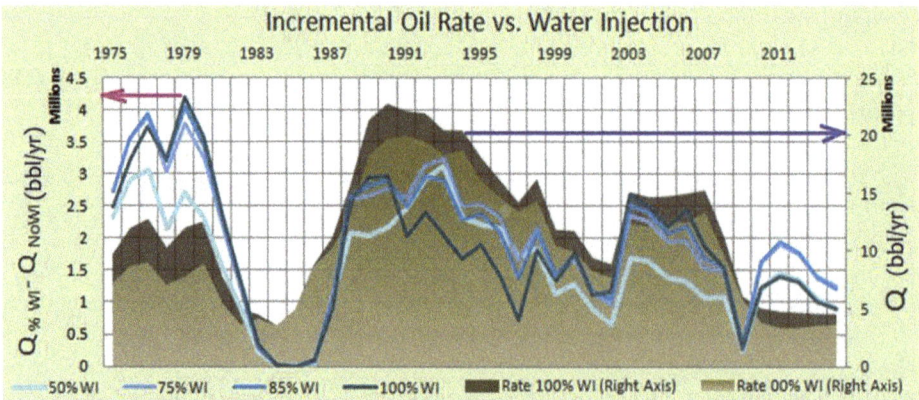

Fig. 56—Water-injection optimization. The shaded areas (right *y*-axis) represent annual oil production as a function of 100 and 0% water injection. Different blue-colored lines (left *y*-axis) represent incremental oil production as a function of different amounts of water production, 100% of what actually was injected and 85, 75, and 50% of what actually was injected.

left Y-axis) also decreases. However, it is clear that during 1991–1999, a smaller volume of injected water would have accomplished more-incremental oil production. This technique can be used in order to create an optimal water-injection schedule for this field in the future.

10.3 Reservoir Characterization

Reservoir characterization within the context of reservoir modeling determines the interaction between wells. Specifically, it becomes quite important to be able to characterize the presence of thief zones (high-permeability streaks) and/or barriers to flow (in the form of sealing faults) in the cases in which the top-down model is being used for mature fields undergoing enhanced recovery and/or water injection. Unlike numerical reservoir simulation models that usually identify and interpret such characteristics in advance and are incorporated into the geological model, during the post-modeling analysis of TDM, such characteristics usually end up being an outcome of the model. Top-down models that are history matched can be used as a tool for reservoir characterization, identifying the contribution of injection wells to the production of oil and therefore providing a high-level map of fluid flow in the reservoir. The interaction and relationship between wells (producer/producer or producer/injector) play important roles in managing reservoirs.

Figs. 57 and 58 are examples of identifying the connectivity between injection and production wells using a completed (history-matched and validated) top-down model for an onshore field in the Middle East. In Fig. 57, only the five closest (Euclidean distance) injectors are considered in the analysis, while in Fig. 58, all the injectors, regardless of their distance to the producer, are considered. In these figures, ease of communication between an injector/producer pair determines the reservoir conductivity (a combined effect of permeability and reservoir net thickness) between the two wells.

The thickness of the lines between producer and injector in these figures is an indication of the strength of the communication between the paired wells. Mapping the strength of these lines on the existing Cartesian grid will provide a distribution of reservoir conductivity that has been interpreted using the TDM technology and is a result of injection/production behavior of the reservoir. This is in contrast to numerical reservoir modeling where such maps and distributions are usually the result of a combination of interpretation of seismic surveys and geostatistical population of reservoir characteristics. In other words, one may conclude that while reservoir characterization is the result of a static data interpretation in numerical modeling, it is, in fact, the result of a dynamic data interpretation in TDM. The author believes that the best result of reservoir characterization can be achieved by (a) independent analysis of TDM and numerical simulation, and (b) by combining (comparing and contrasting) the results from the two methods.

When static reservoir pressure values are available as a function of time and space, they can be used to history match and validate the capabilities of the top-down model and then the top-down model can be used in the forecast mode to predict static reservoir pressure distributions in the reservoir as a function of different production strategies. **Fig. 59** demonstrates such an exercise in an offshore field in the Gulf of Mexico.

10.4 Determination of Infill Locations

During the development of TDM, all the wells in the field are history matched. A high-level geological model is developed that represents the reservoir characteristics while the interactions between wells are accounted for. The top-down model accommodates drilling new wells in the field and completing them either fully or partially. Upon introducing a new well in the top-down-model environment, the modeler can then identify operational constraints and put the well on production to examine its productivity. The well productivity (oil, water, and gas production) is determined by a combination of reservoir characteristics at the location where the well is drilled, the operational constraints that are imposed on the well, presence of fluid (hydrocarbon) at the location (and surroundings) where the well is being placed, and the interaction between the well and its offsets.

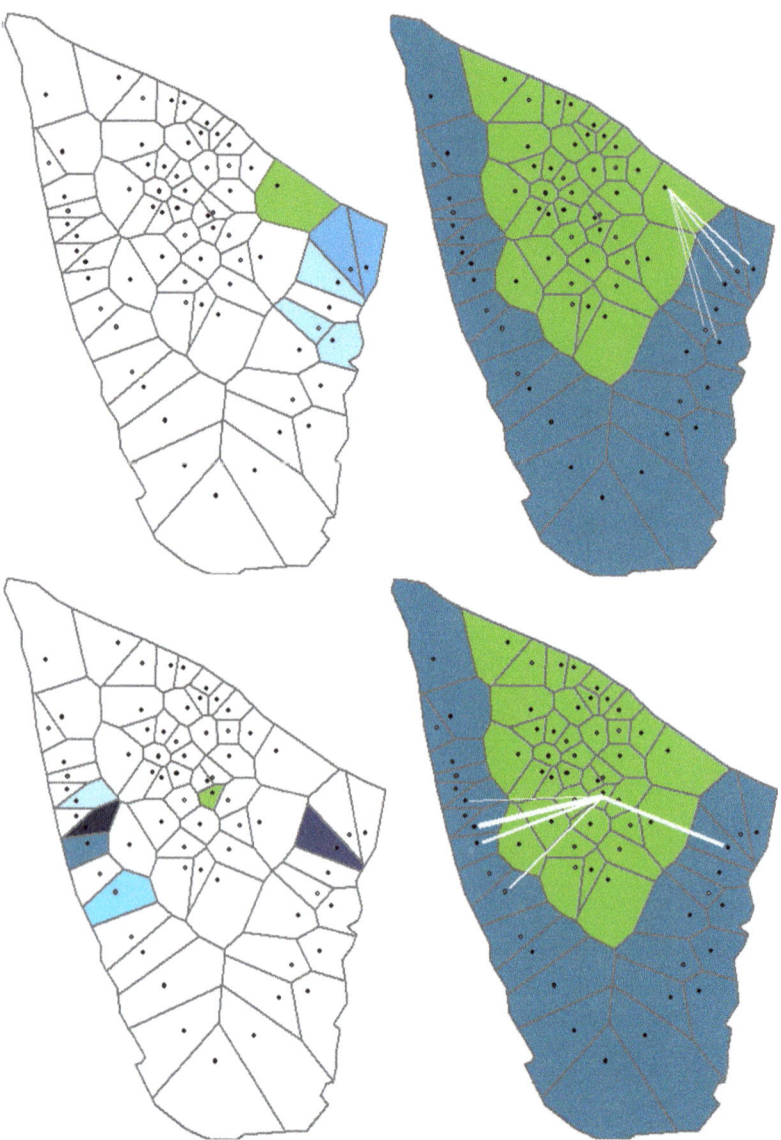

Fig. 57—Identifying the impact of water injection of individual injection wells on each production well. Only the closest five injection wells to each production well are included in the analysis. Injection wells in the polygons with darker background indicate more influence (left). Thickness of the connection lines indicates mode influence (right).

The process mentioned above for drilling and producing a new well in the top-down-model environment is very efficient and has a very small computational footprint. The small computational footprint during the infill drilling is a result of the top-down model being essentially a sector model. Therefore, it is quite efficient to build an automatic well-location determination algorithm (essentially a search and optimization routine) that can examine a very large number of potential well locations (one at a time so that they will not interact with one another, unless multiple infill locations are sought) and identify and rank the most-appropriate infill locations at any given point in time.

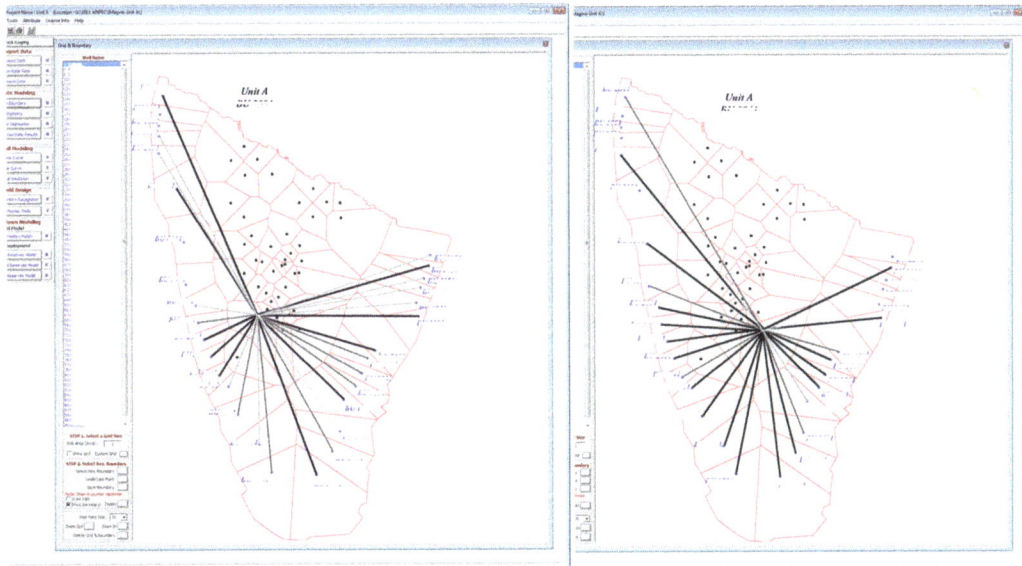

Fig. 58—Identifying the impact of water injection of individual injection wells on each production well. All injection wells in the field are included in the analysis. Lines with the darker color indicate more influence.

Furthermore, this infill-location identification algorithm can be coupled with uncertainty analysis (see Section 10.7 Uncertainty Analysis) in order to generate a more robust routine that includes quantification of uncertainties associated with reservoir characterization regarding new locations in the field.

10.5 Recovery Optimization

Because distribution of static reservoir pressure and fluid saturation throughout the reservoir can also be achieved by the top-down model (as shown in **Figs. 59 and 60**), it can be used for the purposes of maximizing oil recovery in a given field. Once the top-down model is history matched

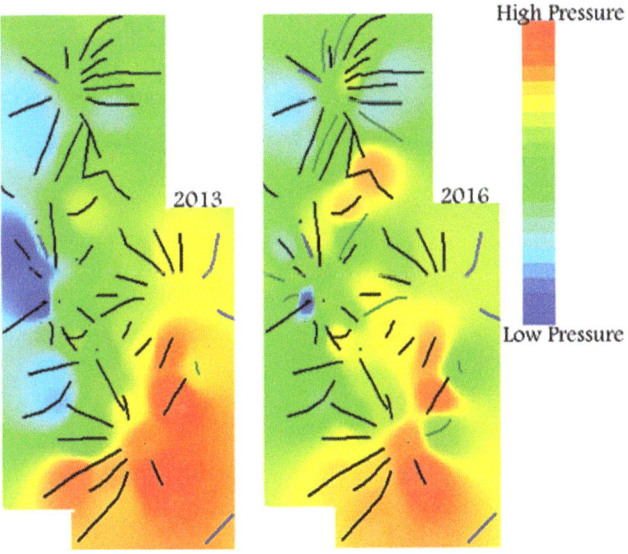

Fig. 59—History-matched (left) and predicted (right) pressure distributions in an offshore field in the Gulf of Mexico.

118 Data-Driven Reservoir Modeling

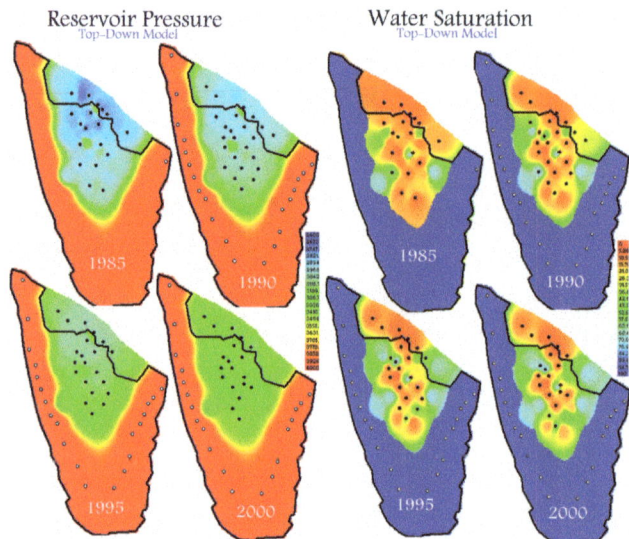

Fig. 60—Top-down model, reservoir pressure, and water saturation distribution throughout one of the production units for the years 1985 to 2000. This distribution was generated by geostatistics after history matching the reservoir pressure at individual-well locations.

using the optimal infill locations (see Section 10.4 Determination of Infill Locations), the modeler can use the top-down model to identify the plateau extension, and by continuously examining the reservoir pressure and saturation distribution, performed iteratively, this process can result in generating best development strategies for a given field.

10.6 Type Curves

A history-matched top-down model can be used to develop type curves. Production profiles (rate vs. time) can be generated for wells in a certain location in the field. The type curves are capable of showing the impact of initial condition, reservoir characteristics, or operational constraints on the production profile for a typical well.

The type curves can be developed for specific locations, or for an area (segment) of the field, or for the entire field. During the development of the type curves, the user gets to examine three parameters simultaneously. Two of the parameters are fixed [as the x (usually the time) and the y (usually the oil-, water-, or gas-production rates) axes]. The production rate (oil, water, or gas) as a function of time is presented as the production profile. The type curves will then be a collection of multiple curves. Each curve will represent a certain value of a selected third parameter that is being examined.

Figs. 61 and 62 are examples of type curves generated by TDM. Fig. 61 shows a series of production-profile type curves for a given well where water saturation at the well location is modified. These curves show the sensitivity of oil production to water saturation. Fig. 62 shows another set of oil-production-profile type curves emphasizing the oil-production sensitivity of a given well to formation permeability. In both figures, the lack of smoothness of the production profiles is a result of wellhead pressure modifications imposed by the surface facility.

10.7 Uncertainty Analysis

Upon completion (training, calibration, and validation) of the top-down model, it was deployed in the forecast mode so that it could predict production (or any other model output) at any location in the future. This, for example, can be production from an infill well or the value of static reservoir

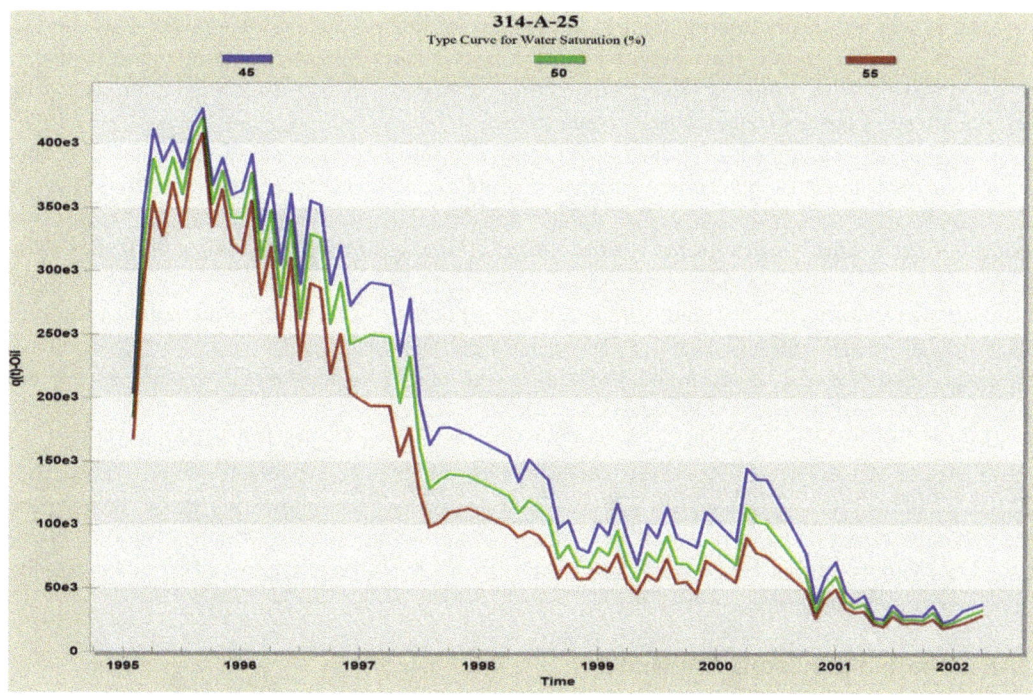

Fig. 61—Example of a set of type curves generated using the top-down model.

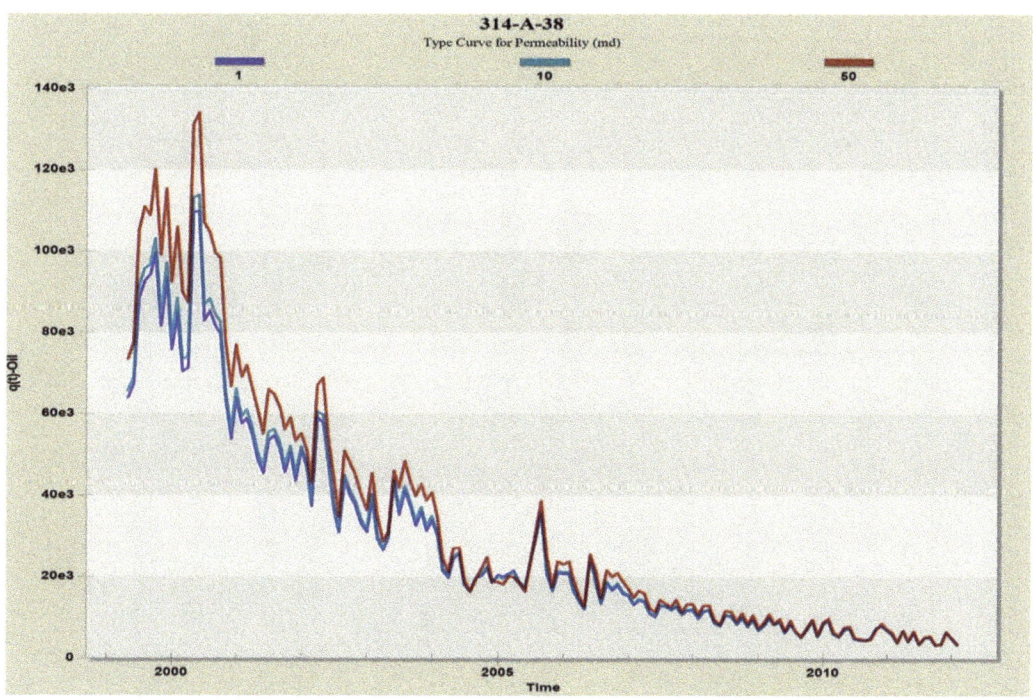

Fig. 62—Oil-production-profile type curves for different values of permeability.

pressure and/or water saturation in a given location in the field. Since these outputs that are generated by the top-down model use reservoir characteristics (or any other parameter in the input space) as input, and since the values of these parameters are uncertain, TDM is capable of quantifying the uncertainties that are associated with its predictions.

The uncertainty quantification is performed using the Monte Carlo simulation technique. In this technique, the value of each uncertain parameter is replaced with a probability distribution function that includes a range of values rather than a single number. Then, the objective function that is being evaluated (in this case, the completed top-down model) is executed approximately 1,000 times, each time randomly selecting one value (from the available range mentioned before) for each parameter that is being analyzed for uncertainty and generates one output. Upon completion of this procedure, the top-down model has generated 1,000 outputs rather than one single output. The 1,000 output values are then plotted in the form of a probability distribution function and P10, P50, and P90 are identified. This is demonstrated in **Fig. 63**.

When the Monte Carlo simulation is applied to a production profile (for example, oil rate vs. time), instead of a single value (for example, initial production, or reservoir pressure or water saturation in a specific location), the results will indicate a profile range, as shown in **Fig. 64**. To generate the curve (representing the production profile) and the shade (representing the range of uncertainty associated with the production profile), each point in time has been evaluated 1,000 times, and the collective result is shown in the figure.

10.8 Updating the Top-Down Model
Updating a top-down model essentially means to retrain, recalibrate, and revalidate one or all of its data-driven models. This may seem pretty drastic at first glance. But in reality, it is a simple and easily achievable task. Once a top-down model is developed (trained, calibrated, and

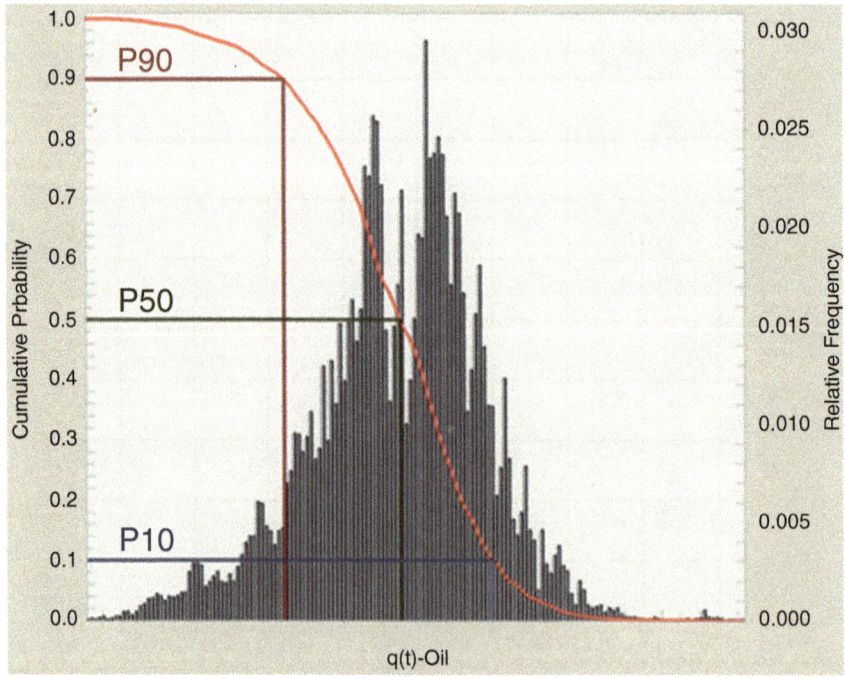

Fig. 63—Probability distribution function generated for the value of initial oil production, identifying P10, P50, and P90. This is the result of a Monte Carlo simulation using the top-down model as its objective function.

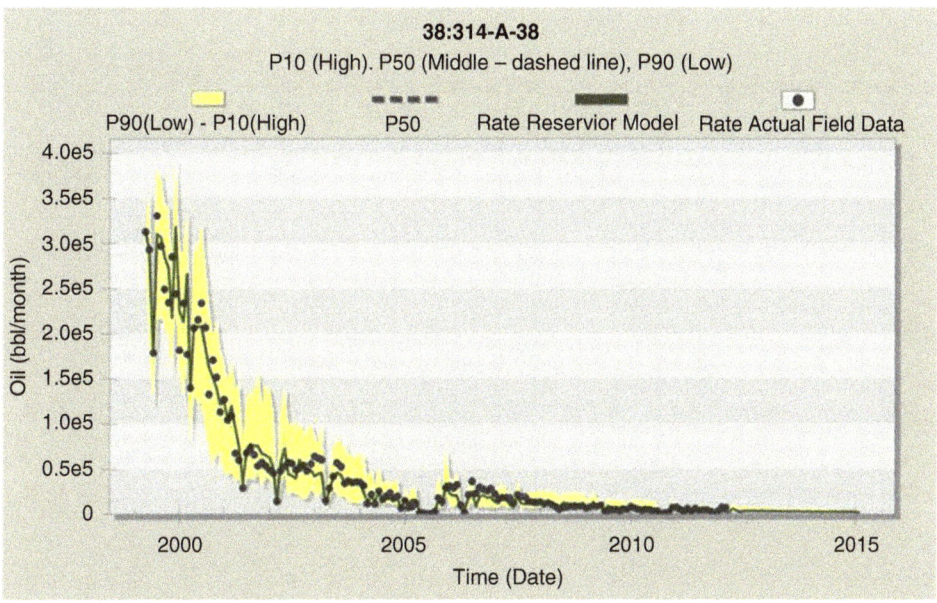

Fig. 64—Result of Monte Carlo simulation performed on the complete production profile generated from a completed top-down model.

validated), there is already a structure in place. This structure includes the following important components:

1. *The data structure:* These are the details of the type and format of the data that have been assimilated in the spatio-temporal database. Therefore, the modeler knows exactly what type of data (and in what format) is necessary for the top-down model. The field measurements are collected and transformed to the predetermined format and uploaded in a database that has already been prepared and is ready to receive new data. All this can be accomplished automatically or manually through a set of written scripts or computer codes.
2. *The input vector:* During the original development of the top-down model, all the parameters that need to be used as input into the data-driven models have already been identified. These data are automatically accessed from within the spatio-temporal database.
3. *The structure of the data-driven models:* All the data-driven models (neural networks) have already been trained, calibrated, and validated once. This means the structure and the topology of the models are already known. No time needs to be spent on this component of the top-down model.
4. *The intelligent agents:* Since we already have a functioning top-down model, this means all the intelligent agents have been identified and completed.
5. *The structure of the top-down model:* Again, because we already have a functioning top-down model, this means that all the data-driven models and intelligent agents have already been connected to each other in a way that fulfills the needs of the project (see example in Figs. 14 and 15), and they do not need to be re-examined.

Ideally, the updating process can easily be coded so that it can be carried out on a routine and regular basis with minimal human interaction. Once new data become available, the first step is to check to see how well the existing top-down model predicts the performance of the wells or performs other tasks that it is programmed to do. If the results are satisfactory, there is no need for updating of the top-down model. However, if it is observed that the top-down model's predictive capabilities are degrading, at some point in time the decision needs to be made to update and retrain the top-down model to enhance its performance.

The top-down model has an organic and evergreen nature, and it can improve with time and as more data become available.

Chapter 11

Examples and Case Studies

Any modeling technology is only as good as its performance in the real world. Furthermore, new reservoir-modeling technologies should not be held to a higher standard than their predecessors. Top-down modeling (TDM) is no exception. A top-down model does not need to prove that it is better than numerical reservoir simulation and modeling. Such a claim has never been made. TDM needs to prove that it is a valid technology that is capable of developing a comprehensive reservoir model that enjoys internal consistency and has the potential to provide useful information (add value) about the field. The fact that TDM can achieve all its objectives in a short period of time and with many fewer dedicated resources (compared with any other reservoir-modeling technology) will demonstrate its value to the industry.

There are a number of articles that include information and case studies regarding TDM. Chronologically speaking, the efforts that resulted in TDM as a data-driven reservoir-modeling work flow started with production data analysis (Jalali et al. 2006; Gaskari and Mohaghegh 2006). These efforts continued when we realized that if other available data can be added to the process, they can enrich the analysis. However, designing the system in such a way that other multiscale data from the field can be integrated with the production data proved not to be a trivial endeavor. In reality, this integration was the most challenging part of the TDM development. It took many years of research and development to arrive at what it is today. Initially, to test the ideas, numerical reservoir simulation models were developed and treated as the ground truth. Then, data were generated from the numerical simulation model to be used in developing top-down models. For consistency purposes, only the type and amount of data that are usually available from an actual field were extracted from the numerical model in order to assess the top-down model's work flow capabilities (Mata et al. 2007; Gomez et al. 2009; Khazaeni and Mohaghegh 2011; Mohaghegh 2009).

In some cases, the real data, as many of them as were available, were integrated with some other reservoir analysis techniques and then the TDM was applied as a combining technology (Kalantari-Dahaghi and Mohaghegh 2011). The very first top-down model was applied to a limited amount of data that were available from a field in the Middle East (Kalantari-Dahaghi et al. 2010). This process opened the door to test the technology with a couple of shale fields (Grujic et al. 2010; Zargari and Mohaghegh 2010; Mohaghegh and Bromhal 2010). The first article that was presented in a conference (published in the conference *Proceedings*) included the application of TDM to the Marcellus Shale (Esmaili et al. 2012). This paper was later published in a refereed journal (Esmaili and Mohaghegh 2016). On different occasions, public data were used to demonstrate the application of TDM when only public data are used to develop a reservoir model (Gaskari et al. 2007; Maysami et al. 2013; Mohaghegh et al. 2012; Haghighat et al. 2014). The very first comprehensive top-down model was developed for an onshore asset in the Middle East (Mohaghegh et al. 2014). This particular case study is also presented in this book as Case Study No. 3. Since then, TDM has been applied to multiple onshore and offshore fields all over the world.

In this section, case studies about this reservoir-modeling technology are presented to show several of its key advantages. Three case studies are presented here. First comes an onshore field in Central America; the second is an offshore field in the North Sea; and finally the most comprehensive case study will be presented for an onshore field in the Middle East. The first two case studies show how TDM was used to build a reservoir model and history match the production from the field. The third study will go beyond history matching and demonstrate the use of the history-matched model in order to make more analyses and help in field development planning.

11.1 Case Study No. 1: A Mature Onshore Field in Central America

This mature Central American onshore field has been in production since the mid-1980s. Being a prolific asset for the operator, significant amounts of resources had been dedicated to develop a numerical reservoir simulation model for this field. A large number of wells, multiphase production, and complex geology are among the factors that have made the development of a geological model, upscaling it to accommodate the flow model, and history matching oil and gas production in this field very challenging.

After limited success in reaching a satisfactory history match with numerical simulation of this field, the operator decided to examine an alternative route of reservoir modeling in order to see if there was a possibility to simultaneously history match both oil and gas production profiles for each well in this field, and to predict future fluid-flow behavior. This mature field has been divided into six different areas on the basis of structural and flow behavior that had been observed throughout the years. **Fig. 65** shows a schematic of this mature onshore field, including the six areal sections identified by the operator.

As mentioned in the previous chapters, one of the first steps during the development of a top-down model is the generation of two sets of grid systems and overlaying them on the field. **Fig. 66** shows the location of the wells drilled in this field since its inception in the mid-1980s. The Cartesian grid along with the Voronoi polygons are also shown in this figure. These two grid systems help determine the spatial resolution that is required for TDM.

It is obvious and expected that human intervention and other operational issues have convoluted the production behavior (signals) in almost all wells in this field throughout its history. **Fig. 67** provides examples of such commonly occurring incidents. This figure shows two examples to demonstrate convoluted production behavior. Similar production behavior is observed in all the wells in this field. It should be noted that this type of convoluted production behavior is very much expected in all mature fields, and TDM is conditioned to expect and to deal with these complex behaviors.

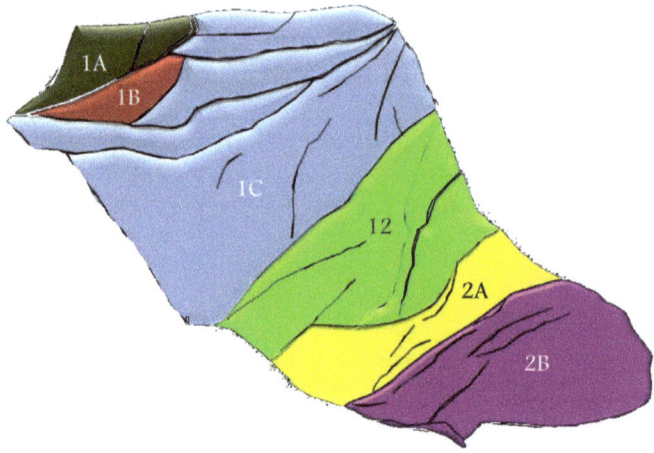

Fig. 65—Onshore mature field in Central America that is divided into six distinct sections separated by structural faults.

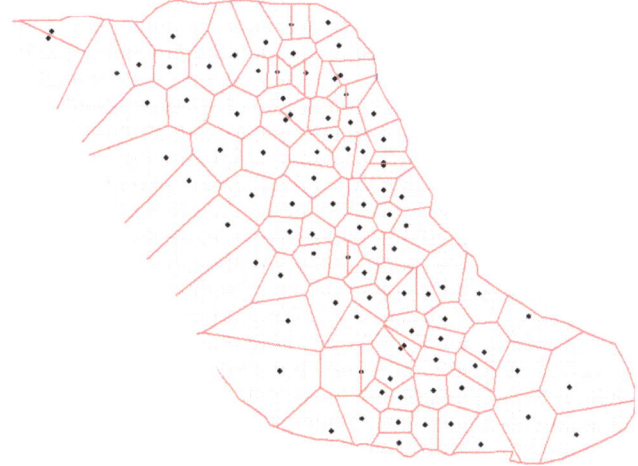

Fig. 66—Voronoi polygons are defined for the wells in each reservoir. Multiple reservoirs are stacked on top of each other, and wells are producing from multiple reservoirs.

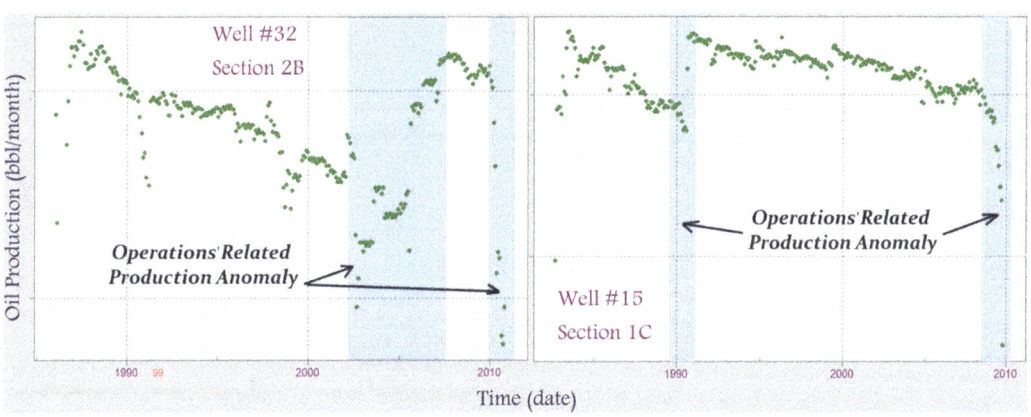

Fig. 67—The well producing from the mature onshore field in Central America, like many other wells, displays convoluted production behavior that needs to be understood and communicated with the top-down model.

In order to put the complexities associated with the production behavior in a particular field in perspective, it is highly recommended that at the start of developing a top-down model the modeler plot and examine (become familiar with what to expect from this particular field) all production profiles of every individual well in the field. Such examination of the production behavior of each individual well is necessary because through this process the modeler learns what types of activities have probably taken place in the field during its production history.

Fig. 22 (Page 56 - Chapter 7) is an example of such a practice for two wells producing from the mature onshore field that is the subject of this case study. In this figure, each well includes seven plots. All these plots have the same x-axis [Time (date)]. From the top, these plots demonstrate

1. Oil rate (field measurements and top-down model match)
2. Gas rate (field measurements and top-down model match)
3. Gas/oil ratio (GOR)
4. Flowing bottomhole pressure (FBHP)
5. Choke size

6. Completion footage
7. Injection rates: (a) nitrogen and (b) sour gas

Therefore, for this field, there are eight different production-related parameters (nitrogen and sour gas as injected fluid each count as a separate parameter) that need to be carefully examined. From a production engineering data-quality-control point of view, plotting all these parameters along the same x-axis [Time (date)] serves an important purpose. If by looking at these plots a petroleum engineer cannot (in general) make sense of the production process, then it may be unreasonable to expect the top-down model to learn much from these data.

A petroleum engineer should be able to look at these plots for each well and be able to understand them, or at least not be completely confused by them. For example, if you see that the choke setting is set to be closed (it happened in both cases shown in Fig. 22), then you should not see any oil and/or gas production. If you do see production, then something is wrong, and that is most probably a typographical error in the value of choke setting that needs to be corrected. It is important for the top-down model to learn that when the choke is closed no production can be observed. One may see this as trivial, but it is not. It is important for machine-learning algorithms to learn even the simple, common-sense issues that we take for granted. Not taking such issues into account can, at a minimum, confuse the algorithm and make it take much longer to converge to a solution that makes sense.

Top-down modelers must keep in mind that the information they are looking at (Fig. 22) is ultimately what is going to be used to train the top-down model. Therefore, chances are that if a certain obvious behavior in production of a well cannot be explained (in general terms) by a petroleum engineer by looking at all the available data, such behavior would confuse the top-down model as well. A good example in Fig. 22 can be pointed to in the production behavior of the well on top (Well No. 24). About one-third into the life of the well, we notice an increase in production. It is important to teach the top-down model that production generally decreases in a well if it is not interfered with. Therefore, if an increase in production is observed, there must be some reason. Looking at the FBHP, one can see a change in this parameter that most probably is the cause of the production increase. The modeler need not present a deterministic equation for this change; as long as the change makes logical sense and is not the result of data being recorded wrongly, the machine-learning algorithm will be able to create the connection and draw its own conclusions.

Once the top-down model is trained and validated, as explained in detail during the past several sections in this book, it is able to history match the oil and gas production from this field and consequently predict its future behavior. **Figs. 68 and 69** are two examples of individual wells that have been history matched in this field. In these figures, monthly production volumes as well as cumulative productions are shown. The monthly production volumes are shown by dots (for field measurements) and lines (for top-down-model-generated production), and the cumulative productions are shown by means of shaded areas (orange shade for field measurements and green for the top-down model).

The history match of Well No. 22 is shown in Fig. 68. Both oil and gas production history matches are included in this figure. It is important to notice the dramatic fluctuation in oil and gas production in this well, which happens almost continuously throughout its life, a common characteristic of almost all real cases. It is noticeable how nicely such fluctuations in production volumes are matched by the top-down model. The same is true of the production from Well No. 53 shown in Fig. 69. Furthermore, it should be mentioned that during the design of the top-down model (as shown in Figs. 14 and 15) the modeler can make sure that gas production volumes are a dependent variable to the oil production volumes.

Once the production volumes from all wells are history matched individually, then the oil and gas production from all the wells can be summed in order to see the quality of the history match for the entire field. **Fig. 70** shows the quality of the history match for oil and gas production, including a couple of years of forecast for the entire field. The forecast for this field shows that unless the operation is modified, the field will experience a decline in oil production with a simultaneous increase in gas production. In this figure, the number of active wells is also shown.

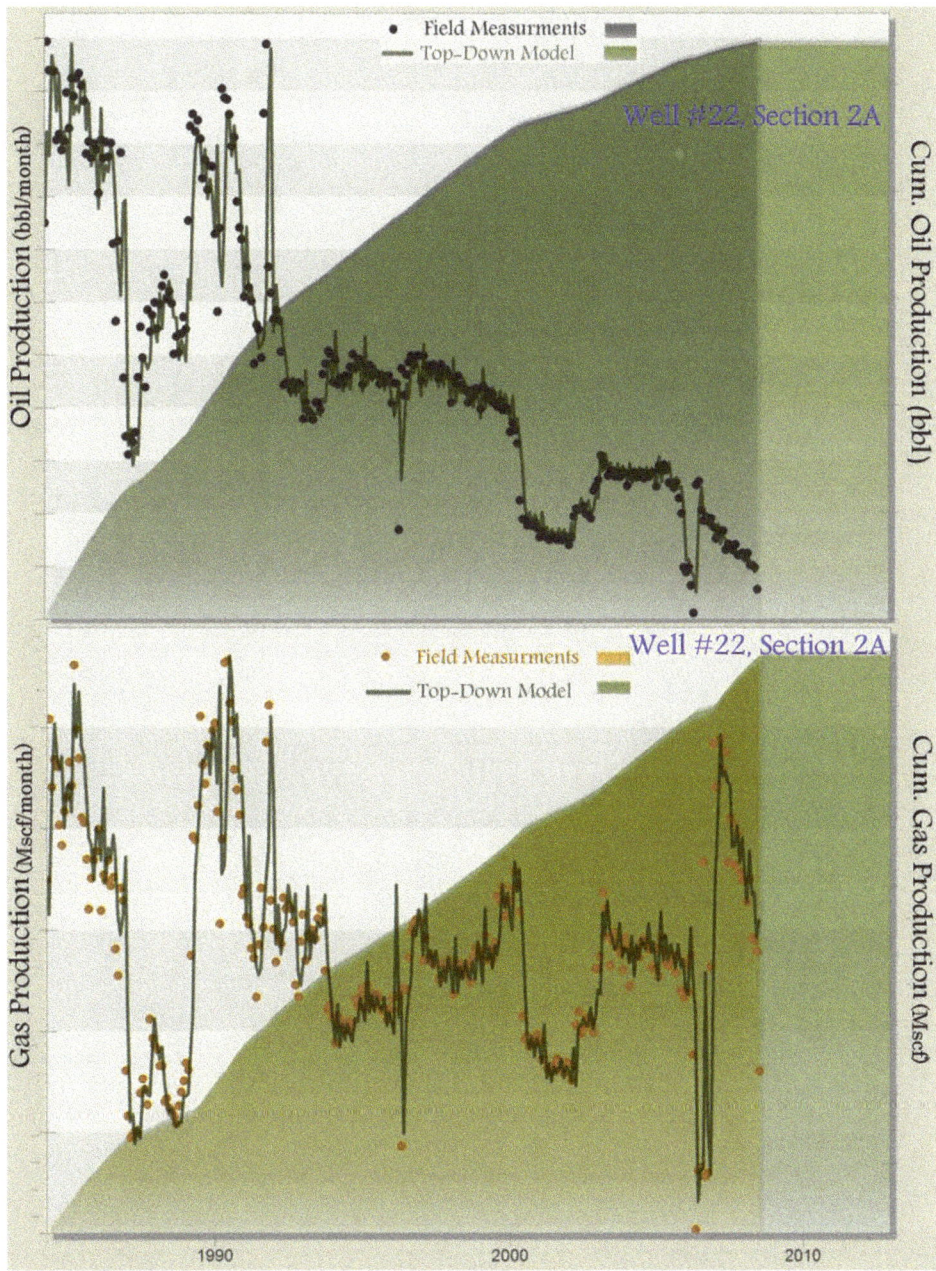

Fig. 68—Oil and gas monthly rate and cumulative production match for Well No. 22 with the surface location in Section 2A. This well was completed in multiple stacked reservoirs—onshore mature field in Central America.

11.2 Case Study No. 2: Mature Offshore Field in the North Sea

This mature offshore field is located in the north-central part of the North Sea. Production from this asset started in the early 1990s. The field is developed from a single platform with multiple injectors and producers as shown in **Fig. 71a**. Fig. 71b shows the completion along each of the wells, and Fig. 71c shows the polygons that are assigned to each completion in the field.

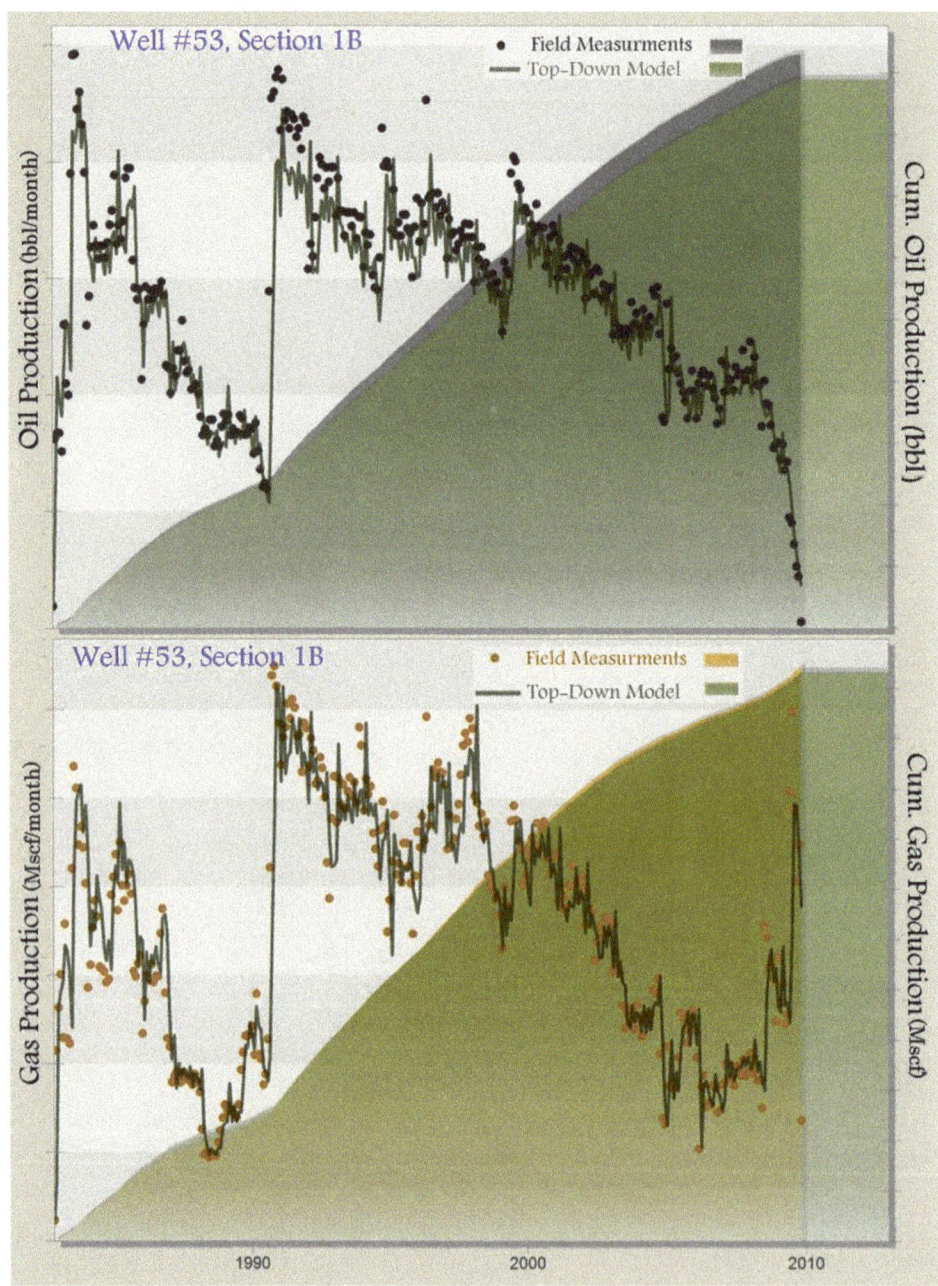

Fig. 69—Oil and gas monthly rate and cumulative production match for Well No. 53 with the surface location in Section 2A. This well was completed in multiple stacked reservoirs—onshore mature field in Central America.

Both gas and water were injected very early in the life of the field. Gas production decreased substantially after a few years of injection and finally came to an end in 2003. Water injection was sustained until 2006 at high levels and then decreased to lower values. **Fig. 72** shows the total volume of gas and water injection in the field as a function time. **Fig. 73** shows the volumes of injection as a function of time for a single injection well in the field. Total oil and gas production from this field is shown in **Fig. 74**. Oil production peaked only a few years after the initial production and started to decline from 1996.

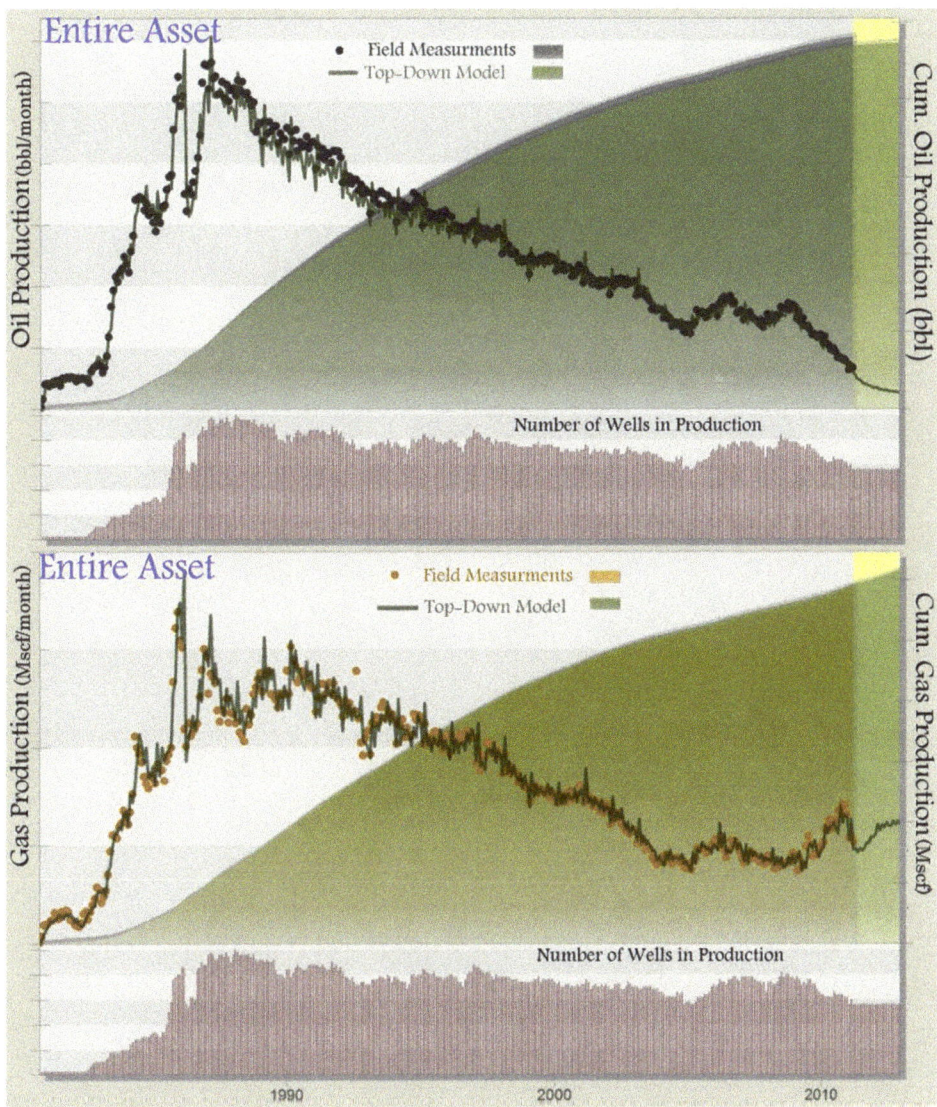

Fig. 70—Oil and gas monthly rate and cumulative production match for the entire asset—onshore mature field in Central America.

The list of the parameters that were used to develop the top-down model for this mature offshore field in the North Sea is shown in **Fig. 75**. The "Well Logs" that are mentioned in Fig. 75 include gamma ray, resistivity, neutron porosity, density porosity, spontaneous potential, temperature, and caliper logs. Data were available from both injection and production wells as shown in Fig. 75.

This field included a total of 28 producers from which only seven were in production at the time of the development of this top-down model. Another 21 producers were shut in sometime during the life of the field. The field also included 14 injection wells, of which only three were active at the time of the development of this top-down model.

The top-down model was developed for this field, and the historical production was history matched on a well-by-well basis for all the producers, including those that were already shut in. The project was carried out in mid-2012, and the top-down model was deployed to predict the production from the active producers until 2015. **Figs. 76 and 77** show two examples of the history match

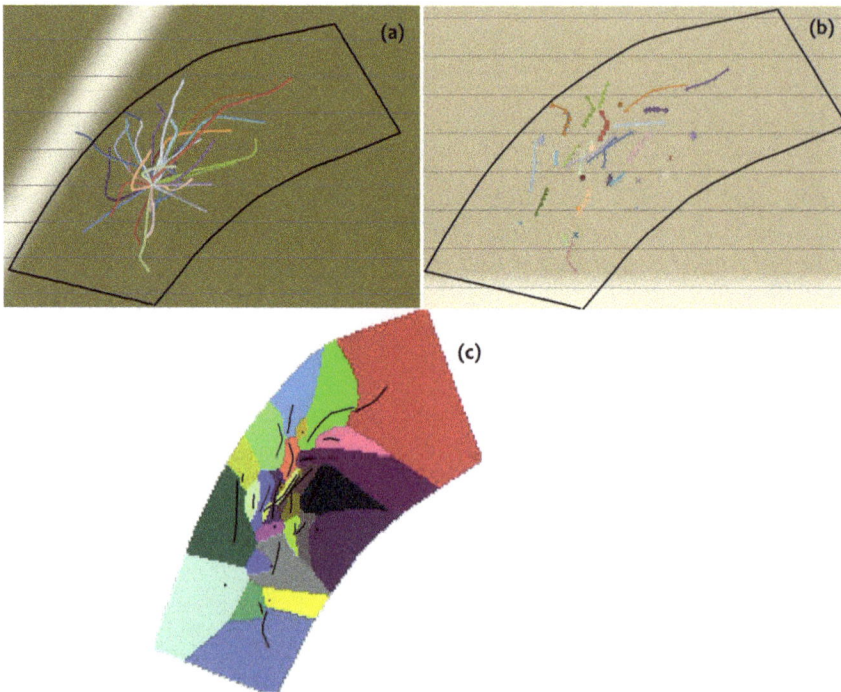

Fig. 71—Preparation for top-down model. (a) Schematics of the wells drilled off a single pad in the North Sea field. (b) Schematic of completions for all the injectors and the producers. (c) Reservoir delineation for each of the completions.

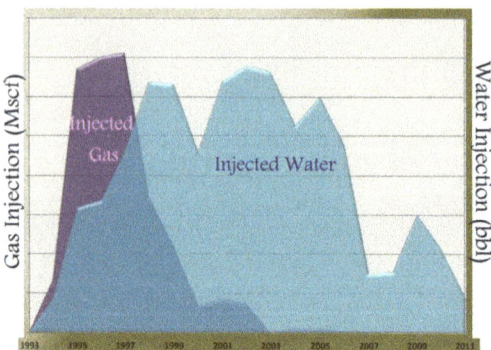

Fig. 72—Total gas and water injected throughout the life of the field.

achieved by the top-down model for two of the production wells. Fig. 76 is for an active well, and therefore production for this well was forecast into the future. However, the well that is shown in Fig. 77 was shut in during 2003, and therefore, it had no production after that time. Therefore, no production forecast was made for this well.

In Figs. 76 and 77, oil production is shown on the top graph and associated gas production is shown on the bottom graph. In both cases, the monthly production volume (circles for field measurements and solid lines for the top-down model) and the cumulative production (for oil, gray shade represents field production and green shade represents the top-down model; for gas, orange shade represents field production and green shade represents the top-down model) are shown in these figures.

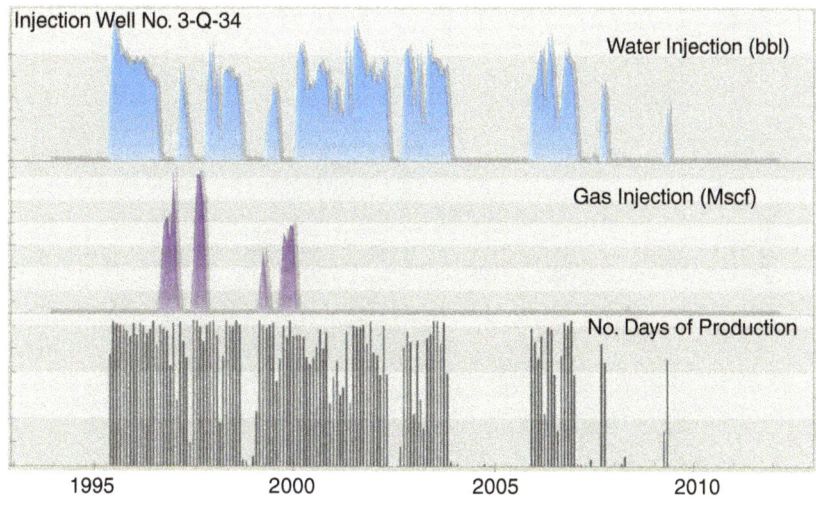

Fig. 73—Water- and gas-injection schedule and amount for one of the injectors in the field.

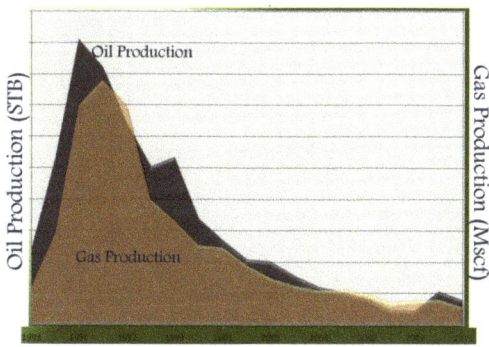

Fig. 74—Total oil and gas production from the field.

Production Well	
Static Data	Dynamic Data
Location - X	CP (t)
Location - Y	CP ($t-1$)
Azimuth	Choke (t)
Inclination	Choke ($t-1$)
Drainage Area	Gas Life (t)
Date of First Production	Gas Life ($t-1$)
Depth	Q-Oil ($t-1$)
Pay Thickness	Q-Oil ($t-2$)
Completion	Q-Gas ($t-1$)
Permeability	Q-Water ($t-1$)
Porosity	
Water Saturation	
Well Logs …	

Offset Injection Well	
Static Data	Dynamic Data
Location - X	Days of Injection (t)
Location - Y	Days of Injection ($t-1$)
Drainage Area	Water Injection (t)
Distance	Water Injection ($t-1$)
Depth	Gas Injection (t)
Pay Thickness	Gas Injection ($t-1$)
Permeability	
Porosity	
Water Saturation	

Fig. 75—List of parameters that were used to develop the top-down model for the mature offshore field in the North Sea. CP = Casing Pressure

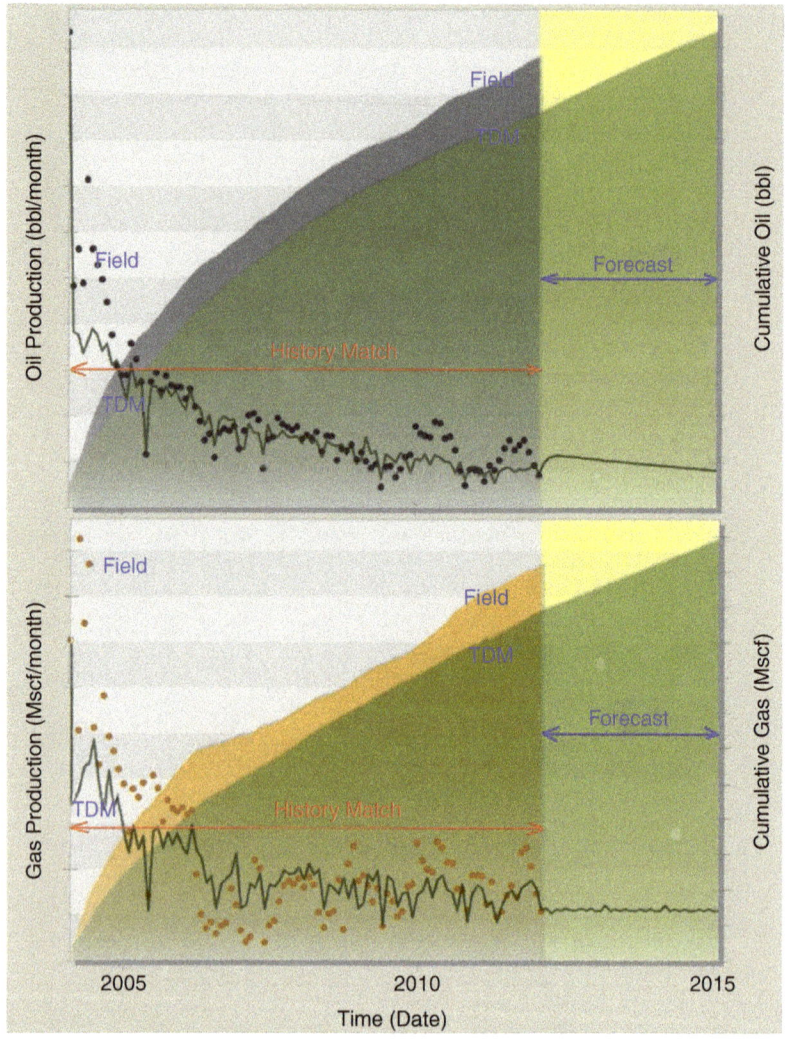

Fig. 76—Oil and gas production history match for one of the active producers in the offshore mature field in the North Sea.

Once oil and gas production for every well was history matched individually (and forecasts were made for active producers), oil and gas production from all the wells was summed to calculate and plot the oil and gas production for the entire field. **Fig. 78** shows the results of history matching the production from the entire field. The plot on the top shows oil production, while the plot on the bottom shows gas production. Both plots include the number of active wells for each month of production.

Fig. 79 shows the response of the top-down models to the uncertainties associated with the production from two of the wells in this field. Because the top-down model has a small computational footprint, quantification of uncertainties associated with any calculations and modeling is an easy and practical exercise. For example, if the uncertainties associated with the reservoir characteristics are to be quantified, then one can include a probability distribution for each of the uncertain parameters instead of a unique value. A Monte Carlo simulation can then be run, and the top-down model will yield a range for each of the production values instead of a single number.

By calculating and plotting the P10, P50, and P90 along with the actual predictions of the top-down model, one can easily, and in a short period of time, generate plots that are shown in Fig. 79 for all the wells in a field. In this figure, historical field measurements for oil production from two

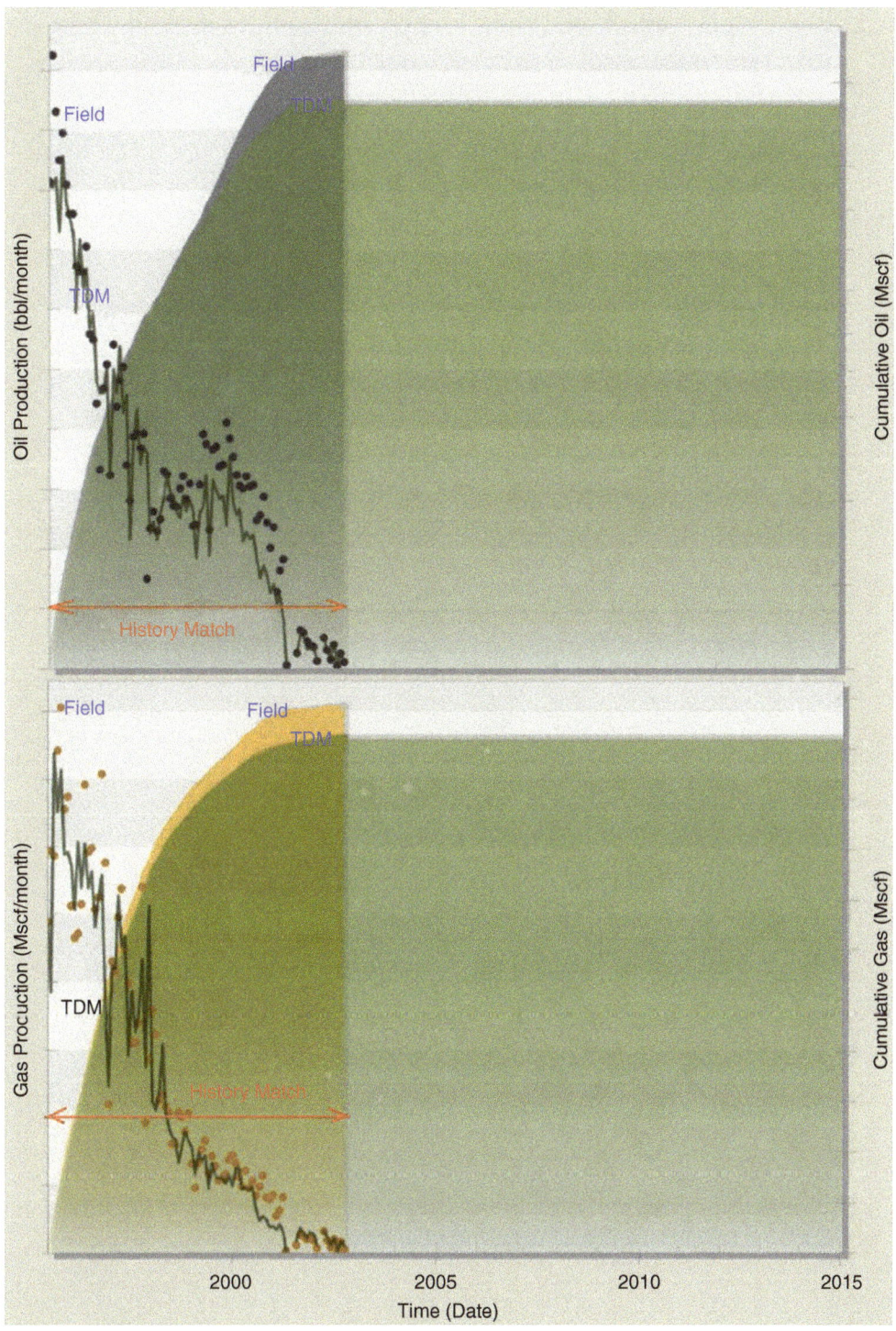

Fig. 77—Oil and gas production history match for one of the inactive producers in the offshore mature field in the North Sea.

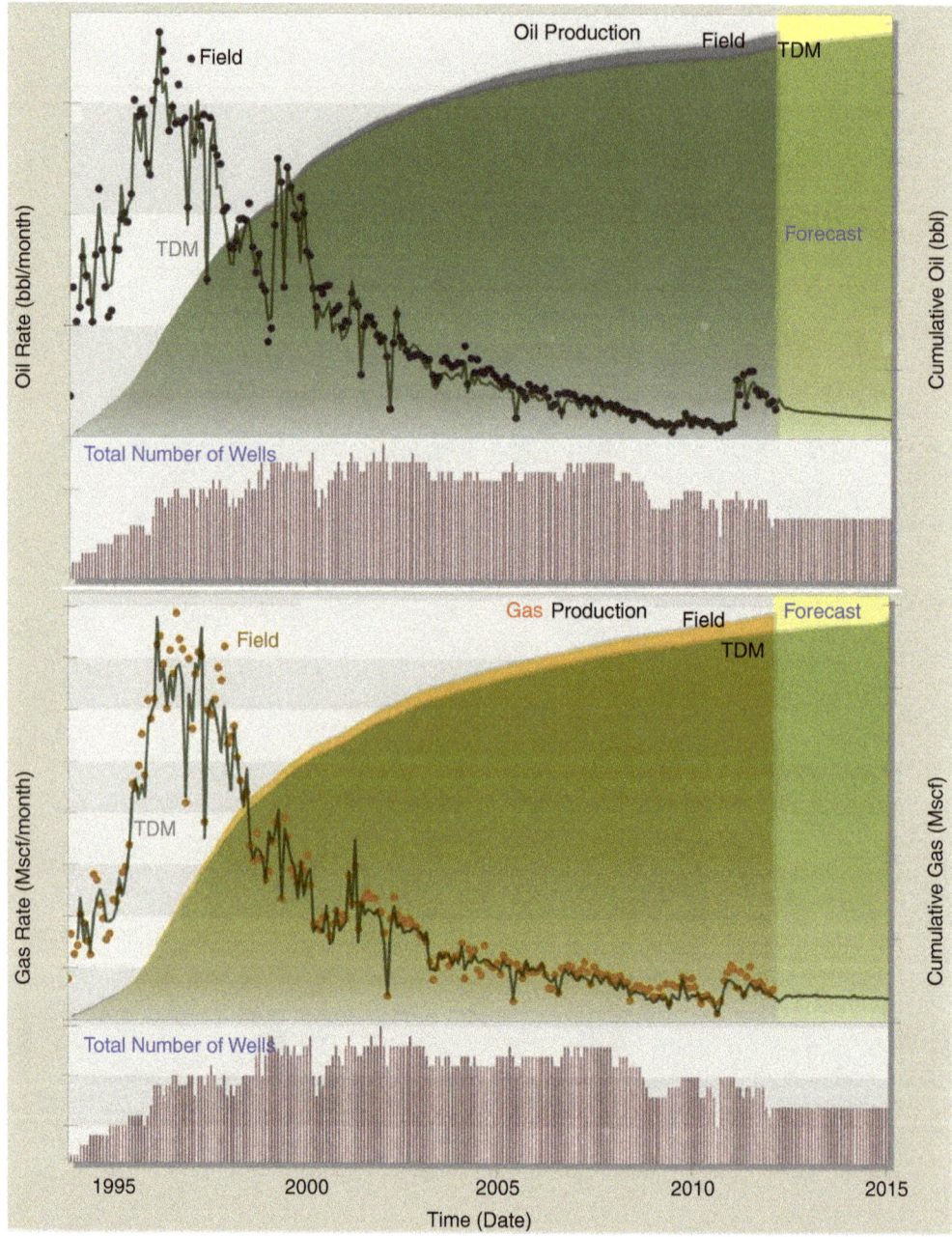

Fig. 78—Oil and gas production history match for the entire field (summation of all individual history matches), along with production forecast. Total number of producers is also shown at the bottom of each plot.

wells in this field are plotted against the top-down model's history match as well as the results of a Monte Carlo simulation for the forecast production by the top-down model until 2015.

Besides forecasting production from existing producers, the top-down model provides the ability to drill new (virtual) wells in the field in order to examine further productivity of the field and eventually optimize infill-drilling programs. **Fig. 80** shows an example of production from a new infill well in this field. The production profile for this well includes the uncertainties associated

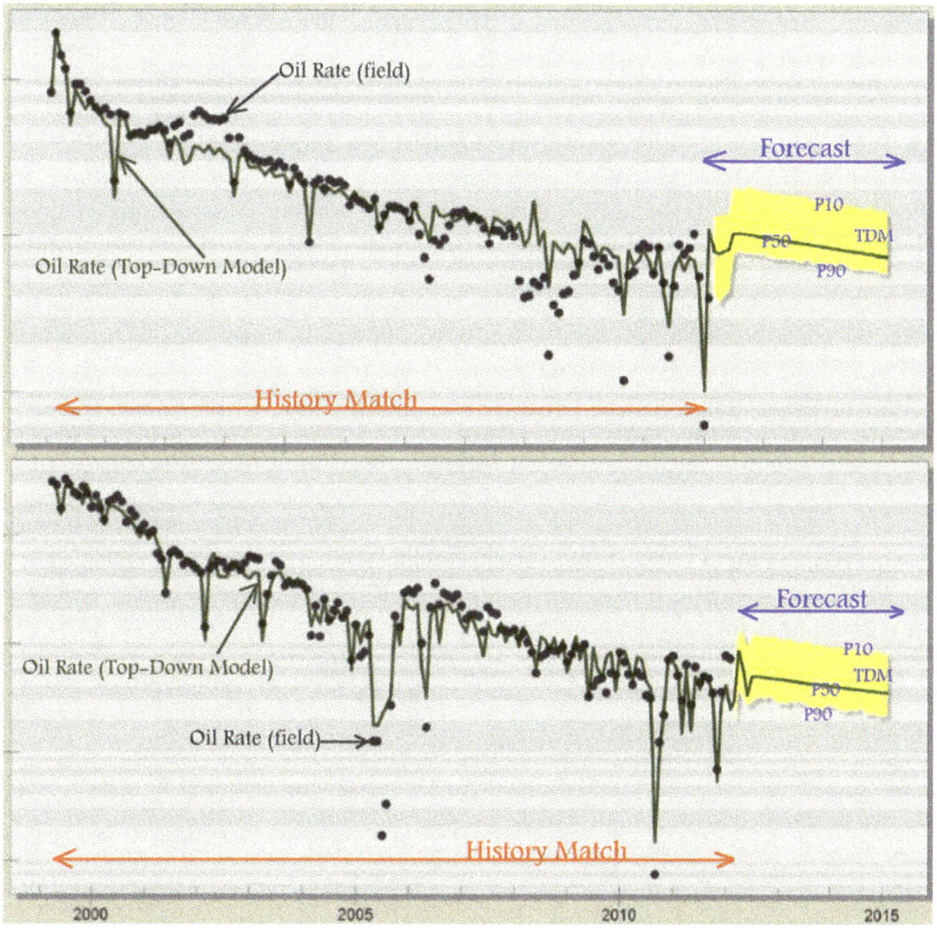

Fig. 79—History match along with the production forecast for two producers in the offshore North Sea field. The forecast includes an uncertainty band.

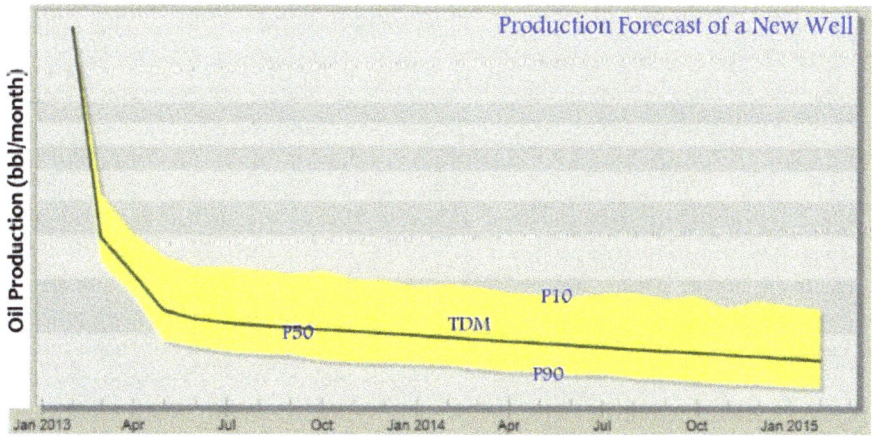

Fig. 80—Production forecast of a new well along with the uncertainty band.

with reservoir characteristics, specifically in a new location in the field where no measured reservoir characteristics are available. Also, it is important to note that because the operational constraints are kept constant throughout the forecast period, the production presents smooth characteristics.

11.3 Case Study No. 3: Mature Onshore Field in the Middle East

In this case study, TDM was applied to a giant mature onshore oil field in the United Arab Emirates. The oil field is located in the Rub-Al-Khali Basin on the eastern shelf of the Arabian Platform. It is included in a geological setting characterized by thick sedimentary deposits, primarily carbonates, and it is accumulated and deformed by intermittent tectonic movements that have resulted in relatively gentle folding, faulting, and salt movement. The field is an ovate anticline with a north/south major axis approximately 22 miles long, producing from Lower Cretaceous buildups with estimated reserves of 20 billion bbl of oil (Alsharhan 1993).

The asset produces from multiple reservoirs. The reservoir being studied in this project is well-known to be one of the most complex and heterogeneous reservoirs in the region. As expected, this asset has a long history of multiple numerical simulation modeling studies, with various degrees of success. Needless to say, there were many reasons that a completely data-driven modeling effort was commissioned for this asset. The top-down model was applied to the south-central portion of the field as shown in **Fig. 81**. This field produces from five different formations called Units No. 1 through No. 5, with Unit No. 1 being the shallowest of the five. The five units may or may not be present everywhere in the field because they may pinch out in some locations and reappear in other locations. Many of the wells in this asset are completed in multiple units. Each horizontal or slanted completion in a unit is called a string. There are wells that include multiple strings (are completed in all the five units along with wells that are completed in any combination of the units) and those that include only a single string (are completed only in one unit).

Fig. 82 shows the number of producer and injector strings completed in each of the units. Even though many of the producers may not be active at the present time, during the development of the top-down model all the wells that have been completed in the asset and have contributed to the injection or the production at some time during the life of the asset are included in the model and are history matched.

11.3.1 Data Used During the Top-Down-Model Development. Because this was a prolific mature field with more than 35 years of production and injection history from more than 430 wells (strings), a very large pool of data was available for this asset. The available data included detailed production and injection history from every single well (string) along with a large number of well logs, well tests, conventional and special core analyses, pulsed neutron logs, seismic, and others. The mere size of this data set with its multiple scales (which is a good example of the recently coined phrase Big Data), although providing a wealth of potential information, usually creates a data tsunami that will overwhelm most reservoir modelers engaged in traditional numerical simulation.

All 438 strings (264 producers and 174 injectors) were included in the model. Production data were available from 1975, and water-injection data were available from its inception in 1980. Well construction data (vertical, slanted, and horizontal) and changes in perforations throughout the history of each well were also included in the model.

Static data incorporated in the model were extracted from well logs and petrophysical calculations included formation tops and thicknesses (for each of the units), porosity, and saturation (**Figs. 83 and 84**). Permeability and relative permeability data were available from core analyses. Well tests had been performed throughout the history of the field on multiple wells. The interpretation of these well tests provided information regarding the changes in static reservoir pressure (at the location of each well) as a function of time. Furthermore, pulsed neutron logs that were run on multiple wells at different times in the history of this asset provided much-needed information about the changes in water saturation throughout the reservoir, as a function of time.

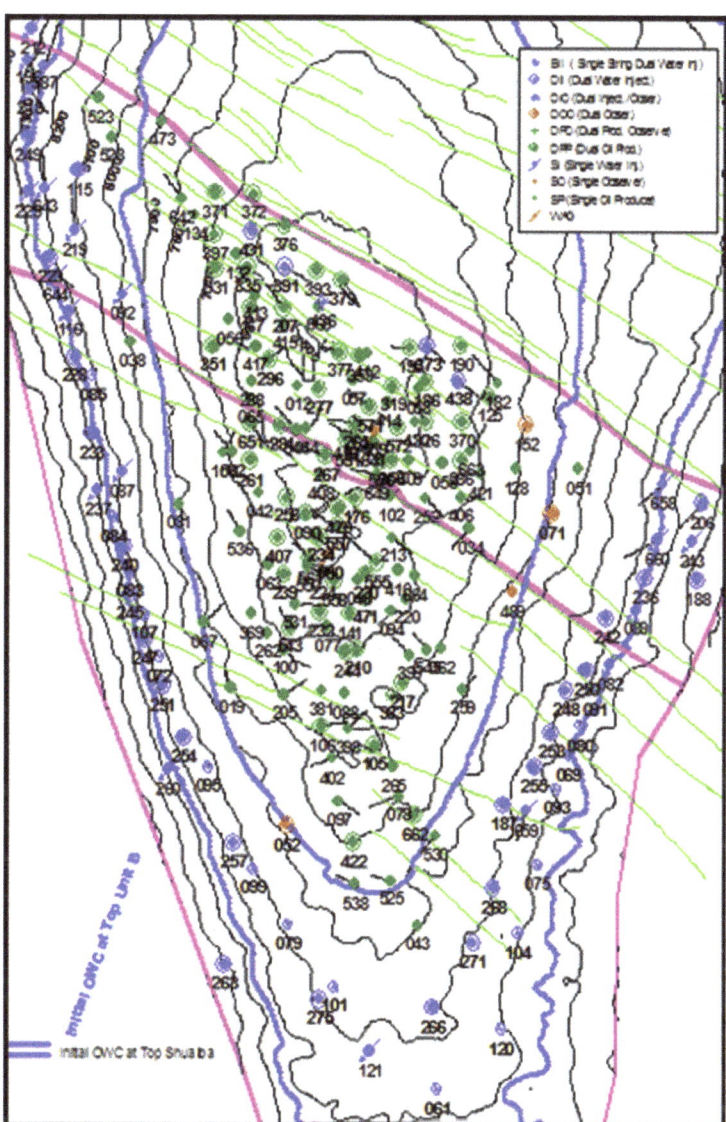

Fig. 81—Map of the south-central portion of the asset used for TDM.

Wells Used in the TDM Project			
Units	Producers	Injectors	Active Producers
Unit #1	43	31	31
Unit #2	65	41	36
Unit #3	39	31	13
Unit #4	71	46	36
Unit #5	46	25	31
Total	**264**	**174**	**147**

Fig. 82—Number of wells used in the TDM study.

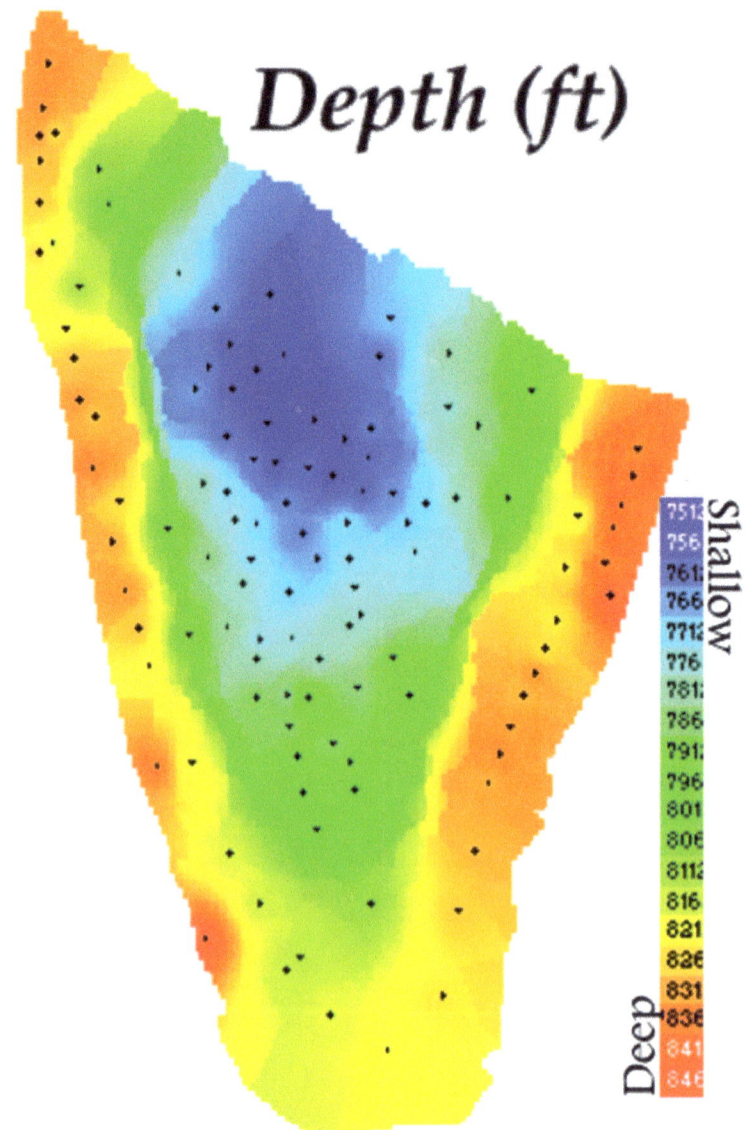

Fig. 83—Geostatistical distribution of formation depth for one of the production units.

Fig. 85 shows four different pulsed neutron logs performed on a particular well from 1983 to 1989. This figure shows measured changes in water saturation as a function of time at this well. These changes reflect the impact of static reservoir characteristics as well as oil, water, and gas production and water injection throughout the reservoir and specifically in the area surrounding this well and its offset injection and production wells. Similar logs were available at multiple locations in the asset.

As far as the static reservoir characteristics are concerned, available information may reflect a specific point in the reservoir (i.e., the well) when, for example, well logs are being considered, and sometimes they may be representative of a larger volume of the reservoir (including the well) as in a well test. Using an allocation algorithm that was developed by integration of Voronoi graph theory (Dickerson et al. 2011) and fuzzy cluster analysis (Höppner et al. 1999), as shown in **Fig. 86**, the reservoir is divided into polygons in order to accommodate this incompatibility of scales.

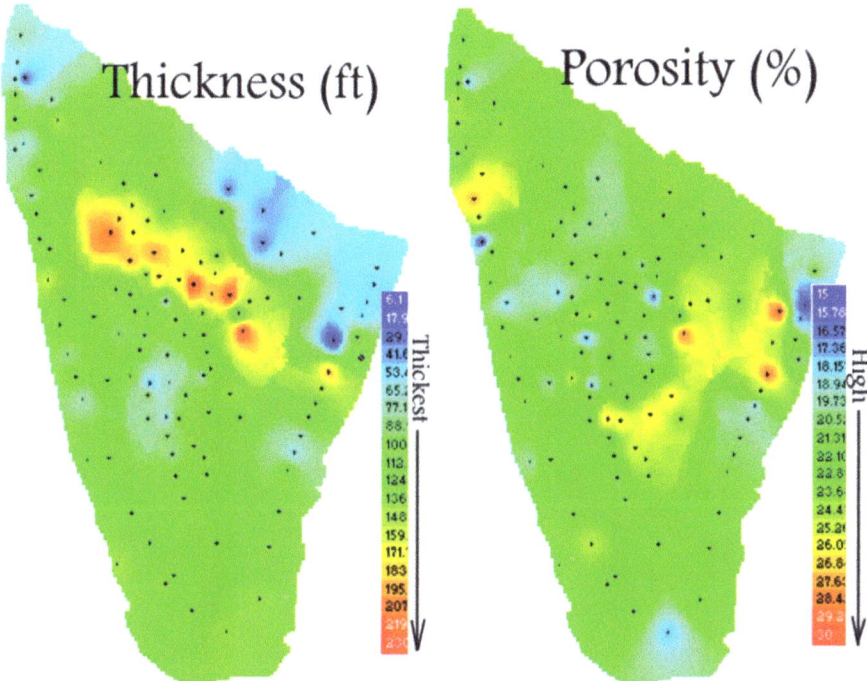

Fig. 84—Geostatistical distribution of formation thickness and porosity for one of the production units.

The data used for the development of the top-down model in this project are organized into three categories: static data, dynamic data, and reservoir response. Each of the categories is then further divided into several subcategories. **Fig. 87** shows the list of the data that were available and used during the development of the top-down model.

Although from a reservoir engineering point of view the static reservoir pressure and water saturation throughout the reservoir, as a function of time and space, are advantageous, they provide a serious challenge to the numerical reservoir simulation modelers, because simultaneous history matching of production from the wells along with static reservoir pressure and time-lapse water saturation markedly increase the complexity of the history-matching process.

One of the main reasons for reaching out to a new and different reservoir simulation and modeling technology such as TDM in this particular asset was the massive challenges associated with performing such a complex, simultaneous, and multiobjective (production, static pressure, and time-lapse saturation) history matching on more than 260 wells producing from five different units.

Attempts to correlate production and injection in this asset, without paying the necessary attention to the fundamentals of fluid flow in porous media, at best provide superficial results that cannot be trusted to generate fundamentally sound and repeatable results. These attempts are usually made using over-the-counter statistical packages that have not been custom developed to handle such challenging tasks. These tools, at the very most and when used appropriately, can provide multiple visualization schemes that are as useful in the oil and gas industry as they are in the pharmaceutical, social networking, retail, or any other industry, for that matter. However, these generic and mainly statistical tools lack the vital component of domain relevance that must be appropriately used by the domain experts.

11.3.2 Top-Down-Model Training and History Matching. Once the assimilation of the spatio-temporal database is completed, a series of pattern-recognition and data-mining exercises is performed. These data-mining and pattern-recognition exercises serve multiple purposes. They are a crucial step in understanding and learning about the reservoir that is being modeled. They reveal the

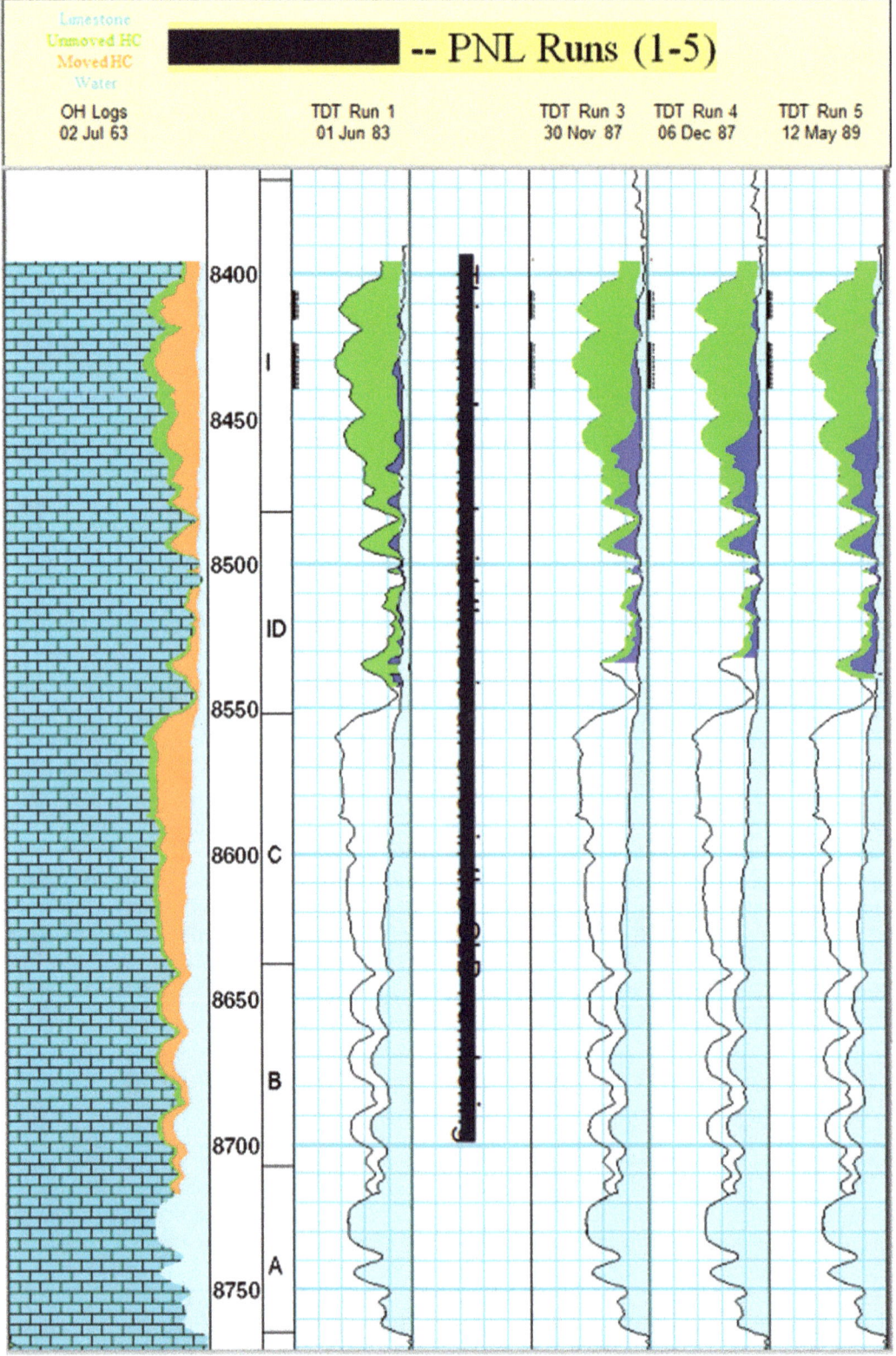

Fig. 85—Example of the pulsed neutron log available for several wells at different points in time. For example, four pulsed neutron logs were available for this particular well.

Fig. 86—Map of one of the units indicating the location of the producer and injector wells. The asset has been delineated using an algorithm that incorporates Voronoi graph theory and fuzzy cluster analysis.

influence of different parameters in the production from the asset. They help the modeler to understand the impact of reservoir characteristics as opposed to the design parameters in the particular asset. Data mining and pattern recognition exercises shed light on all these and eventually help in identifying the best set of parameters to be used as input into the data-driven models that will be developed as part of the top-down model.

For example, for this case study, the project objectives determined the number of data-driven models that needed to be developed and used in sequence in order to form the final top-down model. **Fig. 88** shows the flow chart for the top-down model in this study. In this flow diagram, it is shown that a data-driven static pressure model had to be developed first and its results (with other data in the spatio-temporal database) had to be used in order to develop the data-driven water saturation model. The results of the data-driven static pressure model and the data-driven water saturation model along with other data in the spatio-temporal database were used to develop the data-driven production rate model.

The final top-down model for this asset included three data-driven models that would run in sequence (this is called the cascading scheme, as shown in Fig. 88) in order to provide the required results for this asset. For example, static data from the spatio-temporal database along with dynamic data (mainly operational constraints) from the spatio-temporal database at time t are needed (as well

142 Data-Driven Reservoir Modeling

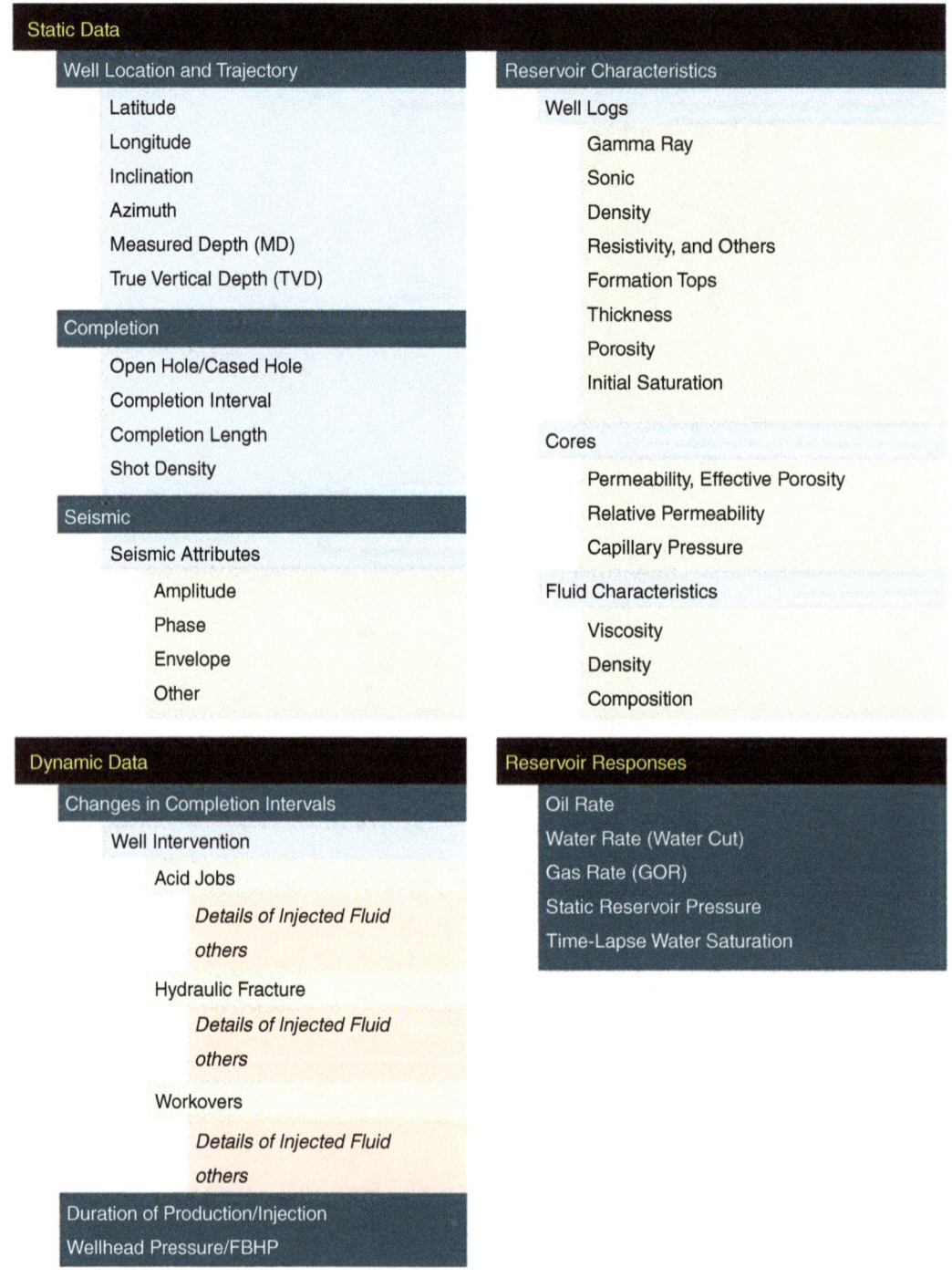

Fig. 87—Partial list of data that were used during the development of the top-down model.

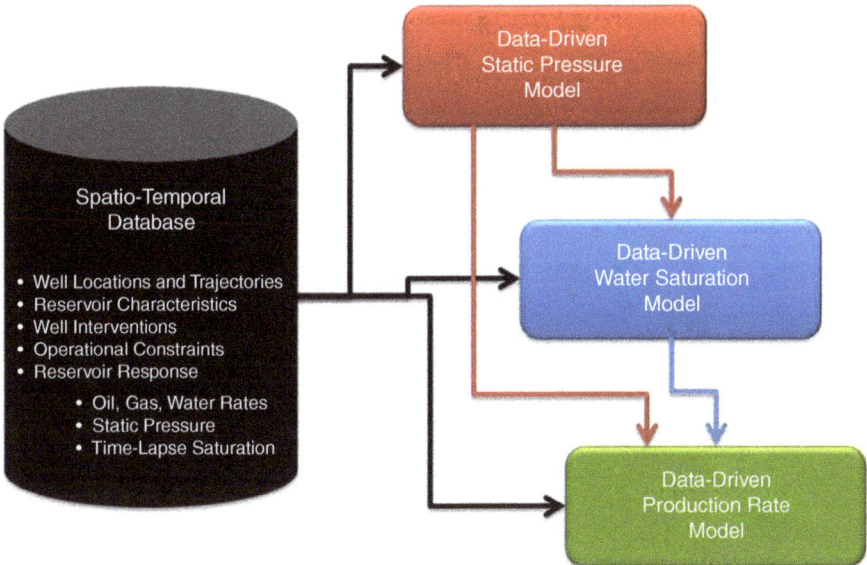

Fig. 88—General flow chart of the top-down model design for this specific asset.

as the "Static Reservoir Pressure" at time $t-1$) to generate the "Static Reservoir Pressure" at time t for all the wells in the asset.

Next, static data along with dynamic data at time t (mainly operational constraints), as well as recently calculated static reservoir pressure at time t, are required as input to the data-driven water saturation model (as well as the water saturation at time $t-1$) in order to calculate water saturation at time t for all the wells in the asset. Similarly, to calculate the production rates at each well at time t, static data along with dynamic data from time t as well as recently calculated static reservoir pressure and water saturation at time t (along with production rate from time $t-1$) are required to be used in the data-driven production rate model.

Data from this asset were available from 1975 to 2010. Production, injection, static pressure, and water saturation data from 1975 to 2001 were used to train and history match the top-down model, while similar data from 2002 to 2009, although available, were not used during the training and history-matching process. This segment of the historical data was put aside to be used after the training and history matching of the top-down model were completed.

These so-called blind history-matching data were to be used as a blind validation data set to measure the goodness and the robustness of the top-down model and identify the degree of confidence that can be placed in the forecasts that are made by the top-down model upon deployment in forecast mode. The top-down model is then used to forecast reservoir pressure, water saturation, and production volumes into the future. The timelines used for modeling and history matching of the top-down model, blind history matching, and forecasting are shown in **Fig. 89**.

Results of training, history matching, blind history matching, and forecasting of the top-down model are shown in **Figs. 90 through 92**. Each of these figures includes detailed history matching of two individual wells. In these figures, the results are shown for individual string (completions in a given geological-formation unit). In each of the figures for a given string, three graphs are shown. In all three graphs, the x-axis is time (date) that extends from the initial production date (1973) to the forecast time of 2015.

The time in the x-axis is divided into three segments (recognized by different background colors) identifying the period of time used for training and history matching of the top-down model

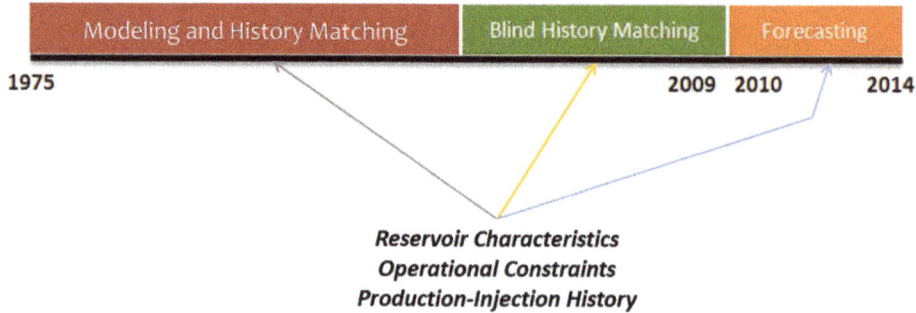

Fig. 89—History-matching strategy for the onshore mature field in the Middle East.

(1973 to 2001—white background), the period of time used for blind history matching (2002 to 2009—light-brown background), and the period of time used for forecasting (2010 to 2015—blue background).

In each of the graphs in Figs. 90 through 92, field measurements are shown using red dots, while the results from the top-down model are shown as solid blue lines. In these figures, the top graph shows the water saturation (measured using time-lapse pulsed neutron logs) as a function of time. The middle graph shows the static reservoir pressure (at the given well) as a function of time. The bottom graph shows oil production as a function of time. In the bottom graph, wellhead pressure values are used as the constraints (input to the model) in order for the oil production rates to be calculated. The TDM results from a total of six strings are displayed in these three figures.

These figures clearly show that TDM is quite powerful when it comes to history matching past production measurements from every individual well/string in the field. As demonstrated throughout this book, the top-down model does this by learning the reservoir and well-production behavior using the internal correlations that it builds between static and dynamic parameters with production from each well, taking into account production constraints and injection and production from offset wells. This is accomplished one record at a time and then is put together to present production from a well and ultimately production from the entire field, as shown in **Fig. 93**.

It has also been demonstrated that the correlation that is built during this process may be successfully used to predict water saturation, static pressure, and oil production volumes from each well during the portion of the date that is left out as blind history match. The accuracy of the top-down model during the blind history match, as demonstrated in Figs. 90 through 93 is an impressive accomplishment, especially when it is compared with results from numerical reservoir simulation.[64]

To further demonstrate the capabilities of the top-down model developed for this asset and the accuracy of the correlations to which it has converged (that this is a clear demonstration that the model has learned the complexities of fluid flow in this particularly complex carbonate field with hundreds of production and injection wells), two more figures are presented.

Figs. 94 and 95 show water saturation, static reservoir pressure, and oil production volumes history matched for two wells. What is interesting about these two wells and distinguishes them from other wells shown in the previous figures is that these two wells were drilled and put in production during the blind history matching period of this project. In other words, the top-down model was not trained with data from these wells, but the accuracy of the top-down model's predictions is quite impressive. Furthermore, it must be noted that there were approximately a dozen wells completed in multiple units that had these characteristics, and the top-down model's performance for all of them was quite consistent.

---

[64]Unfortunately, because of confidentiality issues, results of such comparisons cannot be shown here.

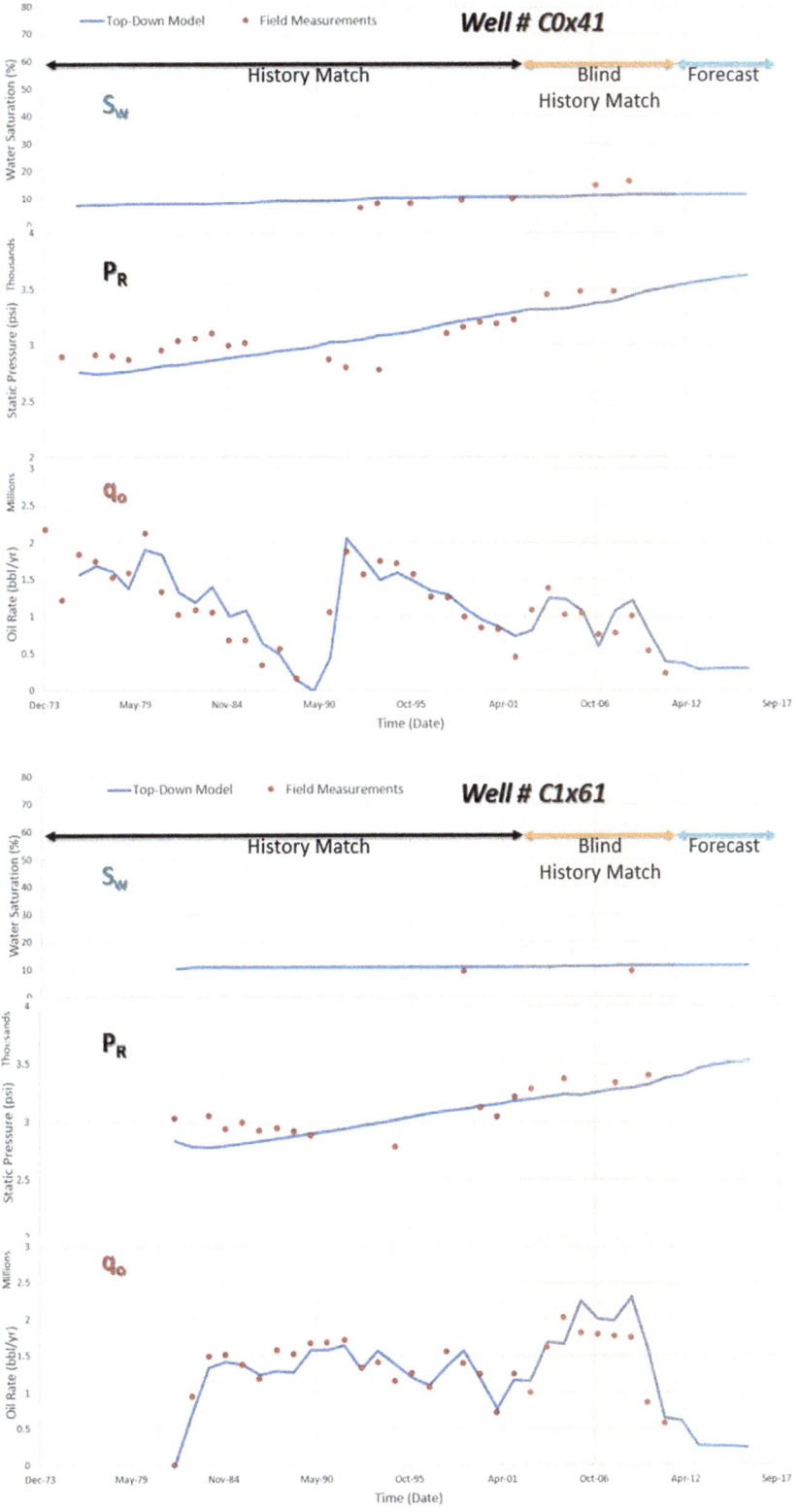

Fig. 90—Complete history-matching results for Wells No. C0x41 and No. C1x61.

146 Data-Driven Reservoir Modeling

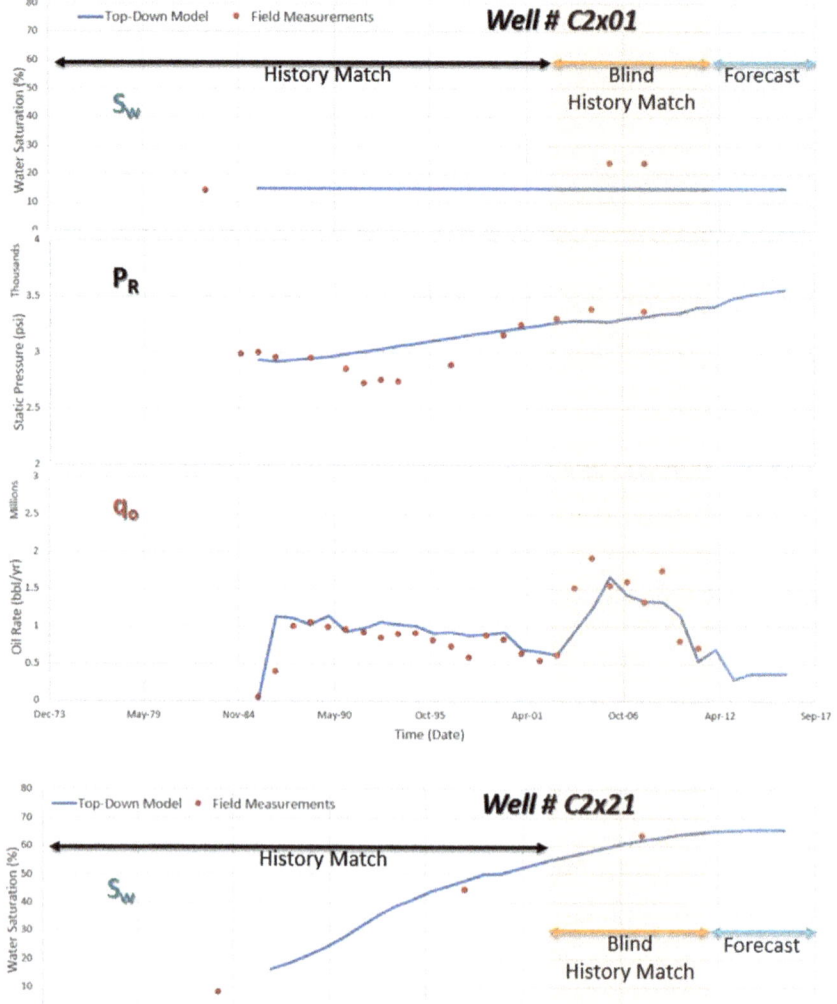

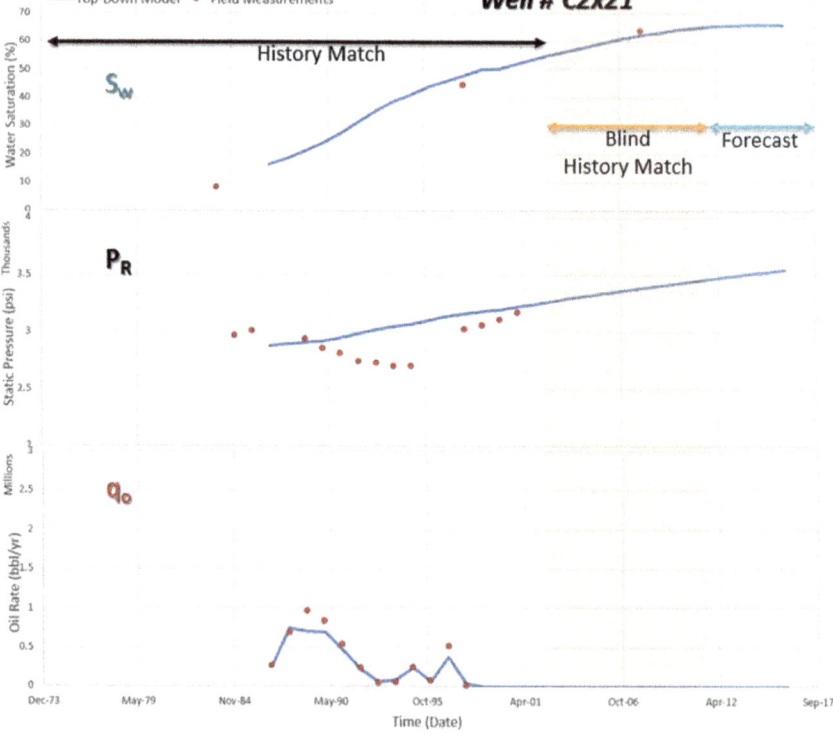

Fig. 91—Complete history-matching results for Wells No. C2x01 and No. C2x21.

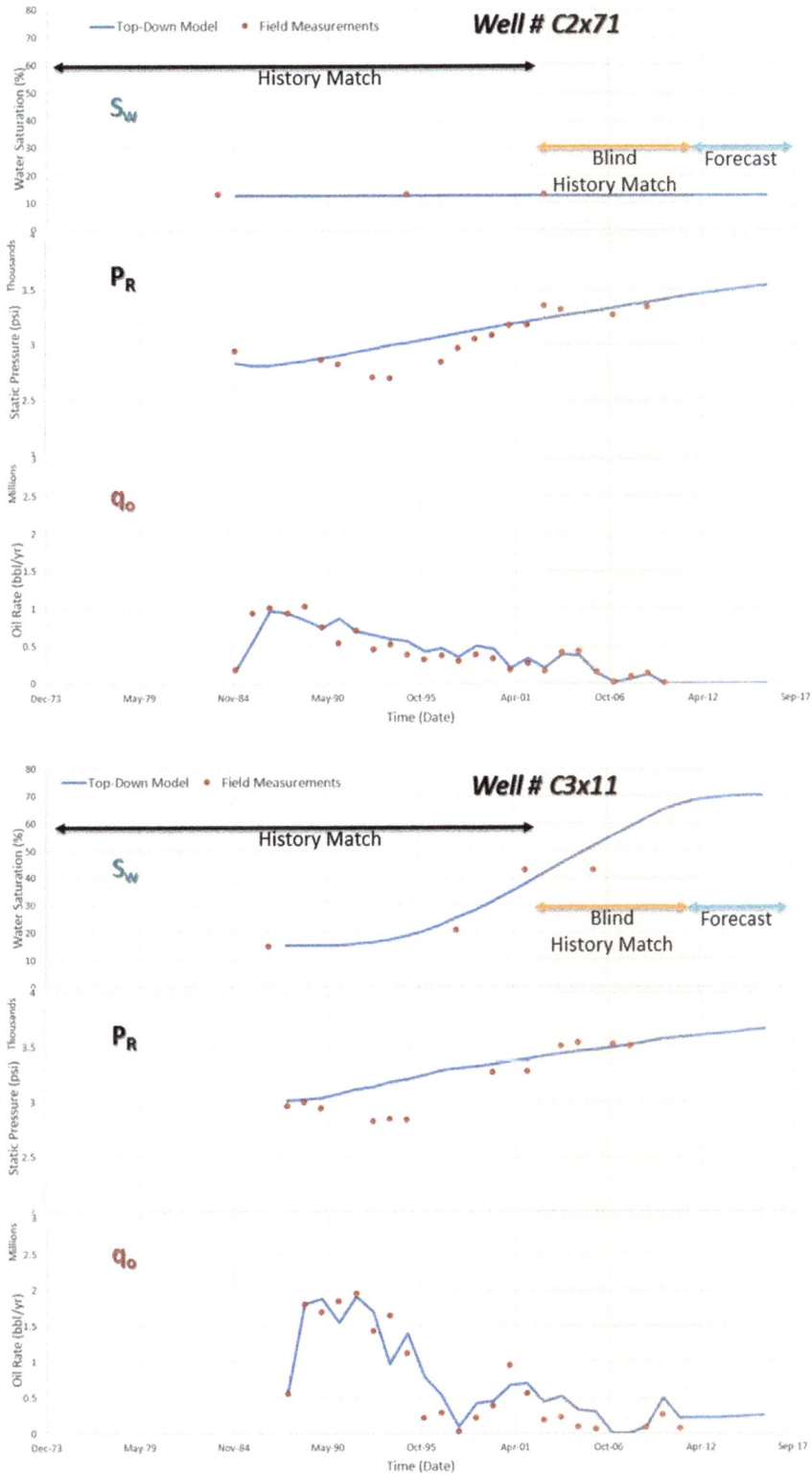

Fig. 92—Complete history-matching results for Wells No. C2x71 and No. C3x11.

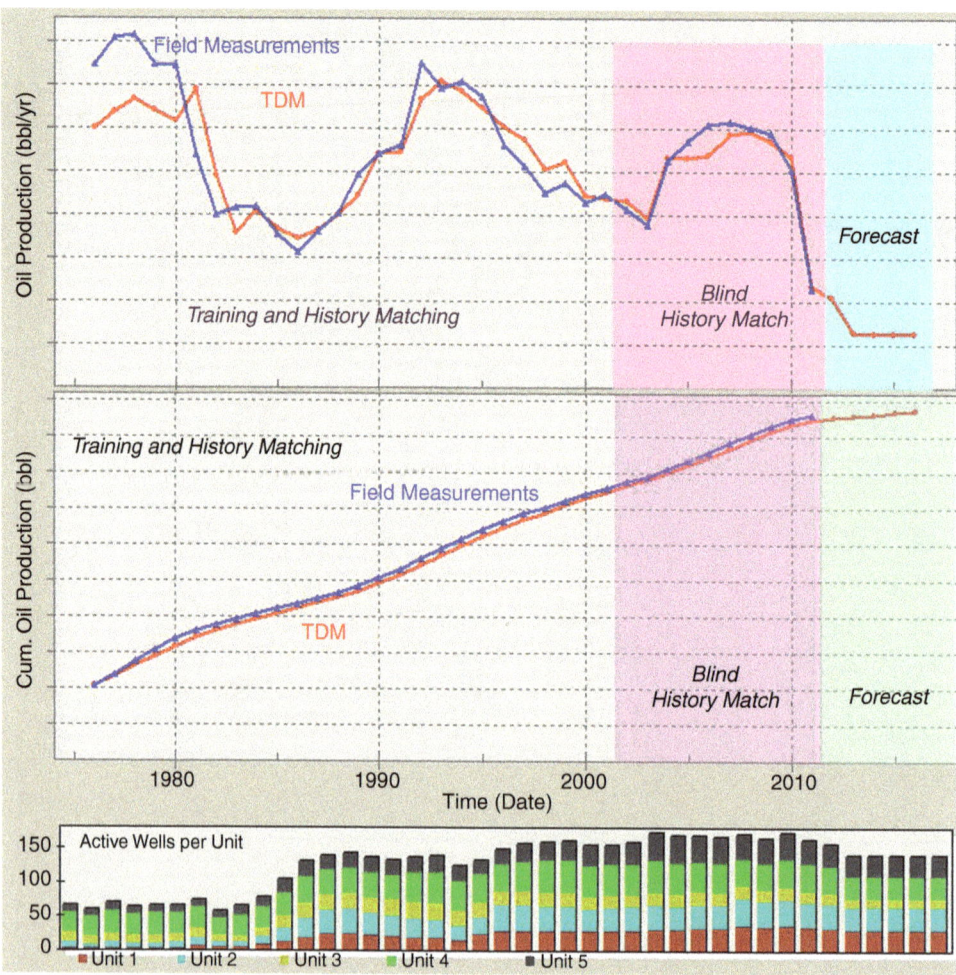

Fig. 93—Production history matching of the annual oil production rates (top) and cumulative oil production (middle) for the complete asset, including the number of active wells in each year for each of the production units (bottom). The sequential history-matching process included 7 years of blind history matching.

Once history matching static reservoir pressure and water saturation (simultaneously with oil production rates) is completed, the model can then be used to generate the distribution of these parameters throughout the reservoir. Fig. 60 shows the distribution of static reservoir pressure and water saturation generated by the history-matched top-down model throughout the reservoir for one of the units in this field.

Visualization of the distribution of parameters such as static reservoir pressure and water saturation can play an important role in understanding the dynamics of fluid flow in this reservoir and assist engineers in planning future development.

11.3.3 Post-Modeling Analysis. Once the top-down model is trained, history matched, and validated for accuracy (by performing blind history matching), the top-down model is used to plan future operations in the field. It can be used to identify the best locations for infill wells, to identify the most efficient mode of production that can be imposed on the producers, or to optimize the schedule and the amount of the injection, identifying how much water should be injected in which injection wells in order to maximize production with the minimum amount of injected water.

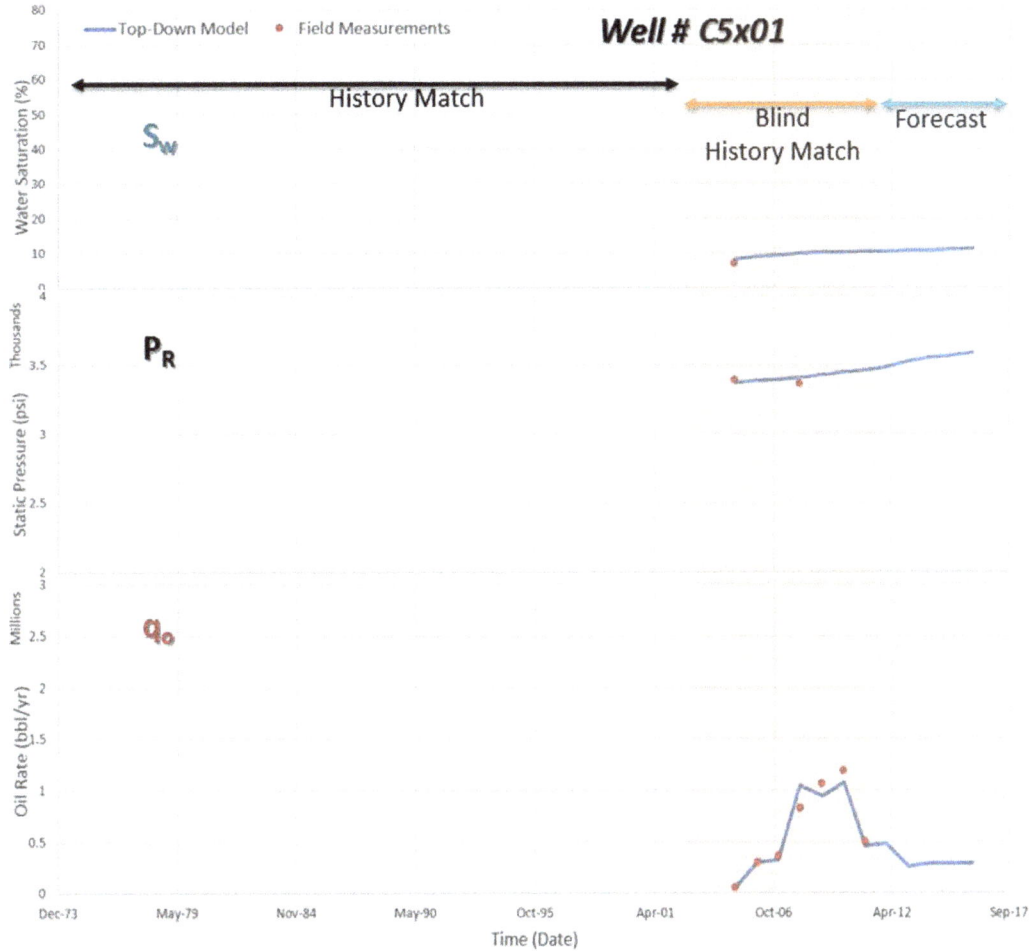

Fig. 94—Complete history-matching results (history matching, blind history matching, and forecast) for one of the new wells in the asset (Well No. C5x01). The top-down model included history matching water saturation (top), static reservoir pressure (middle), and oil production rate (bottom) for every string of every producer in the field. Please note that this well was completed and put in production during the blind history-matching period.

Furthermore, TDM can identify and map reservoir conductivity from the interaction between injection and production wells. To briefly demonstrate one of the capabilities of the top-down model in the post-modeling analysis phase, one of the many exercises that can be performed is shown here. In this post-modeling exercise, one can identify the contribution of the total amount of injected water to the oil production. This is done by identifying the degree of contribution from each injection well to the producers. Then, by performing an optimization routine, one is able to schedule optimal water injection to maximize oil production in the field, while minimizing the risk associated with high water cut in the producers that would eventually result in killing the well.

Fig. 96 shows the characteristics of historical water injection in this field. This figure shows the number of active injection wells (bars) as well as the total injected volume (line) for each year since 1975. To examine the utility of the top-down model and to perform post-modeling analysis in order to understand the characteristics of the reservoir, TDM was executed (in forecast mode) for the entire history of the field (1975–2010), but during this run, only 75% of the historical volume of water was injected.

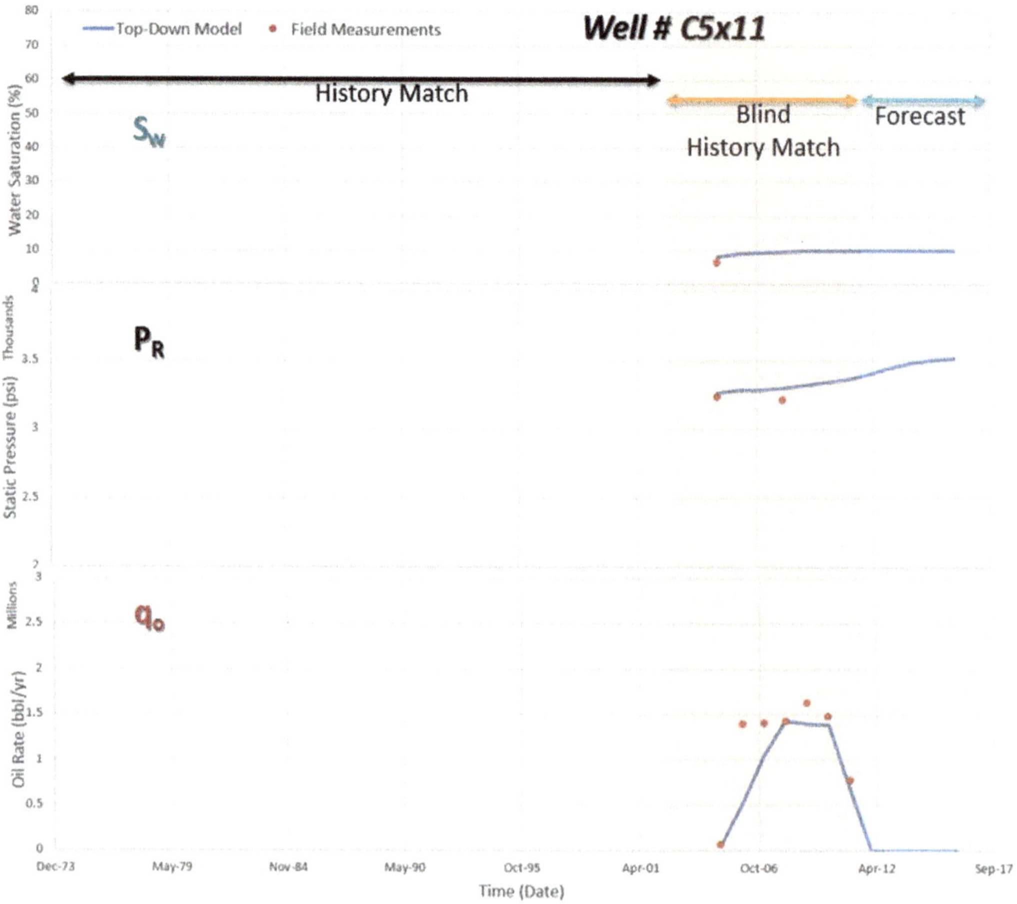

Fig. 95—Complete history-matching results (history matching, blind history matching and forecast) for one of the new wells in the asset (Well No. C5x11). The top-down model included history matching water saturation (top), static reservoir pressure (middle), and oil production rate (bottom) for every string of every producer in the field. Please note that this well was completed and put in production during the blind history-matching period.

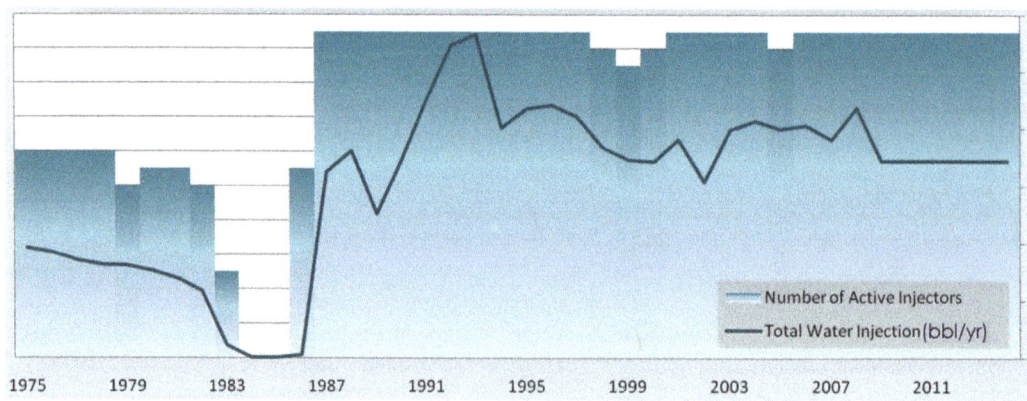

Fig. 96—Total historical (schedule and volume) water injection in the asset.

This was done to examine the impact of water injection on oil production. **Fig. 97** shows the water saturation distribution throughout the history of one of the reservoir units under two different scenarios. The water saturation distribution maps on the left are the result of 25% less water injection (compared with the historical total) and are compared with water saturation distribution at the historical total. In this figure, water saturation is shown in blue and oil saturation in red.

Fig. 98 shows the impact of different water-injection scenarios on oil production. It is interesting to note that during the earliest time period (1975 to 1992) higher water-injection volume results in higher incremental oil production. However, from 1992 to 1999, there is no significant impact on oil production when 15% less water is injected (85% of total volume). Furthermore, these analyses show that after 2009 less water injection (25% less) results in more oil production.

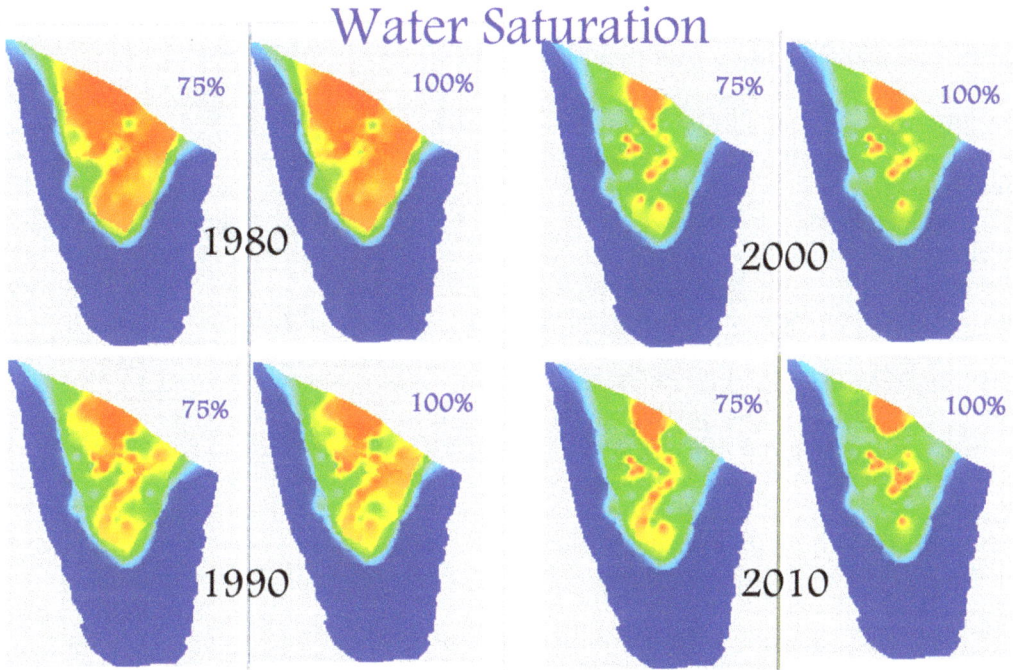

Fig. 97—Water-saturation distribution throughout the reservoir (between 1980 and 2010) in one of the production units. Comparison between actual historical water injection (100%) and the scenario in which 25% less water would have been injected (75%).

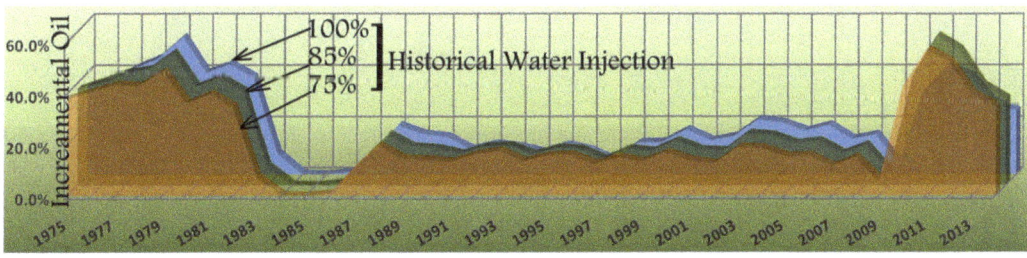

Fig. 98—Assessing the impact of lower water injection on oil production. Percent incremental oil production as a function of water injection in the field throughout years—results from the top-down model.

This figure emphasizes the well-known principle in reservoir engineering that the impact of water injection in a reservoir as a tool for sweep enhancement and pressure maintenance is dynamic and needs to be analyzed, understood, and optimized, throughout the life of the field. In continuation of this exercise, **Fig. 99** shows that throughout the history of water injection in this field, 15% less water could have been injected (this adds up to 182 million bbl of water), which would have resulted in approximately 2% more oil production (approximately 10 million bbl of oil).

Another advantage of the trained and validated top-down model is its ability to identify the impact of each water-injection well, individually, and in comparison with other injectors. **Fig. 100** shows the result of this exercise when it is applied to one of the reservoir units in this field. In this figure, the areas with darker color show a higher impact of the injection well. Having a tool such as this can help reservoir managers design a much more effective water-injection program that will result in substantial cost savings.

11.3.4 Performing a "Stress Test" on the Top-Down Model.

A "stress test" is a medical term that describes testing the limits of a healthy organ to see when it starts behaving abnormally. The term was also used by the US government after the 2007–2008 economic recession to test the financial efficacy of large US banks. In the context of reservoir modeling, stress tests can be used to test and validate the predictive capabilities of a reservoir model beyond the blind tests performed during the model development. The stress test would be the ultimate test of the reservoir model, to see if it can predict reservoir dynamics for several years in the future. To be useful, the stress test must be performed not upon completion of the reservoir model, but years after its development when actual field measurements that have been predicted by the reservoir model are available for comparison. If and when a reservoir model passes such a test, then it can be judged as a viable tool for making reservoir management decisions. This is far more complex and "stressful" for a model than the blind history match that was shown in the previous chapters of this book.

The top-down model presented in this section (built and validated through blind tests in 2010) was recently put through a stress test. The operator decided to examine the quality of the top-down model predictions, 5 years after the model was completed (and not updated with new data) to see if its prediction would stand a stress test. The stress test would be between the predictions made by the top-down model and actual field measurements made years after the model was completed and submitted.

The operator examined the predictions made by the top-down model for static reservoir pressure and water saturation of 23 wells that were drilled and completed after the completion of the project in 2010. The 23 wells were completed in all five units (reservoir) in this field; a list of them is shown in **Table 1**.

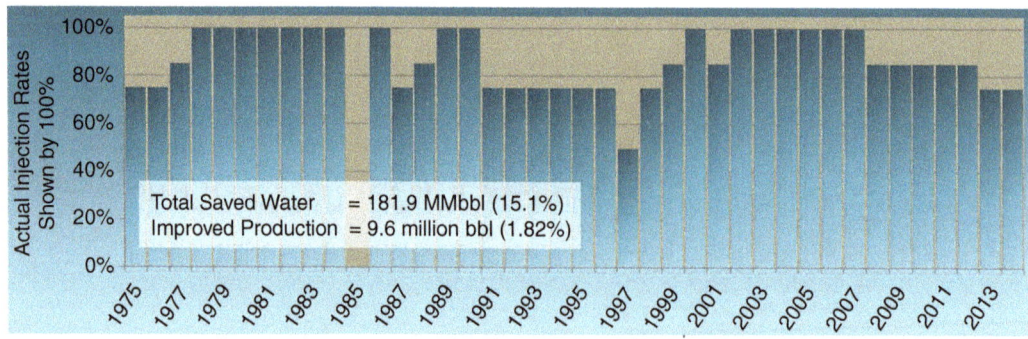

Fig. 99—Historical assessment of the water injection in one of the units in the field. On the basis of the top-down model's results, this unit could have produced 10 million bbl more oil (an increase of approximately 2%) if 180 million bbl (approximately 15%) less water had been injected.

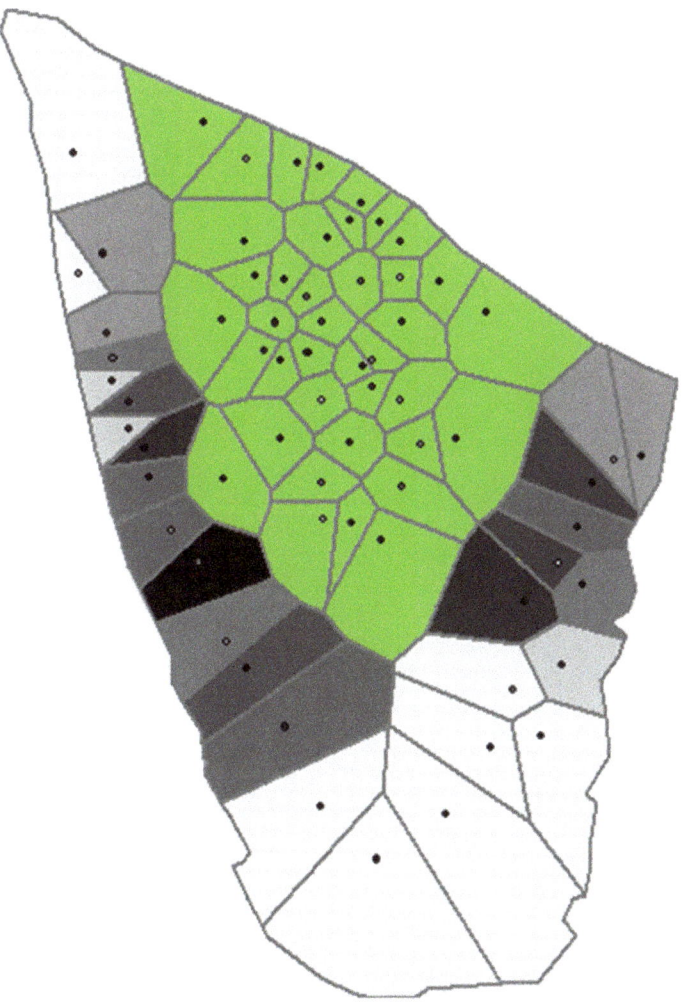

Fig. 100—Influence of injection wells in incremental oil production. Darker color means greater impact.

TABLE 1—LIST OF WELLS DRILLED AND COMPLETED IN EACH OF THE UNITS.

Units	Number of Wells Drilled Since 2010
Unit No. 1	2
Unit No. 2	4
Unit No. 3	4
Unit No. 4	10
Unit No. 5	3
TOTAL	23

Figs. 101 and 102 show the results of this stress test. Locations of these wells were used to drill and complete virtual wells in the top-down model, and the static reservoir pressure and water saturation at these locations were estimated by the top-down model and presented to the operator. The operator then compared the top-down model's predictions with the actual measured values from the field. We are not aware of similar tests that might have been performed using the numerical simulation model that was developed for this field.

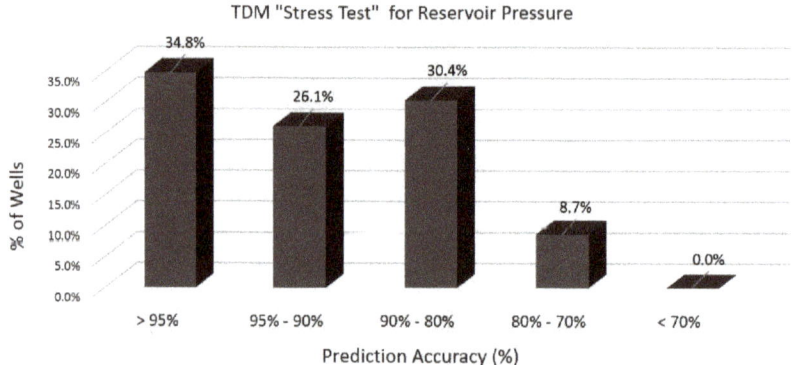

Fig. 101—Result of the top-down-model stress test. The top-down model's predictions are compared to actual field measurements, 5 years after its development (static reservoir pressure).

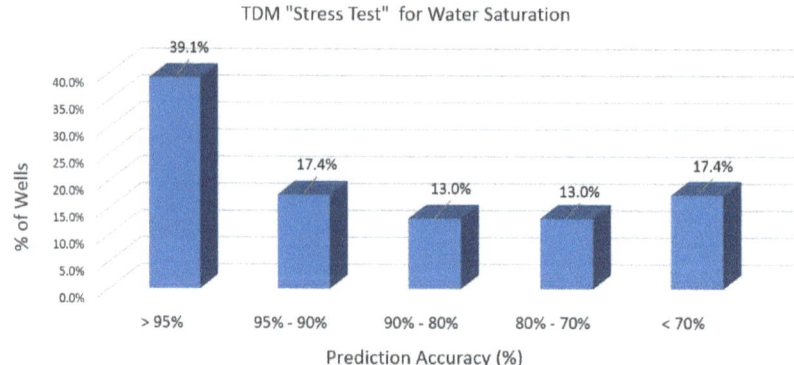

Fig. 102—Result of the top-down-model stress test. The top-down model's predictions are compared with actual field measurements, 5 years after its development (water saturation).

As can be seen from these figures, more than 90% of static reservoir pressure and 70% of water saturation predictions made by the top-down model are within 20% of the reality (field measurements), 5 years after the completion of the model. This clearly demonstrates the robustness and predictive capabilities of TDM.

Chapter 12

Limitations of Data-Driven Reservoir Modeling

Like any other technology that is developed for specific purposes, top-down modeling (TDM) has many limitations, and it is most powerful when it is used under the right circumstances. One limitation of TDM is that it is only as valid as the degree to which the available data are representative of the fluid flow through the reservoir that is the subject of the TDM. This is an important issue because in data-driven modeling, we are limited by the physics that is historically present in the operations and is captured by the data.

That said, it is important that we not take this statement superficially. In other words, if operators only refer to their traditional experience and education with reservoir and operational characteristics as they apply to reservoir modeling and fluid flow through porous media, then operators may conclude that since they do not have permeability measurements from many locations in the field, and since knowledge about formation permeability is critical in estimating flow (production), TDM cannot be applied. This is an incorrect interpretation of the limitation of the TDM that is being addressed here. The reason is that because TDM uses artificial intelligence to make its estimations and to learn the fluid flow behavior in a reservoir, it can use other data, such as well logs, gamma ray, density porosity, neutron porosity, sonic, spontaneous potential, and resistivity, to create an internal representation of formation permeability and then correlate these data to production from the reservoir.

The next limitation of TDM has to do with the age of the field. Data-driven reservoir modeling should be applied to fields with a certain amount of production history. Approximately 20 to 30 wells and at least 2 years of production history would probably be the minimum requirements for the development of the top-down model. As the number of wells in a field increases and as the age of the field increases, the field becomes a better and better candidate for a TDM study. Therefore, TDM is not applicable to greenfields and fields with a small number of wells and short production history.

Another limitation of TDM that needs to be taken into consideration concerns an application when the physics of the fluid flow in a reservoir changes considerably. Once the physics of the flow changes in a reservoir, an already developed top-down model will no longer be applicable. For example, once a top-down model is developed for a field under primary recovery, with no history of water injection, then the model cannot be applied to predict the impact of water injection. Or when only one kind of fluid has been injected to serve as a displacement fluid, or a pressure maintenance agent, then using the TDM that has been developed for such a history and trying to learn from it the impact of injecting another fluid (for example, gas instead of water) would not be an ideal way of using this technology. In such cases, TDM needs to be updated (retrained) using new measurements that reflect the new fluid-displacement mechanism.

Chapter 13

The Future of Data-Driven Reservoir Modeling

Top-down modeling (TDM) is in its infancy. It has been introduced as a new paradigm in developing reservoir models that are not based on first-principles physics and deterministic equations, but rather on the data collected as field measurements. As such, there is an extensive future in front of it. It is expected that this technology will be expanded on multiple fronts, some of which can be estimated now, but many advances cannot be forecast yet. The new generation of reservoir engineers and geoscientists will be armed with a new way of looking at almost everything, and they must take this technology and elevate it to its limits. What is presented here, today, as the future of this technology, is only the author's speculation at this point in time.

New generations of sensors will provide vast amounts of information and data from the subsurface in real time. It is inconceivable that our models that are based on first-principles physics and are solved numerically will be able to handle and make sense of the amount of data and information that will become available not too far into the future. We will have little choice but to start looking outside of our comfort zones to reach new solutions.

Permanent downhole gauges provide continuous measurements of the state of pressure in a well. Distributed temperature sensors and distributed acoustic sensors that are now being installed along long lateral wells can provide information regarding the flow of fluid into the wellbore that can be analogs to a continuous production-logging tool. Flow-control valves will provide the means of controlling the portion of the completion that can be open to flow at any given point in time. Once we can easily have access to real-time information from the interface between the well and the reservoir, we can understand what type of fluid is coming from which portions of the wellbore. This information can be used to make decisions to selectively open and close portions of the wellbore to the flow in order to control and ultimately optimize production, gas/oil ratio, and water cut.

We need the software tools that can handle the very large amounts of data that are generated with this new generation of sensors and tools in the oil industry and can respond at the same time scale at which data and information are being generated. One thing is for sure: Deterministic approaches do not stand a chance of providing engineers and scientists with the type of software applications that can fulfill such requirements. A good example are autonomous, self-driving cars. These cars collect and process massive amounts of information and data in fractions of a second and need to make decisions and react on the same time scales (fractions of a second). If it were not for artificial intelligence and its ability to process large amounts of data and make decisions in real time, self-driving cars would never have been developed.

The same argument can be made for the upstream oil and gas industry. We are not too far from the days when reservoir models that represent very large fields at very high resolution can be run in real time in order to process all the incoming data and information, can combine them with state-of-the-art knowledge, and can react with optimal decisions and actions in real time, so much so that there will be no need for a reservoir engineer to continuously monitor the activities of the field. This "smart field" can start moving toward reality only when the industry understands and completely embraces the art and science of artificial intelligence. The same will be true for entirely automated, autonomous, self-drilling rigs.

References

Agarwal, R. G., Gardner, D. C., Kleinsteiber, S. W. et al. 1998. Analyzing Well Production Data Using Combined Type Curve and Decline Curve Analysis Concepts. Paper presented at the SPE Annual Technical Conference and Exhibition, New Orleans, 27–30 September. SPE-49222-MS. https://doi.org/10.2118/49222-MS.

Alsharhan, A. S. 1993. Bu Hasa Field—United Arab Emirates, Rub al Khali Basin, Abu Dhabi. In *Structural Traps, Vol. 8: Treatise of Petroleum Geology*, ed. N. H. Foster and E. A. Beaumont, 99–127. Tulsa: Atlas of Oil and Gas Fields Series, AAPG.

Arnsdorf, I. 2014. Shale Boom Tested as Sub-$90 Oil Threatens U.S. Drillers. BloombergBusiness.com, 7 October 2014 (updated 8 October 2014). http://www.bloomberg.com/news/2014-10-07/shale-boom-tested-as-sub-90-oil-threatens-u-s-drillers.html (accessed 9 January 2017).

Arps, J. J. 1945. Analysis of Decline Curves. In *Transactions of the Society of Petroleum Engineers*, Vol. 160, Part 1, SPE-945228-G, 228–247. Richardson, Texas: Society of Petroleum Engineers. https://doi.org/10.2118/945228-G.

Aurenhammer, F. 1991. Voronoi Diagrams: A Survey of a Fundamental Geometric Data Structure. *ACM Computing Surveys* **23** (3): 345–405. https://doi.org/10.1145/116873.116880.

Barlow, H. B. 1989. Unsupervised Learning. *Neural Computation* **1:** 295–311.

Bell, G., Hey, T., and Szalay, A. 2009. Beyond the Data Deluge. *Science* **323** (5919): 1297–1298. https://doi.org/10.1126/science.1170411.

Black, M. 1937. Vagueness: An Exercise in Logical Analysis. *Philosophy of Science* **4** (4): 427–455. http://www.jstor.org/stable/184414.

Box, G. E. P. 1976. Science and Statistics. *Journal of the American Statistical Association* **71** (356): 791–799. https://doi.org/10.2307/2286841.

Bruce, W. A. 1943. An Electrical Device for Analyzing Oil-Reservoir Behavior. In *Transactions of the Society of Petroleum Engineers*, Vol. 151, SPE-943112-G, 112–124. Richardson, Texas: Society of Petroleum Engineers. https://doi.org/10.2118/943112-G.

Chevron Corporation. 2012. Reservoir Management (updated May 2015). http://www.chevron.com/deliveringenergy/oil/reservoirmanagement/ (accessed 9 January 2017).

Datta-Gupta, A. and King, M. J. 2007. *Streamline Simulation: Theory and Practice*. Richardson, Texas: SPE Textbook Series Vol. 11, Society of Petroleum Engineers.

Davis, J. C. 2002. *Statistics and Data Analysis in Geology*, third edition. New York City: Wiley.

Dickerson, M. T., Goodrich, M. T., Dickerson, T. D. et al. 2011. Round-Trip Voronoi Diagrams and Doubling Density in Geographic Networks. In *Transactions on Computational Science XIV*, Vol. 6970, 211–238. https://doi.org/10.1007/978-3-642-25249-5_9.

Duong, A. N. 2011. Rate-Decline Analysis for Fracture-Dominated Shale Reservoirs. *SPE Res Eval & Eng* **14** (3): 377–387. SPE-137748-PA. https://doi.org/10.2118/137748-PA.

Eberhart, R. C., Simpson, P. K., and Dobbins, R. W. 1996. *Computational Intelligence PC Tools*. Boston, Massachusetts: Academic Press Professional.

Esamili, S. and Mohaghegh, S. D. 2016. Full Field Reservoir Modeling of Shale Assets Using Advanced Data-Driven Analytics. *Geoscience Frontiers* **7** (1): 11–20. https://doi.org/10.1016/j.gsf.2014.12.006.

Esmaili, S., Kalantari-Dahaghi, A., and Mohaghegh, S. D. 2012. Modeling and History Matching of Hydrocarbon Production From Marcellus Shale Using Data Mining and Pattern Recognition Technologies. Presented at the SPE Eastern Regional Meeting, Lexington, Kentucky, USA, 3–5 October. SPE-161184-MS. https://doi.org/10.2118/161184-MS.

Fausett, L. V. ed. 1994. *Fundamentals of Neural Networks: Architectures, Algorithms, and Applications*. Upper Saddle River, New Jersey: Prentice Hall.

Franklin, S. and Graesser, A. 1997. Is It an Agent, or Just a Program? A Taxonomy for Autonomous Agents. In *Intelligent Agents, Vol. 3: Agent Theories, Architectures, and Languages*, ed. J. Müller, M. J. Wooldridge, and N. R. Jennings, 21–35. Berlin/Heidelberg: Springer.

Freeman, E. ed. 1983. *The Relevance of Charles Peirce*, 157–158. La Salle, Illinois: Monist Library of Philosophy.

Gaskari, R. and Mohaghegh, S. D. 2006. Estimating Major and Minor Natural Fracture Pattern in Gas Shales Using Production Data. Paper presented at the SPE Eastern Regional Meeting, Canton, Ohio, USA, 11–13 October. SPE-104554-MS. https://doi.org/10.2118/104554-MS.

Gaskari, R., Mohaghegh, S. D., and Jalali, J. 2007. An Integrated Technique for Production Data Analysis With Application to Mature Fields. *SPE Prod & Oper* **22** (4): 403–416. SPE-100562-PA. https://doi.org/10.2118/100562-PA.

Gomez, Y., Khazaeni, Y., Mohaghegh, S. D. et al. 2009. Top-Down Intelligent Reservoir Modeling (TDIRM). Presented at the SPE Annual Technical Conference and Exhibition, New Orleans, 4–7 October. SPE-124204-MS. https://doi.org/10.2118/124204-MS.

Grujic, O. S., Mohaghegh, S. D., and Bromhal, G. S. 2010. Fast Track Reservoir Modeling of Shale Formations in the Appalachian Basin. Application to Lower Huron Shale in Eastern Kentucky. Presented at the SPE Eastern Regional Meeting, Morgantown, West Virginia, USA, 13–15 October. SPE-139101-MS. https://doi.org/10.2118/139101-MS.

Haghighat, S. A., Mohaghegh, S. D., Gholami, V. et al. 2014. Production Analysis of a Niobrara Field Using Intelligent Top-Down Modeling. Presented at the SPE Western North American and Rocky Mountain Joint Meeting, Denver, 17–18 April. SPE-169573-MS. https://doi.org/10.2118/169573-MS.

Haykin, S. 2009. *Neural Networks and Learning Machines*, third edition. Upper Saddle River, New Jersey: Prentice Hall.

Hertz, J. A., Krogh, A. S., and Palmer, R. G. 1991. *Introduction to the Theory of Neural Computation*. Redwood City, California: Addison-Wesley.

Höppner, F., Klawonn, F. Kruse, R. et al. 1999. *Fuzzy Cluster Analysis: Methods for Classification, Data Analysis and Image Recognition*. New York City: Wiley IBM PC Series, Wiley.

Ilk, D., Anderson, D. M., Stotts, G. W. J. et al. 2010. Production-Data Analysis—Challenges, Pitfalls, Diagnostics. *SPE Res Eval & Eng* **13** (3): 538–552. SPE-102048-PA. https://doi.org/10.2118/102048-PA.

Jalali, J., Mohaghegh, S. D., and Gaskari, R. 2006. Identifying Infill Locations and Underperformer Wells in Mature Fields Using Monthly Production Rate Data, Carthage Field, Cotton Valley Formation, Texas. Paper presented at the SPE Eastern Regional Meeting, Canton, Ohio, USA, 11–13 October. SPE-104550-MS. https://doi.org/10.2118/104550-MS.

Jamshidi, M., Vadiee, N., and Ross, T. J. eds. 1993. *Fuzzy Logic and Control: Software and Hardware Applications*. Englewood Cliffs, New Jersey: Prentice Hall.

Jensen, J. L., Lake, L. W., Corbett, P. W. M. et al. 2000. *Statistics for Petroleum Engineers and Geoscientists*, second edition. Amsterdam: Elsevier.

Jolliffe, I. T. 2002. *Principal Component Analysis*, second edition. New York City: Springer Series in Statistics, Springer.

Kalantari-Dahaghi, A. and Mohaghegh, S. D. 2011. A New Practical Approach in Modelling and Simulation of Shale Gas Reservoirs: Application to New Albany Shale. *Int. J. Oil, Gas and Coal Technology* **4** (2): 104–133. https://doi.org/10.1504/IJOGCT.2011.038925.

Kalantari-Dahaghi, A., Mohaghegh, S. D., and Khazaeni, Y. 2010. New Insight Into Integrated Reservoir Management Using Top-Down, Intelligent Reservoir Modeling Technique: Application to a Giant and Complex Oil Field in the Middle East. Presented at the SPE Western Regional Meeting, Anaheim, California, USA, 27–29 May. SPE-132621-MS. https://doi.org/10.2118/132621-MS.

Khazaeni, Y. and Mohaghegh, S. D. 2011. Intelligent Production Modeling Using Full Field Pattern Recognition. *SPE Res Eval & Eng* **14** (6): 735–749. SPE-132643-PA. https://doi.org/10.2118/132643-PA.

Kosko, B. 1993. *Fuzzy Thinking: The New Science of Fuzzy Logic*. New York City: Hyperion.

Kuhn, T. 1996. *The Structure of Scientific Revolutions*. Chicago: University of Chicago Press.

Kuhn, T. S. 1977. *The Essential Tension: Selected Studies in Scientific Tradition and Change*. Chicago: University of Chicago Press.

Lee, W. J. and Sidle, R. 2010. Gas-Reserves Estimation in Resource Plays. *SPE Econ & Mgmt* **2** (2): 86–91. SPE-130102-PA. https://doi.org/10.2118/130102-PA.

Lukasiewicz, J. 1963. *Elements of Mathematical Logic (Elementy logiki matematycznej)*. New York City: International Series of Monographs on Pure and Applied Mathematics 31, Pergamon Press.

Mata, D., Gaskari, R., and Mohaghegh, S. D. 2007. Fieldwide Reservoir Characterization Based on a New Technique of Production Data Analysis: Verification Under Controlled Environment. Presented at the SPE Eastern Regional Meeting, Lexington, Kentucky, USA, 17–19 October. SPE-111205-MS. https://doi.org/10.2118/111205-MS.

Maysami, M., Gaskari, R., and Mohaghegh, S. D. 2013. Data Driven Analytics in Powder River Basin, WY. Presented at the SPE Annual Technical Conference and Exhibition, New Orleans, 30 September–2 October. SPE-166111-MS. https://doi.org/10.2118/166111-MS.

McCord Nelson, M. and Illingworth, W. T. 1990. *A Practical Guide to Neural Nets*. Reading, Massachusetts: Addison-Wesley.

McCulloch, W. S. and Pitts, W. 1943. A Logical Calculus of Ideas Immanent in Nervous Activity. *Bulletin of Mathematical Biophysics* **5** (4): 115–133. https://doi.org/10.1007/BF02478259.

McNeill, D. and Freiberger, P. 1993. *Fuzzy Logic*. New York City: Simon & Schuster.

Mills, F. and Stufflebeam, R. 2005. Introduction to Intelligent Agents. Consortium on Cognitive Science Instruction. The Mind Project. 23 June. http://www.mind.ilstu.edu/curriculum/ants_nasa/intelligent_agents.php (accessed 9 January 2017).

Minsky, M. L. and Papert, S. A. 1969. *Perceptrons*. Cambridge, Massachusetts: MIT Press.

Mohaghegh, S. D. 2009. Top-Down, Intelligent Reservoir Modeling (TDIRM): An Alternative Reservoir Modeling Technique; Integrating Classic Reservoir Engineering With Artificial Intelligence and Data Mining Techniques. Adapted from oral presentation at the AAPG Annual Convention and Exhibition, Denver, 7–10 June.

Mohaghegh, S. D. 2011. Reservoir Simulation and Modeling Based on Artificial Intelligence and Data Mining (AI&DM). *Journal of Natural Gas Science and Engineering* **3** (6): 697–705. https://doi.org/10.1016/j.jngse.2011.08.003.

Mohaghegh, S. D. 2017. *Shale Analytics*. Springer International Publishing AG, Switzerland. https://doi.org/10.1007/978-3-319-48753-3

Mohaghegh, S. D. and Bromhal, G. 2010. Top-Down Modeling; Practical, Fast Track, Reservoir Simulation & Modeling for Shale Formations. Presented at the AAPG/SEG/SPE/SPWLA Hedberg Conference, Austin, Texas, USA, 5–10 December.

Mohaghegh, S. D. and Gaskari, R. 2009. An Intelligent System's Approach for Revitalization of Brown Fields Using Only Production Rate Data. *International Journal of Engineering* **22** (1): 89–106.

Mohaghegh, S. D., Al-Mehairi, Y., Gaskari, R. et al. 2014. Data-Driven Reservoir Management of a Giant Mature Oilfield in the Middle East. Paper presented at the SPE Annual Technical Conference and Exhibition, Amsterdam, 27–29 October. SPE-170660-MS. https://doi.org/10.2118/170660-MS.

Mohaghegh, S. D., Grujic, O., Zargari, S. et al. 2012. Top-Down, Intelligent Reservoir Modelling of Oil and Gas Producing Shale Reservoirs: Case Studies. International Journal of Oil, Gas and Coal Technology 5 (1): 3–28. https://doi.org/10.1504/IJOGCT.2012.044175.

Rosenblatt, F. 1958. The Perceptron: A Probabilistic Model for Information Storage and Organization in the Brain. *Psychological Review* **65** (6): 386–408. https://doi.org/10.1037/h0042519.

Ross, T. J. 1995. *Fuzzy Logic With Engineering Applications*. New York City: McGraw-Hill.

Rumelhart, D. E. and McClelland, J. L. 1986. *Parallel Distributed Processing, Volume 1. Explorations in the Microstructure of Cognition: Foundations*. Cambridge, Massachusetts: MIT Press.

Sayarpour, M., Kabir, C. S., and Lake, L. W. 2009. Field Applications of Capacitance-Resistance Models in Waterfloods. *SPE Res Eval & Eng* **12** (6): 853–864. SPE-114983-PA. https://doi.org/10.2118/114983-PA.

Shannon, C. E. 1948. A Mathematical Theory of Communication. *Bell Labs Technical Journal* **27** (3): 379–423, 623–656. https://doi.org/10.1002/j.1538-7305.1948.tb01338.x.

Stubbs, D. 1988. Neurocomputers. *MD Comput* **5** (3): 14–24.

Swan, A. R. H. and Sandilands, M. 1995. *Introduction to Geological Data Analysis*. Oxford, UK: Blackwell Science.

Thakur, G. C. 1996. What Is Reservoir Management? *J Pet Technol* **48** (6): 520–525. SPE-26289-JPT. https://doi.org/10.2118/26289-JPT.

Widrow, B. 1962. Generalization and Information Storage in Networks of Adaline Neurons. In *Self-Organizing Systems*, eds. M. D. Yovits, G. T. Jacobi, and G. D. Goldstein, 435–461. Washington, DC: Spartan Books.

Zadeh, L. A. 1965. Fuzzy Sets. *Information and Control* **8** (3): 338–353. https://doi.org/10.1016/S0019-9958(65)90241-X.

Zargari, S. and Mohaghegh, S. D. 2010. Field Development Strategies for Bakken Shale Formation. Presented at the SPE Eastern Regional Meeting, Morgantown, West Virginia, USA, 13–15 October. SPE-139032-MS. https://doi.org/10.2118/139032-MS.

Zurada, J. M., Marks, R. J., and Robinson, C. J. eds. 1994. *Computational Intelligence: Imitating Life*. Piscataway, New Jersey: IEEE Press.

INDEX

A
Adeline, 19
artificial intelligence, 10
    applications, 18
    artificial neural networks, 18–23
    characteristics, 30
    definition, 18
    fuzzy logic, 23–28
    pitfalls, 30
artificial-lift optimization, 113
artificial neural networks
    activation functions, 22
    backpropogation, 19, 23
    convergence, 102–103
    data set partitioning, 94–95
    healthy training process, 101
    input parameters selection, 93–94
    mean square error (MSE) *vs.* number of training, 98–100
    measured output *vs.* neural network prediction
        for calibration data set, 101, 102
        for training data set, 101, 102
        for validation data set, 101, 103
    memorization, 98
    multilayer network, 20
    neurons structure, 19–20
    structure and topology, 95–98
    supervised learning, 92
    supervised neural networks, 21
    three-layer neuron network, 21
    training process, 21–23
    unhealthy training process, 101, 102
    unsupervised neural networks, 21

B
backpropagation, 19, 23
Big Data solution, 3, 35

C
capacitance/resistance modeling (CRM), 34
Central America, onshore mature field
    areal sections, 124
    history matching, 126–128
    oil and gas monthly rate and cumulative production match, 126, 129
    production behavior, 124–126
    production-related parameters, 125–126
    Voronoi polygons, 124, 125
choke-setting optimization, 113

comprehensive data-driven reservoir-modeling technology. *See* top-down modeling (TDM)
computational fluid dynamics, 11
CRM. *See* capacitance/resistance modeling (CRM)

D
Darcy's law, 87
Data-Driven Models Arrangement and Sequence module, 42–43
data-knowledge fusion, 63
data mining, 10, 17
Data Science, 9
decline curve analysis, 3, 34, 112
defuzzification procedures, 28
development and analysis phases, 17
diffusivity equation, 4
discrete calculus, 13
distributed acoustic sensors, 7, 157
distributed temperature sensors, 7, 157

E
empirical models, 33–34

F
fact-based reservoir management
    advantages, 33
    comprehensive and cohesive model, 33
    decision-making process, 31
    economic recovery, 31
    updation, 32
feature reduction, 47–48
feature selection, 47–48
functional relationships, 87, 88
fuzzy logic
    applications, 24
    approximate reasoning, 26–27
    father of, 24
    fuzzy set theory, 24–26
    inference methods, 27–28
    Yin-Yang symbol, 24
fuzzy set theory, 24–26

G
geocellular model, 13

H
history matching process, 39
    numerical reservoir simulation models, 14–15, 88

TDM, 88
- artificial neural networks, 92–103
- dynamic parameters, 104
- for individual wells, southern Mexico, 89–90
- for mature offshore field, North Sea, 90
- mixed history matching, 108–109
- random history matching, 107–108
- sequential history matching, 104–106
- validation, 109–110
- well production behavior, 90, 91

hydrocarbon pore volume (HPV), 48

I
IMagine™, 5
infill-location identification algorithm, 115–117
intelligent agents, 43–44

K
Kalman filter, 24

L
logging while drilling (LWD), 6

M
machine learning, 29–30
Mamdani's inference method, 27–28
material balance check, 109–110
mature fields, 6
measurement while drilling (MWD), 6
Middle East, onshore mature field
- data-mining, 139, 141
- flow diagram, 141, 143
- fuzzy cluster analysis, 138, 141
- history matching, 143–149
- pattern-recognition, 139, 141
- post-modeling analysis, 148, 149, 151–153
- producer and injector strings, 136, 137
- production data, 136
- pulsed neutron logs, 138, 140
- south-central portion, 136, 137
- static data, 136, 138, 139
- stress test, 152–154
- TDM development, data list, 139, 142
- Voronoi graph theory, 138, 141

mixed history matching, 108–109
Monte Carlo simulation technique, 120, 121, 132, 134
MWD. *See* measurement while drilling (MWD)

N
North Sea, offshore mature field
- completions, injectors and producers, 130
- drilled well schematics, 130
- historical field measurements, 132–133
- history matching, 129–130, 132–135
- infill-drilling programs, 134, 135
- injected total gas and water, 128, 130
- Monte Carlo simulation, 132, 134
- parameters, 129, 131
- reservoir delineation, 130
- total oil and gas production, 128, 131
- uncertainties, 132
- water-and gas-injection schedule, 128, 131

numerical reservoir simulation models
- accuracy and precision, 14
- characteristics, 36
- computational footprint, 14
- discrete calculus, 13
- history-matching process, 14–15
- *vs.* TDM, 37

P
paradigm shift, 5–7
permanent downhole gauges, 157
post-modeling analysis
- infill-location identification algorithm, 115–117
- production optimization
  - artificial-lift optimization, 113
  - choke-setting optimization, 113
  - definition, 113
  - water-injection optimization, 114–115
- recovery optimization, 117–118
- reservoir characterization, 115–117
- type curves, 118–119
- uncertainty analysis, 118, 120, 121

R
random history matching, 107–108
reservoir simulation models, 7

S
seismic surveys, 10
self-driving cars, 157
sequential history matching, 104–106
shale assets, production, 7
smart completions, 7
smart fields, 7
smart wells, 7
solution space, 2
spatio-temporal database, 17
- automatic timestep scheme, 70
- completion data, 66–67
- data quantity and quality, 83, 85
- dynamic data, 59, 64–66
- general structure, 81
- offset wells, 77–79
- for onshore field, Middle East, 81–84
- parameters, 38
- practical communication, 62
- production profile, 60
- resolution in space
  - Cartesian grid system, 71, 72, 81
  - Phase One production, 72–73
  - Phase Three production, 75, 76
  - Phase Two production, 74–76
  - timestep, 70–71
  - 2D grid system, 71–72
- resolution in time, 76–77
- schematic diagram, 62

static data
    average porosity, 59
    coarser grid, 64
    dynamically modified static data, 59
    finer grid system, 64
    hydrocarbon pore volume, 63
    reservoir, storage and transport capacities, 64
    truly static data, 59
TDM, 38–39
time resolution, 70
2D vs. 3D reservoir modeling, 68–69
well trajectory, 66, 67
SRMs. *See* surrogate reservoir models (SRMs)
streamline simulation, 79–80
supervised learning, 92
supervised neural networks, 21
surrogate reservoir models (SRMs), 16

T
top-down modeling (TDM)
    advantages, 35, 60
    Big Data solution, 3, 35
    correlation and causation, 48–50
    curse of dimensionality, 47–48
    data-driven models, 42–43
    data QC and QA
        artificial intelligence, 52
        data mining, 52
        examples, 52–53
        noise types, 54
        oil production profile in Persian Gulf, 54–55
        preliminary items, 51
        production data, Central America, 55–57
    decline curve analysis, 112
    definition, 3
    deployment, 46
    diffusivity equation, 4
    dynamic variables, 4, 45
    execution time, 36
    feature selection, 42
    field development strategies, 40
    flow chart, 40
    forecast period, 112
    formulation, 44–46
    gas/oil ratio (GOR), 111
    goal, 37, 61
    history matching process (*see* history matching process)
    intelligent agents, 43–44
    limitations, 5, 155
    vs. numerical reservoir simulation, 37
    offshore mature field, North Sea, 126–136
    oil production forecast, 111, 112
    onshore mature field, Central America, 124–129
    onshore mature field, Middle East, 136–154
    optimization problems, 113
    outcomes, 5, 39
    post-modeling analysis (*see* post-modeling analysis)
    production/injection data, 3
    reservoir-modeling tasks, 35–36
    size determination, 5
    small computational footprint, 5, 35
    software tool, 5
    spatio-temporal database (*see* spatio-temporal database)
    static variables, 4, 45
    and streamline simulation, 79–80
    structure of, 41
    updating process
        data-driven model structure, 121
        data structure, 121
        input vector, 121
        intelligent agents, 121
        structure of TDM, 121
    validation, 41
    water cut (WC), 111

U
UNIX-based systems, 13
unsupervised neural networks, 21

V
Voronoi graph theory, 72, 81, 82, 138, 141

W
water-injection optimization, 114–115

Y
Yin-Yang symbol, 24

Printed in the USA
CPSIA information can be obtained
at www.ICGtesting.com
CBHW060001090724
11332CB00017B/285